THE HAN
DYNASTY

Michèle Pirazzoli-t'Serstevens

THE HAN DYNASTY

translated by Janet Seligman

RIZZOLI
NEW YORK

**This English translation is dedicated
to the memory of my mother, 1891–1982. — J. S.**

French-language edition, *La Chine des Han:*
Copyright © 1982 by Office du Livre S.A. Fribourg, Switzerland

English translation:
Copyright © 1982 by Janet Seligman

English translation published in 1982 in the United States of America by:
*R*IZZOLI INTERNATIONAL PUBLICATIONS, INC.
712 Fifth Avenue/New York 10019

Library of Congress Cataloging in Publication data
Pirazzoli-t'Serstevens, Michèle.
    The Han Dynasty.

    Translation of: La Chine des Han.
    Bibliography: p.
    Includes index.
    1. China—History—Han dynasty, 202–B.C.–220 A.D.

I. Title.
DS748.P5713   1982   931'.04   82–50109
ISBN 0-8478-0438-0

Printed and bound in West Germany

Contents

Introduction

During the four centuries of its history the Han dynasty (206 B.C.–A.D. 220) prepared the ground for the main political, economic, social and cultural structures that were to characterize the Chinese world for two millennia. The Han empire was China's imperial Rome. Like its western counterpart, the Han, inheriting the unified territory of the Qin, founded a system of government, enacted laws, laid the foundations of a social organization and promoted intellectual enquiries that were to serve as models not only to future dynasties in China itself, but also to those countries of the Far East that came under the influence of Chinese civilization.

An autocratic monarchy, strongly centralized and hierarchical, it depended upon a syncretic Confucian ideology that became the true uniting principle and moral regulator of society. The educated élite, the majority of whom adhered to this ideology, gradually formed itself into a powerful social class and monopolized the administrative offices and the economic machinery of the State. The bureaucracy that resulted outlived the Han dynasty and became one of the factors that ensured the continuity and stability of Chinese society up to the twentieth century.

From the second century B.C. onwards, with unification consolidated, the power of the Han opened up vast new territories from Korea in the north-east to Central Asia in the west and Vietnam in the south. This expansion, China's reaction to the barbarian menace, led to the establishment of indirect commercial relations with the west, to the incorporation of numerous barbarian groups into the empire, and to the development and spread of Chinese influence in the newly occupied regions.

The rise of agriculture, craftsmanship, communications and trade that coincided with the military expansion of the reign of Wudi (140–87 B.C.) helped to bring about a radical transformation of society. The Han dynasty had at first relied upon the mass of the minor peasantry, who were conscripted. But those who had grown rich in the service of the State (the future class of educated officials and the new nobility) or in industry and trade invested increasingly in land—the best investment possible in a very mobile society. This resulted in the creation of great estates monopolized by rich landowners. As land was taken over, the countryside became more and more impoverished, and shortage of land in a country with a fast-growing population led the dispossessed peasantry into uprisings that sometimes degenerated into serious political disruption.

During the first two centuries of the Han era, a gulf began to open between a peasant proletariat, to whom the formation of the great estates had brought abject poverty and dependence, and a class of landowners of mounting power and independence. This deterioration culminated in great popular insurrections that weakened the central power, caused conflict at court, and brought about the fall of the dynasty and the splintering of the empire.

The Han period is therefore at once an age of consolidation, of change, and of experiment; in four centuries the immense effort devoted to agriculture, the improvement and diffusion in the field of technology, and great movements of population totally transformed the economic scene. Autocratic government, the desire to centralize power, the ascendancy of Confucian ideology and social revolution brought changes in outlook. The available information concerns mainly the intellectual and political élite. The Han historian did not write about peasants, artisans or small traders, classes that, in his view, had no history. Archaeology makes up in part for the silence of the texts; nevertheless, in so far as we can apprehend it, Han civilization remains that of the prosperous classes who gravitated round the court, held the best appointments in government, and possessed rich estates.

The Han emperors endeavoured to centralize culture as they centralized power. The influence of Chang'an and later of Luoyang is comparable only to that of ancient Rome. The historians, expositors and scholars whose writings were to remain authoritative for nearly twenty centuries worked in the capital. Again, it was the imperial court, and to a lesser extent certain princely courts, that set the tone in the fields of poetry and the plastic arts, and this remained true to the very end of the dynasty, when the centre of gravity was slowly passing from Luoyang to the provinces.

Dynamic and vigorous, an age of conquest and initiative, of tremendous social inequality and violence in political life, the Han period was one of borrowing from the past and of syncretism as well as of innovation and creativity in almost every area of culture. Behind its formidable intellectual certainty it was also a period of superstition, anguish and aspiration that neither the official ideology nor the growing formalism could satisfy.

It may appear presumptuous to attempt a survey of this period. Since the beginning of the present century classical literary sources, already abundant, have been supplemented by the discovery of thousands of Han texts, mostly written on wooden slips. Remarkable work has been done on deciphering and interpreting these slips by E. Chavannes (1913) and H. Maspero (1953) for Dunhuang, by Lao Kan (1944–60), Chen Mangjia, Zhang Chun-shu and M. Loewe for Juyan—to name only a few, for these finds are still being made in almost every region. But rich though they are in the fields of history, institutions, economic life, philosophical and religious thought, and literature, these texts tell us little about material life, technical developments and art. For these fields archaeology is the best source. And during the past thirty years archaeological campaigns in the People's Republic of China have become much more numerous, and the resulting discoveries have continued to renew, enrich and modify our image of the various moments and aspects of Chinese civilization. But this abundant new information is not always simple to use, partly because of its volume—there are thousands of new sites for the Han period alone—partly because it is scattered over a vast area, and especially because of the lengthy work of interpretation and of comparison with the historical facts that it necessitates. Faced with this extraordinary harvest we must not forget that, in the short term, many of the finds and much of the evidence pose more problems than they solve. Furthermore, the number of finds does not always, *ipso facto,* lead to a better understanding in depth of phenomena and systems. Thus, although light is being thrown on many aspects of Han civilization, we are still in the dark as regards vast geographical, social and cultural areas. Our knowledge of many spheres of the Han world is still fragmented, incomplete and therefore simplistic.

Despite these abiding difficulties we have tried to capture the movement of the Han empire by considering the political, economic, social and cultural evolution of a world that changed greatly in the course of four centuries. We have decided to present the material chronologically, as this seemed to be the only way of conveying the complexity, dynamism and trends of the period without too many repetitions; the second advantage of this method is that it shows the continual clashes between the different sectors of activity in Han society. In conclusion we have returned to certain currents and the major cultural legacies of the Han dynasty in a more global manner.

The sole aim of the present study is to serve as an introduction to one of the most exciting moments in the history of civilizations. But we are well aware that the book owes everything—except its omissions, errors and deficiencies, for which we are responsible—to the great body of work that Chinese, Japanese and western scholars have devoted to the Han empire.

To avoid overloading the bibliography we have put all references to articles in Chinese archaeological journals on certain subjects and on every important site into notes, which appear at the first mention of the site. Only site reports in book form and some exhibition catalogues have been mentioned in the general bibliography.

The romanization of Chinese used here is the official transcription used by the People's Republic of China since 1958.

Qin and Han Emperors

Qin Shi Huangdi 246–210 B.C. Ershi Huangdi 209–208	Qin dynasty
Gaozu [or Gaodi] 206–195 Huidi 194–188 Dowager Empress Lü 188–180 Wendi 179–157 Jingdi 156–141 Wudi 140–87 Zhaodi 86–74 Xuandi 73–49 Yuandi 48–33 Chengdi 32–7 Aidi 6–1 B.C. Pingdi A.D. 1–5 Wang Mang (regent) 6–8	Dynasty of the Former (Western) Han
Wang Mang (reigned) 9–23	Xin dynasty
Guangwudi 25–57 Mingdi 58–75 Zhangdi 76–88 Hedi 89–105 Shangdi 106 Andi 107–25 Shundi 126–44 Chongdi 145 Zhidi 146 Huandi 147–67 Lingdi 168–89 Shaodi 189 Xiandi 190–220	Dynasty of the Latter (Eastern) Han

Part I

China at the Accession of the Han:
The Legacy of the Qin (206–141 B.C.)

Chapter I

The Qin Empire (221–207 B.C.)

In 221 B.C., after bitter struggles against rival states, the first Qin emperor (Qin Shi Huangdi) completed the unification of China. Brutal though they may appear, the ground for the measures that he immediately imposed on his new empire had been prepared by two centuries of profound change and of struggles for hegemony. Indeed, this period of tumult, known as the Period of the Warring States (453–221 B.C.), saw the reorganization of Chinese society as feudal royalty passed to a more modern style of government.

Already in decline at the death of Confucius (479 B.C.), who had worked so vigorously to defend it, the old feudal system finally broke down in the third century. Following the reformers of the Legalist school, personal government, favoured by the Confucians, and based on custom and the rites, was replaced by a much more rigid concept in which law alone—impersonal, impartial and universal—was supreme.

The rise of Qin, an outlying kingdom of the north-west with its centre in the present-day province of Shaanxi, was the work of Shang Yang (390?–338 B.C.), a statesman and reformer of broad vision. He arrived in Qin in 361 B.C. and proceeded to redistribute land, divide the country into administrative districts, modify forms of taxation, and establish extremely severe penal laws based on collective responsibility and compulsory denunciation.

The aim of the Legalists, whose principles were applied by the Qin from the mid-fourth century B.C. onwards, was to deprive the traditional aristocracy of its territorial or hereditary privileges and to make it subject to the law and the hierarchy of merit. As they dispossessed the aristocracy of its land and its discretionary rights over the peasants, the statesmen of the time aimed to develop agriculture to the maximum, to channel the growing wealth of the artisans and traders and to subjugate the people. They also made efforts to modernize technology, standardize weights and measures and unify writing.

Having lost their place close to the sovereign to a new, centralized bureaucracy composed of paid and removable officials, the aristocracy were also compelled to yield to strategists in the wars of the period and especially to the vast infantry forces. The infantry was composed of the peasants who, promoted simultaneously to the rank of independent farmers and soldiers, formed the foundation of the economic and military power of the new state.[1]

It was against this background of social revolution, economic growth, technological development and radical change of outlook, that the expansionist policy of the Qin State asserted itself and succeeded in unifying the empire in 221. The modern province of Sichuan was occupied in 311; Hubei, the former territory of the state of Chu, was conquered in 277. In 249 Qin seized the royal domain of the Zhou in the province of Henan and put an end to the ancient dynasty that had reigned, in name at least, since the eleventh century B.C. Finally, between 230 and 221, Qin annexed successively the states of Han, Zhao, Wei, Chu, Yan and Qi, i.e. the six states that, with Qin itself, had been fighting for supremacy.

With China thus united, King Zheng (246–210 B.C.) of Qin proclaimed himself First Emperor of the Qin (Qin Shi Huangdi). Zheng's reign saw the continuation and systematic extension to all parts of the country of the reforms undertaken in the fourth century based on Legalist principles.

To the Legalist thinkers, the most important of whom was Han Fei (280?–234 B.C.), efficiency was the supreme criterion, and realism and objectivity were therefore the major virtues. They rejected the Confucian concept of the mandate of heaven and the divine right of the monarchy and recognized only a sovereignty founded by men. Finally, royalty became with them a totalitarian imperialism in which the prince was the incarnation of the state.

The Legalist government substituted force and law for morality and mutual responsibility. For Han Fei, as for Li Si (d. 208 B.C.), counsellor to Qin Shi Huangdi, the functioning of the state was based on a certain number of regulations that were objective, public and applicable to all without distinction. Likewise, everyone was judged and classed by the yardstick of his actions, performance and merits. The end-product of this was a social hierarchy in which every subject was a servant of the State. Those whose activities were considered essential, such as agricultural workers and fighting men, were favoured at the expense of the unproductive, potential agitators and profiteers, and those pushers of useless commodities: the craftsmen, traders, vagrants and philosophers. This social order, in which there was no place at all for free individual initiative, was maintained by force of law, that is to say, a severe penal code applied by administrative tribunals. These repressed crime less for its effect on private persons than for the disorder it caused.[2]

Certain bamboo slips discovered in 1975 in the tomb of Master Xi, officer of the law in Hubei (d. 217 B.C.),[3] show clearly that the rôle that had devolved upon the judge was to define the crime and to apply the corresponding articles of the code.

Until the fourth century A.D. official documents in China were written on slips of bamboo or wood, for these materials were less expensive and, fortunately, less perishable than silk. The slips varied in size—those illustrated measure between 23 and 28 centimetres—and were tied together by cords to form a kind of book. The texts were written in ink, with a brush; a knife was used to scrape out incorrect characters.

The slips relating to law (over 500) found in the tomb of Master Xi are the earliest as well as the fullest Chinese legal texts to have come down to us in their original versions. In addition to the articles of the law, with explanations, they contain regulations concerning agriculture, artisans, slaves, public works and collections of jurisprudence describing typical cases to which the judge could refer.

These were the foundations, evolved before the accession of Qin Shi Huangdi, on which Han legislation was based.

The Reforms of Li Si

Li Si rather than the emperor himself was responsible for the reforms of Qin Shi Huangdi's reign. Moreover most of these had been conceived in the fourth century—some even earlier—and were merely revived, modified or broadened and rationalized in application. Thus the whole country was forced to adopt the Qin calendar in which the year began with the tenth lunar month.

Shi Huangdi divided the empire into thirty-six commanderies (jun), each comprising several sub-prefectures (xian). Each commandery was governed by a civil administrator and a military governor. The activities of the civil administrator were supervised by an inspector. At the head of each sub-prefecture was an official known as *ling* in sub-prefectures of over ten thousand households and *zhang* in those of fewer. These territorial divisions, established in Qin in the mid fourth century B.C. and revived by the Han, are the direct ancestors of the administrative system of modern China.

Those who remained of the former aristocracy were compulsorily domiciled in the capital Xianyang, to the north-west of modern Xi'an in Shaanxi province. One hundred and twenty thousand families were moved there.

Certain other measures were used to reinforce the unification of the country, e.g. a single type of coin was created: the round cash with a square hole in the centre, the model of which was to endure un-

1

Qin and Han coins: (1) Qin cash *(banliang)*, (2) cash *(banliang)*, 175 B.C., (3) cash *(wushu)*, reign of Wudi (140–87 B.C.), (4) cash *(wushu)*, between 73 B.C. and A.D. 8, (5) currency-knife issued by Wang Mang in A.D. 7, (6) coin in the shape of a spade issued in A.D. 14 by Wang Mang, Xin dynasty, (7) cash *(huoquan)* issued in A.D. 14 by Wang Mang, Xin dynasty, (8) cash *(wushu)* of the Latter Han. Musée Guimet, Paris.

p. 226 til the twentieth century; measurements of volume and length and even of the gauge of the wheel-base of chariots and carts were standardized.

Writing too was modified. Up to this time, i.e. the end of the third century B.C., many regional features had survived. The structure of the characters needed codifying. So, in its turn, the system of writing was unified. Two existing types of writing *(xiaozhuan* or small-seal script and *lishu,* the clerical script) were standardized. These were simplifications of the old scripts; *xiaozhuan* was usually re-

served for inscriptions on stone and the engraving of official texts, while *lishu,* itself a simplified version of *xiaozhuan,* was used in everyday life and lent itself to the use of the brush. Thus the bamboo slips found at Yunmeng are written mostly in the scribal hand *(lishu)* with certain characters in *xiaozhuan,* whereas the stelae erected during Shi Huangdi's tours of inspection in the eastern commanderies are engraved in *xiaozhuan.*

As the hand of the officials, of overworked judges who had perfected a simpler and speedier form, *lishu* was used increasingly at the end of the third century and came fully into its own in the Han era.

76–8

The measure that, more than any other, has called down the wrath of history upon Qin Shi Huangdi was the Burning of the Books. In 213, during a speech preserved for posterity by the great historian Sima Qian (*c.* 145–86 B.C.) in his *Records of the Historian (Shiji),* Li Si proposed that certain books be burned:

> ...In antiquity the empire was divided and disrupted; there was no one who could unify it; that is why the lords reigned simultaneously. When they talk, all the scholars speak of antiquity in order to denigrate the present;... these men stress the excellence of what they have learnt in their private studies in order to denigrate what Your Majesty has instituted.... These men who condemn the laws and directives, as soon as they hear that an edict has been issued, hasten to discuss it, each according to his own principles; when they are at court they disapprove in their heart of hearts; when they have left the court they dispute in the streets;... they influence the common people to fabricate calumnies. Since this is how things stand, if one does not oppose them, then at the top, the authority of the sovereign will diminish, while at the bottom conspiracies will strengthen. A defence is required. Your subject proposes that the official histories, except for the Memoirs of Qin, shall all be burnt. Except for people who are responsible, for scholars of vast knowledge, those who in the empire

venture to hide the *Shi[jing]*, the *Shu-[jing]* or the lectures of the Hundred Schools shall all be compelled to go to the local civil and military authorities to have them burnt. Those who dare to argue among themselves about the *Shi-[jing]* and the *Shu[jing]* will be [put to death and their bodies] exhibited in the public square; those who use antiquity to denigrate modern times will be put to death, with their relatives. Officials who see or hear [that individuals are contravening this order] and do not denounce them will be accessories to their crime. Thirty days after the edict has been issued, those who have not burnt [their books] will be branded and sent to forced labour. The books that will not be proscribed will be those on medicine and pharmacy, on divination by tortoise and yarrow, on agriculture and arboriculture. As for those who wish to study laws and orders, let them take the officials for their masters.[4]

The idea was not new. At the suggestion of Shang Yang, Duke Xiao (361–338 B.C.) of Qin had ordered the burning of *The Book of Songs (Shijing)* and *The Book of Documents (Shujing)*.

Li Si condemned three types of writings: anthologies of verse *(Shijing)* and collections of political and ritual texts *(Shujing)*, historical chronicles of the early states other than Qin and philosophical writings.

The reasons for this auto-da-fé are well known: Li Si hoped to put an end to the dissemination of dangerous ideas and to the manoeuvres of Confucian and feudal reaction. The *Shujing* and the *Shijing* were indeed always cited by the Confucians as mirrors of the golden age of antiquity, when peace and prosperity reigned in the world under the leadership of the sage-kings, who governed by virtue rather than force.

The Burning of the Books was also in keeping with the policy of unification. According to the Qin rulers the various populations of the empire must be made to forget their local traditions and independent histories; rather than feel that they belonged to Chu or Qi, the inhabitants of these regions must consider themselves to be Chinese first

and foremost. By outlawing local literatures, the Qin tried to efface cultural differences from the minds of the inhabitants of a country that was already vast, but they offered no substitute, no positive, new ideal capable of rallying the best minds. By destroying ancient literature all resistance was smothered, and as Jia Yi (*c.* 200–168 B.C.) was to comment in *The Faults of Qin,* the minds of the people were deliberately dulled.

It was the less powerful philosophical trends and the chronicles of the various states of the Zhou period that suffered more than the great Classics, for these were preserved by the schools. However, following the Confucian historians, the consequences of the Burning of the Books have been much exaggerated. During this difficult but short period—the auto-da-fé took place in 213, the Qin dynasty fell in 207—the erudite recited the texts that they knew by heart. Bundles of wooden slips and manuscripts on silk were tucked away and hidden. Furthermore, the exercise did not extend to the works preserved by the 'erudite of great knowledge', i.e. the seventy learned men whom Shi Huangdi kept at his court. The burning of the imperial library by Xiang Yu in 207 and the lack of interest in literature shown by the first Han emperors did more than the auto-da-fé of 213 to bring about the disappearance of many works of the Zhou period.

When the Han emperors did find the time and inclination to interest themselves in cultural matters, the memory of the Burning aroused greater respect for literature, for the written testimony and national history that had so nearly been lost.

Public Works under the Qin

While he was organizing the administration of the empire, Shi Huangdi reinforced his policy with a whole series of vast undertakings, which the Han inherited.

The ancient fortifications constructed at the end of the fourth century in the north by the states of Qin, Zhao and Yan against the invasions of the Xiongnu, the nomadic shepherds of the steppes, were strengthened and extended. This first Great Wall ran in an unbroken line from Lintao in the south of

Gansu province to the north of the Liaodong peninsula (map. p. 222).

In 220 the construction of a network of roads and irrigation canals was begun. Broad roadways were built to aid military campaigns in the north against the Xiongnu in the region of the loop of the Yellow River, in the south in Fujian, Guangdong and Guangxi provinces, and as far as North Vietnam. Each time, the conquered territories were organized in commanderies, peopled with condemned criminals deported for that purpose.

Xianyang, the capital of Qin from 350 B.C., was embellished with new palaces copied from those of the noblemen subjugated by the First Emperor.

Finding his own residence too modest, in 212 Shi Huangdi ordered the building of the Ebang Palace south of the River Wei. Over 700,000 men were conscripted for this and for building the emperor's even more grandiose mausoleum. Shi Huangdi had ordered work to begin on his tomb in 246, at the beginning of his reign. He had chosen a site at the foot of Mount Li, some 50 kilometres east of the capital. The unusually imposing mound stands to this day 5 kilometres east of Lintong. It formed part of an enclosed precinct *(ying)* covering about 2 square kilometres on a north-south axis and surrounded by a rectangular outer enceinte. Encircled by an inner wall, the mound, shaped like a truncated pyramid and measuring about 350 metres at the base and 47 metres high, rises in the centre of the southern half of the precinct.

The gigantic undertaking had begun with the construction of what amounted to an underground palace, above which the mound was built in rammed earth. Sima Qian's description in *Records of the Historian* is certainly accurate in the main. It clearly reflects the megalomania, the love of mystery and of magical conjunctions, as well as the fear of death that haunted the First Emperor: in this underground palace with its treasury of rare and precious objects the rivers of the empire and the vast sea had been traced in mercury, their flow simulated by machines; on the ceiling were images of the stars and planets; torches made of whale-blubber had been specially devised to burn slowly. The interior

2

Tumulus of Qin Shi Huangdi. Lintong, Shaanxi.

16

of the burial chamber was faced with bronze, and the entrance to it was defended by automatic crossbows designed to loose their arrows at would-be intruders. During the funeral celebrations those of the First Emperor's wives who had not borne sons were executed and buried with him. Similarly, the workmen and craftsmen who

3
Figure of a woman seated on her heels.
Earthenware, H. 64.5 cm, discovered in 1964 at Lintong, Shaanxi, near the tumulus of Qin Shi Huangdi, Qin dynasty (221–207 B.C.).

4
Figures of an officer, a charioteer and infantrymen.
Earthenware, with traces of pigment, H. *c.* 1.82 m, unearthed from the burial pits near the mausoleum of Qin Shi Huangdi, Lintong, Shaanxi, Qin dynasty (221–207 B.C.).

had installed the protective mechanisms and arranged the treasures in the tomb had been walled up alive in the passage between the doorway of the burial chamber and the exit. Despite all these precautions it seems probable that, at the fall of the Qin dynasty, the rebel general Xiang Yu opened the tomb and pillaged it.

Although there has so far been no archaeological investigation of the mound, the discoveries made since 1974 in the vicinity exceed anything that the historical texts could lead us to imagine. Many large earthenware statues of servants had previously been found by chance in the neighbourhood of the mound. But in 1974, when sinking a well some 1,500 metres east of the outer enceinte, peasants discovered a first pit, which proved to be 230 metres long (east-west) by 62 metres wide (north-south) by 5 metres deep. This underground construction, made of a wooden framework and rammed earth and comprising eleven parallel passage-ways with access ramps at the sides, had been pillaged and burned. It still contained an army of over 6,000 life-sized earthenware foot soldiers and horses, some broken by the weight of the collapsed structure and soil, together with wooden war chariots and real bronze weapons.

Another pit, 20 metres to the north-west of the first, excavated in 1976–7, has yielded some thousand figures of foot soldiers and horsemen, the horses harnessed to wooden chariots, all ranged in battle formation, as in the first pit.

A third pit contained what seems to have been the military headquarters of this army of some 8,000 men and horses,[5] all of whom—generals, officers, horses and chariot drivers, horsemen, foot soldiers and crossbowmen—faced east.

We shall return to the information about military science, weaponry and the art of sculpture at the end of the third century B.C. provided by this extraordinary army.

As the substitute for his earthly army, this battle formation was intended to protect the deceased emperor and his burial. For us there remains an astonishing gallery of portraits. Suffice it here to draw attention to the human dimension that this find adds to our knowledge of the Qin empire and to the technical virtuosity of these pottery figures, which are of a size and realism previously unknown in China.

The Rebellion and the Accession of the Han

The First Emperor died at the age of fifty in 210, during one of his journeys through the eastern commanderies, journeys which, though disguised as tours of inspection, were no less than quests for immortality. This indefatigable worker and megalomaniac autocrat, the prey of superstition, had become the plaything of those who specialized in the cult of the Immortals. Magicians, men learned in esoteric method from Shandong and Hebei provinces (the former states of Qi and Yan), had for years been promising that he would commune with the Immortals of the Eastern Sea and obtain drugs that would protect him from dying.

The main features of the short reign of his younger son, who was proclaimed emperor with the title of Ershi Huangdi ('second emperor'), were the rising tide of revolution and the execution of the counsellor Li Si. Shi Huangdi's nephew, who succeeded him in 207, occupied the throne for a mere three months and was beheaded when the rebel troops entered Xianyang.

The excessive burden of constructional work imposed by Shi Huangdi, the enormous movements of population, especially to the frontier regions, the extreme harshness of the penal system, the summary executions of those in opposition and the suppression of the ancient aristocracy had rendered the régime intolerable. The rebellion started in eastern China and began as a struggle between local armies commanded by rival generals, some of whom came from the ancient aristocracy, like Xiang Yu (232–202 B.C.), and others from the people, like Liu Bang. Thus, at first, the revolt was both an attempt to restore feudalism and a popular insurrection. However, the aristocracy soon showed itself to be incapable and, faced with this collapse, the people put their trust in men of their own class who worked their way up to the seat of supreme power.

5
Kneeling archer.
Earthenware, with traces of pigment, H. 1.20 m, unearthed from pit No. 2 at Lintong, Shaanxi, near the mausoleum of Qin Shi Huangdi, Qin dynasty (221–207 B.C.).
Shaanxi Provincial Museum.

6
Landscape of central Shaanxi, Chang'an region, near the present city of Xi'an.

The capture of Xianyang at the end of 207 was the signal for the final struggle between Xiang Yu, descended from famous Chu generals, and Liu Bang, a former head of a posting station who had become the leader of a troop and with whom Xiang Yu had allied himself. Civil war continued until Xiang Yu was defeated in 202. Liu Bang then proclaimed himself emperor, established his capital at Chang'an, some 10 kilometres north-east of modern Xi'an, and so founded the Han dynasty. He was to be known to history by his temple name (the name under which he was worshipped in the temple of the dynastic ancestors), Gaozu ('eminent founder') and by his posthumous title of Gaodi ('Emperor Gao').

He must have been about forty years old when the rebellion broke out. His ability to take rapid and firm decisions, to consult others and recognize their talents, to surround himself with men of merit, together with his generosity, had as much to do with his success as external conditions. Unprecendented in Chinese history, his rise left its mark on the popular imagination, especially as he retained the manner of a Chu peasant throughout his life. Nevertheless, the respect for nobility was deep-rooted. So a genealogy going back to Yao, one of the mythical sovereigns of antiquity, was created for the new emperor in order to attract more partisans.

Until his death in 195 B.C. Gaozu spent much time in quelling revolts and in establishing his sons and close relatives in the kingdoms he had liberated. He also ennobled partisans, but this new aristocracy, composed of men who had begun from nothing and had proved themselves in the turmoil of war, was to remain in the emperor's power. Feudalism was restored at the beginning of the Han period in appearance only; the structure of the State, as conceived by the Qin Legalists, remained practically unchanged under the new dynasty.

Chapter II

The Legacy of the Qin:
The Administrative and Legislative Structures

For four centuries, from the end of the third century B.C. to the beginning of the third century A.D. the political and administrative organization remained in broad outline unchanged from the time when the first Han emperors inherited and adapted it from the Qin.

Central Administration

The emperor was assisted by a Grand Counsellor (*Chengxiang*)—sometimes there were two—who acted as prime minister, by a Grand Constable (*Taiwei*) and by the Grand Officer of Censorship (*Yushidafu*). In addition to the rôle of counsellors to the sovereign, these three dignitaries, known as the Three Dukes (*Sangong*), were called upon to centralize and control the whole administrative machine. Of the three, the Grand Counsellor wielded the widest and most absolute power, and he often governed in place of the sovereign.

While the political functions of the Three Dukes were very general, the administrative powers of each of the Nine Ministers (*Jiuqing*) were well defined: the Grand Rector (*Taichang*) was responsible for the rites, astrology, medicine and the schools; the Grand Master of Ceremonies (*Dahonglu*) was in charge of everything relating to the feudatory princes and the barbarians; justice and the prison service were the responsibility of the Constable of the Court (*Tingwei*). Finance was shared between two ministers: the Grand Director of Agriculture (*Dasinong*), who looked after taxes in kind and public finance, and the Privy Treasurer (*Shaofu*), who was responsible for the taxes that fed the private finances of the imperial house. In fact the *Shaofu* had supreme control over all the palace staff, the imperial workshops (*shangfang*), the palace library and archives, the secretariat (*shangshu*), which was responsible for the sovereign's public and private correspondence, the eunuchs, etc. Two other ministers commanded the guards: the Constable of the Guards (*Weiwei*), who was responsible for the palace police, and the *Guanglujun*, who was in charge of the emperor's bodyguard and the gentlemen of the court (*lang*). The Grand Coachman (*Taipu*) administered the stud-farms and arsenals and the duties of the palace horses and carriages. Lastly, the Director of the Imperial Clan (*Zongzheng*), chosen from the members of the ruling family of the Liu, saw to the maintenance of the princes of the blood.

These high officials headed an administrative system of considerable extent. Each ministry comprised several distinct duties, which were themselves divided into offices (*cao*).

Besides this cumbersome centralized administration the emperor had a private secretariat (*shangshu*), run, as we have seen, by the Privy Treasurer. Its duty was to keep the emperor informed, to draft his decisions and see them carried out, and it gradually took the lead over the other great offices of the state.

Provincial and Local Administration

At the beginning of the Han dynasty the empire was divided into commanderies *(jun)* and kingdoms *(guo)*—fiefs given by the emperor to princes, known as kings *(wang)*, and to marquises *(hou)*.

The commanderies (map, p. 222) were administered by a governor *(taishou)* and by a constable general *(duwei)*. Later, in certain commanderies that covered large areas and were poorly served, military command was split between several constables general. The kingdoms were administered by two imperial officials, for the kings and marquises were very soon excluded from governing their fiefs.

All the commanderies, and sometimes the kingdoms, were divided into sub-prefectures *(xian)*, headed, as under the Qin, by a *ling* or *zhang* subprefect according to the importance of the subprefecture (i.e. containing over or under 10,000 households), assisted by civil and military aides. 'The governors of the commanderies and the subprefects represented the emperor and had full religious, civil, legal, financial and military powers. They governed the people, kept an eye on agriculture, judged lawsuits, raised taxes, despatching to the capital the part representing the "tribute" *(gong)*, performed the ceremonies of the official religion at the appointed times, raised and commanded troops and superintended the school in the chief town.'[1]

At least during the period of the Former or Western Han, the numerous employees of the offices of the commanderies and the sub-prefecture were appointed by the governor or the sub-prefect and so were entirely dependent on him.

The sub-prefectures were sub-divided into districts *(xiang)* of some 5,000 families, into *ting,* which were postal relay stations and police posts on the imperial highways, and into communes *(li)* of from 50 to 100 families. At this level local notables superintended the assessment of taxes, conscription, distribution of land and the good attitude of the population; they received a small salary in return. Two of these notables, the *sanlao* and the *tingzhang,* appear frequently in the biographies and documents of the time. The *sanlao,* an elderly man whose rôle was largely moral, directed the at-

tention of the provincial authorities to pious sons, virtuous wives and charitable persons. Roads were policed by the postmaster *(tingzhang)*. He was responsible for stabling, coach-houses and coaching inns where travellers could spend the night and change horses. He was also in charge of the 10 *li* (a little over 4 km) of the road that lay between him and the next inn, of the secondary post situated at the half-way mark, the mail and the free movement of traffic on the road. It was as the humble head of one of these official post-houses of the Qin dynasty that Liu Bang, the founder of the Han dynasty, began his career.

The Inspectors

The civil and military power wielded by the governors of the commanderies was so great that it was essential to supervise their activities. The inspectoral tours, which had already existed under the Qin, were systematized at the end of the second century B.C. A body of twelve inspectors was created, each of whom was responsible for a department *(zhou)* comprising a certain number of commanderies. The inspectors *(cishi)* were answerable to the prime minister. Every year in the eighth month they travelled to their districts, where they audited the accounts and checked the administration of justice and government, returning to the capital to present a report on New Year's day. These men were minor officials (earning 600 *shi* a year), whereas the governors were very high officials whose earnings equalled those of the Nine Ministers (2,000 *shi*).

The Salaries of the Officials

Han officials were paid partly in grain and partly in cash. The whole amount was calculated in *shi,* a cubic measure roughly equal to 20 litres of hulled grain (table, p. 226). The scale of salaries varied from over 4,000 *shi* per annum for the Three Dukes to 100 *shi* per annum for a district official. High officials like the Nine Ministers earned salaries corresponding to 2,000 *shi* and their assistants (departmental heads) the equivalent of from 2,000 to 600 *shi;* the pay of a *ling* sub-prefect varied between 1,000 and 600 *shi,* that of a *zhang* sub-prefect between 500 and 300 *shi.*

Legislation

The first measure adopted by the founder of the Han dynasty was to reduce the severity of Qin law by restricting punishment to crimes of common law and high treason. With these exceptions the Qin penal code remained in force and, at least during the first half of the Han dynasty, law remained public and all were equal before it. Its aim was both political—to maintain the stability and power of the government—and religious—to preserve cosmic harmony, which was thought to be affected by human actions.

The Administration of Justice

Although vendettas seem to have been fairly common during the Han period, they were seriously censured in official circles. In fact, the administration of justice was essentially in the hands of the emperor's representatives. Legal proceedings followed fixed rules: accusation was followed by arrest, imprisonment with or without chains, and interrogation under torture—usually beating on the soles of the feet. Questions and answers were taken down, and the whole proceedings copied in the form of an official document that was read out to the accused by way of confirmation. Much use was made of witnesses, who were arrested by the administration, detained with the accused and doubtless subjected to the same forms of interrogation.

The local official acted as judge, the only judge known to most of the lower classes being the sub-prefect. The governor and inspector were naturally entitled to review the sub-prefect's findings. Above them the duty of the prime minister's director of justice was to denounce illegalities. Similarly, the central assistant in the Office of Censorship *(Yushi zhongcheng)* received reports from the regional inspectors on irregularities in the administration of the commanderies. He also received memoranda, accusations or enquiries from the dif-

ferent ministries and was responsible for difficult judicial questions.

Religious Character of the Gravest Offences

Crimes that were felt by the collective conscience to be sacrilegious and particularly harmful were parricide, incest, the murder of three innocent people in the same family, rebellion, disobedience to the emperor, breach of religious observance, attacks on the imperial majesty (especially imprecations against the emperor and witchcraft aimed against the sovereign). These crimes, which carried the death penalty for the accused and often for his family, were described as impious *(budao, dani)* and harmful *(bujing).* But, as we shall see, these terms were applied fairly loosely and vaguely when someone had to be removed.

The Notion of Collective Responsibility

Collective responsibility of the group for actions committed by one of its members was a salient feature of Han law. Although it became less and less acceptable as moral standards and attitudes changed, it was doubtless retained because it sanctioned a more effective form of repression; the gravity of the misdemeanour determined the number of members of the group—most commonly the family—to be held responsible.

A distinction may be drawn between the several types of collective responsibility. The first implied a presumption of connivance or complicity, as in the case, for example, of counterfeiters and their neighbours. The second, which was religious in origin, was linked to the idea of defilement; the defilement attaching to a crime and to the criminal could only be effaced by exterminating the group, that is to say, the criminal's whole family, which it had in some way contaminated. A third form of collective responsibility associated the local official with the misdemeanours of his subordinates or with natural calamities that occurred in his district. In this case natural disasters looked like manifestations of the accused official's lack of virtue, in the same way as the occurrence and frequency of phenomena such as eclipses and earthquakes revealed lack of virtue on the part of the sovereign.

These different concepts of collective responsibility and solidarity were firmly rooted in the most ancient level of Chinese thought and remained indestructible until the twentieth century.

Sentences

So as to harmonize with the cycle of nature, to which human actions were thought to conform, capital executions had to take place in autumn and winter, the seasons of decline and death. An execution in spring would have hampered the progress of nature and caused catastrophes. By contrast spring was the time for pardons and mercy.

The condemned person was either beheaded or cut in two at the waist, the dead body being afterwards exposed to public view. Executions and exhibitions of the victims took place in market-places and at town gates.

The severest penalty under the Han was the extermination of the condemned person and his family. This included his parents, probably his paternal grandparents, his wife, children and perhaps his grandchildren and his brothers and sisters.

Sentences prescribing mutilation were of four types: castration or the 'sentence of rottenness', abolished in 167 B.C. and later restored as the commutation of the death penalty; amputation of the feet, likewise abolished in 167; amputation of the nose; and tattooing. The last two marks of ignominy were not sentences in themselves but an augmentation of the sentence of forced labour.

Forced labour in its various forms constituted the principal sentence of the Han period. The most severe was a term of five years. Convicts wore irons at the neck and their heads were shaved. They were employed on public works (the building of fortifications and of dikes on the Yellow River), in mines and foundries and in the imperial workshops. They were also used as soldiers in distant wars and in frontier garrisons. Prisoners condemned to forced labour thus constituted a considerable work-force for great governmental projects and therefore played an important part in the economy throughout the period.

The same is true to a lesser degree of the governmental slaves. Reduction to the rank of slave, the severest sentence after the death sentence,

might extend beyond the condemned man to the family of one who had been condemned to death and executed.

Exile was reserved mainly for members of the ruling class, as were dismissal and exclusion from public office, a sentence that could be extended to the relatives, descendants and even the friends of the accused.

Finally, minor offences were punishable by fines.

Political Aspects of Justice:
Ransom for Sentences and Amnesties

It was possible during the Han period in certain cases to avoid a sentence by paying a sum to the Treasury. This type of ransom, to be distinguished from a fine, depended on a special reprieve from the emperor. It took the form of permission granted exceptionally to an accused to pay a sum of money to redeem himself from a sentence that would normally have been served in a different way. The ransom for a nobleman might consist in renouncing his fief or title. Thus in 119 B.C. Gao Bushi was convicted of having fraudulently exaggerated the number of enemy heads captured during a campaign against the Xiongnu. His crime was punishable by beheading, but he was ransomed by being stripped of his marquisate of Yiguan.

The Han emperors granted a considerable number of amnesties. There were many occasions for these. Nearly all the emperors gave an amnesty at their accession, frequently also when they appointed a crown prince, and sometimes when they elevated a wife to the rank of empress. There were other occasions also that lent themselves to imperial mercy such as great religious ceremonies (sacrifices to Heaven, Earth, to the Supreme One, etc.), victories, exceptional harvests, good or bad omens.

There were also amnesties that applied only to a specified region or to a group. Thus when on his travels the emperor passed through a certain region he might grant an amnesty to the convicts of that region. In the same way some amnesties were probably designed to rally hostile clans.

It is hard to say how far an amnesty went. It appears to have implied that a sentence was commuted, rather than remitted in full.[2]

Chapter III

State Resources and the Distribution of Wealth

Chinese Territory before the Han

The empire at the beginning of the Han period was essentially inland territory. The coastal regions were sparsely populated or populated by non-'Han' ethnic groups; the political and economic centre lay in the north-west deep in the interior and remote from the sea, in particular from that other Mediterranean, the South China Sea.

As in the days of the Qin, the heart of the country was still central Shaanxi province, round the capital, now moved to Chang'an, north-west of modern Xi'an. This region (which was then called Guanzhong, 'inside the passes') is securely protected by its natural defences, the Qinling Mountains in the south and the Yellow River to the east. Within this stronghold the valleys of the Wei River and its tributaries form a fertile and densely populated basin.

The historian Sima Qian gives a true picture of the economic supremacy of central Shaanxi in the second century B.C.: 'Guanzhong occupies a third of the territory under Heaven with a population of three-tenths of the total; but its wealth constitutes six-tenths of the wealth of the empire.'[1]

To the south-west of Guanzhong difficult routes across the Qinling Mountains and the valley of the Han River (Hanzhong commandery) led to the rich commanderies of Ba and Shu in modern Sichuan province. This region, which is still not wholly Chinese, was a country of exile at the beginning of the Han period. Yet the eastern basin, and in particular the fertile plain around Chengdu,

already possessed a remarkable irrigation system constructed under the Qin by Governor Li Bing and his son. The most ambitious project was the Guanxian dam, by which the Min River could be divided into two main branches, each ramifying into many secondary canals for irrigation and transport; small businesses using hydraulic power were set up on the banks. The plain around

7
A salt mine.
Impressed brick from a tomb, (left) head frame over the well, (right) salt evaporates over a furnace, Chengdu, Sichuan, second century A.D. (See Zhongguo kexuequan ..., *Xin Zhongguo*, p. 112).

6

map, p. 222

Chengdu owed its fertility to this irrigation system. The region of Shu quickly became one of the three most prosperous centres of the empire, together with Guanzhong and Guandong (the region 'east of the passes'). Its wealth was not only agricultural but also industrial, and included craftsmanship: salt, iron and forests were developed; there were copper foundries, lacquer and bamboo workshop, etc.

The Great Plain stretches to the east of Guanzhong. In those days the mouth of the Yellow River was near the modern city of Tianjin. The vast expanse of country through which it flows (then called Guandong) comprises southern Shanxi, northern Henan, western Shandong and southern Hebei provinces. The second of the centres supplying grain to the capital at the beginning of the Han era, this region, which had been populated very early, gradually supplanted Guanzhong and under the Latter or Eastern Han became the key

economic zone of the empire. In addition to agriculture and the growing of hemp, Guandong developed prosperous industries, including silk-weaving—especially in Shandong—salt-working and iron metallurgy.

To the south of Guandong, the valley of the central and lower Yangzi River, the ancient kingdoms of Chu and Wu (in the modern provinces of Hubei, Anhui, Jiangsu, Zhejiang, Jiangxi and Hunan) had not yet assumed the importance they were to have from the time of the Latter Han. The population of

8
Wine cup *(bei)*.
Lacquered wood, handles plated in gilt bronze, H. 4 cm, L. 19 cm, W. 10.5 cm, painted decoration of birds and spirals, incised inscription surrounding the foot; found during excavations at Lelang, Korea, made in Sichuan province, dated A.D. 3.
Musée Guimet, Paris.

these regions was more scattered than in northern China, and because these areas lay at a distance from the political centre and also because they retained a sense of local identity, they remained a country of exile and colonization for the northerner; nevertheless, the *Records of the Historian,* and, to an even greater degree, archaeological finds testify to their great riches. These included the cultivation of rice in burn-baited and irrigated land, the salt marshes of the coastal plains, copper mines, lake and river fish, forestry and bamboo-work.

Despite the campaigns of Qin Shi Huangdi, the other southern provinces—Fujian, Guangdong, Guangxi, Guizhou and Yunnan—still belonged in *c.* 200 B.C. to independent kingdoms. It took the wars of conquest of the end of the second century B.C. to bring these kingdoms, with which Chinese merchants had long traded, into the Han orbit.

In the north of Guangdong, along and to the south of the Great Wall, Chinese families of soldier-farmers rubbed shoulders with nomadic cattle-breeders. Here again the first Han emperors continued to pursue Qin policy. Convicts, freed slaves, soldiers and peasants who had been victims of disasters were sent to settle and develop the arid ground of the northern confines and defend the frontier.

In 198 B.C. simultaneously with these movements of population to the north and north-west, several rich and influential clans, most of whom belonged to the old states of Chu and Qi, totalling over 100,000 individuals, were moved to the region of the capital. Once uprooted, these old aristocratic families became politically harmless.

State Resources

Taxation

Capitation *(fu)* was levied on the whole population, as it had been in pre-imperial days. The tax was called *soanfu* in the case of adult men and women between fifteen and fifty-six years old and *koufu* in that of children between seven and fifteen years old, and of old men. The *soanfu* (120 cash for an adult) was collected by the public treasury, while the revenue from the *koufu* (20 cash per child

or old man) went into the private treasury of the imperial house. Soldiers, officials above a certain grade and the highest ranks of the nobility were exempt. By contrast, merchants paid a double capitation tax, as did masters for their slaves.

In addition to the capitation there was a land tax *(tianzu)* calculated according to the extent of the area under cultivation. This tax, which was the basis of all the financial resources of the State, was levied in grain by the local authorities. In 203 B.C. the rate of the land tax was fixed at one-fifteenth of the harvest and in 156–155 B.C. reduced to one-thirtieth (33.3%), but no account was taken of the quality of the soil, annual variations in the crop or the type of grain harvested (millet, wheat or rice).

The greater part of this land tax remained *in situ* in the provinces to pay local expenses. The part sent to the capital was put to many uses, including maintenance of troops, salaries of officials of the central administration, provisions for the army when on military campaign, and reserves in case of famine. The annual task of levying and forwarding to the capital part of the local revenue in the form of tribute in grain was considered one of the essential duties of the local officials.

Civil and Military Service

In theory military (or civil) service was universal. Each man was registered in his native place at the age of twenty *sui*. (A person's age *sui* is the current year and not the past one. In China the age of an individual is calculated according to the number of calendar years during which he has lived. Even if he was born on the last day of the year, that year is counted as a year of age; similarly, if he dies on the first day of the new year, that year is counted. Thus twenty *sui* for a living individual is the equivalent of nineteen years by western reckoning. The ages given here follow the Chinese system.) From twenty onwards a man had to do a month's civil service (public works) in his sub-prefecture every year; then at twenty-three and twenty-four a month's military service in the local militia annually. From twenty-five to twenty-six he had to do three days of military service at the frontier annually. These periods of compulsory service might be lengthened by special conscription in the event of war or when some great project was undertaken.

Thus in the spring of 192 B.C. 146,000 men and women were conscripted for 30 days to build the walls of the capital; in the autumn of the same year 20,000 convicts continued the work.

Officials and members of the highest ranks of the aristocracy were exempt from corvées (civil service) and military service. Corvées could be avoided by hiring a substitute at 300 cash a month. As regards military service, there was little sense in short annual periods at the frontier. And whereas in peace-time there was no point in assembling large forces, it was preferable in time of war, or for the frontier garrisons, to employ regular soldiers or, at least, trained men who were used for longer periods. Thus, in practice, only some of the conscripts were sent to the frontiers and then for longer periods. Those who were not included paid a tax designed to maintain substitutes.

Thus from the very beginning of the dynasty application of taxes and compulsory service was extremely uneven. Either by right or *de facto,* the privileged classes (the aristocracy, officials and rich contractors) escaped simply by virtue of their social position, or else money enabled them to pay for substitutes. The peasants, artisans and small tradesmen were left to bear the burden of taxation and compulsory service.

Nevertheless, as we shall see, the first sixty years of the dynasty were characterized by an economic recovery, and taxation of all sorts was relatively light in comparison to what it would become later.

The Army

At the beginning of the Han dynasty, from 206 to 130 B.C., the composition of the army and its weaponry remained unchanged from the reign of Qin Shi Huangdi. The army then consisted of an enormous body of infantrymen who surrounded the chariots and were supported by cavalry.

The astonishing formation unearthed near the mausoleum of Qin Shi Huangdi, with its statues of warriors and horses modelled in earthenware, the remains of its wooden chariots and what has survived of its bronze weapons, is unquestionably the best source for the study of the military organization and equipment of the period.

It shows that the infantry was defended by an advance guard of archers and foot soldiers without armour and by horsemen on the flanks and at the rear. The chariots were placed between the advance guard and the main body of the infantry. The fact that there were almost equal numbers of chariots and cavalry (e.g. in pit No. 2: 89 chariots, 116 horsemen, 562 foot soldiers) shows that the cavalry had not reached the position of supremacy that it was to occupy in the Han army from the second century B.C.

Suitable for combat in open country, chariots had been the main force of the Shang (sixteenth to eleventh century B.C.) and the Western Zhou (1027–771 B.C.) dynasties. But from the sixth century B.C. onwards foot soldiers assumed increasing importance in the battles fought by the kings.

Cavalry was introduced into China by the king of Zhao at the end of the fourth century to combat the horsemen of the steppes who harried the northern marches of his state. He created a body of mounted bowmen who, like the nomads, could shoot from horseback. He ordered the long, cumbersome Chinese robe to be replaced by the trousers and tunic of the horsemen of the steppes.

Chariots required flat, dry ground for their manoeuvres, as well as a body of foot soldiers to defend them. Being far more mobile, cavalry could be used in very rapid engagements and on uneven ground that would have been inaccessible to chariots. Although during the third and second centuries B.C. the chariot remained the symbol of authority and continued to be used by staff officers, its tactical rôle gradually diminished.

All that remains of the real wooden chariots that accompanied the army at the mausoleum of Qin Shi Huangdi is their imprint and some bronze trappings. Vestigial though they are, these remains enable us to reconstruct the form of the chariots, which does not differ significantly from that of the chariots of the Period of the Warring States (fifth to third century B.C.). The light body was square (between 1.30 m and 1.50 m wide by 1.20 m long) and was surrounded by a balustrade on the front, sides and part of the rear, from which the chariot

9
Cavalrymen.
Earthenware, painted, H. (individual figures) c. 68.5 cm, discovered at Yangjiawan, Xianyang, Shaanxi, c. 179–141 B.C.

28

was entered. The two wheels measured 1.80 metres in diameter. The chariot was drawn by four horses attached to the shaft by a cross-piece supporting yokes in the shape of inverted Vs for the two inside horses, while the two outside horses were harnessed by means of leather traces.

The chariot carried a driver and one or two armoured fighting men, one of whom was often an officer, and was defended by a body of infantry of from eight to thirty-two men and sometimes by cavalry as well. The chariot-driver, whose social status remained superior to that of the infantryman—as is shown by the different sizes of the statues (1.75 m to 1.86 m for infantrymen; 1.82 m to 1.92 m for chariot drivers; 1.96 m for the largest statue, that of the commanding officer)—wore a calf-length gown over trousers. His chest and sometimes the upper side of his arms and hands were protected by armour.

The cavalrymen wore tunics over long, straight trousers. A short armoured vest reaching to the waist and not covering the top of the arms was worn over the tunic. The horse wore a leather saddle resting on a saddle blanket hung with little bells and ribbons. The saddle was secured by two girths and a crupper, but there were no stirrups. In fact stirrups did not make their appearance in China until after the Han period, and the earliest known representation dates from the year A.D. 302.[1] Cavalrymen were armed with swords and some with crossbows as well.

In the Qin army draught and riding horses were both of the same race, recognizable by its thick-set body, short legs and broad neck.

The cavalry remained the weak point of the army in the early days of the Han in their encounters with the Xiongnu. The Chinese government possessed only a handful of large stud farms in the western and north-western commanderies (Tianshui, Longxi, Anding, Beidi, Shang and Xihe). Most of the 320,000 men who made up the Chinese forces during Emperor Gaozu's ill-fated campaign against the Xiongnu in 201 were infantrymen. Gaozu assessed the superiority of the mobile Xiongnu cavalry over the Chinese infantry and realized that he would have to bring his army up to equal strength. But the economic situation precluded any idea of horse-breeding on a large scale. So half measures were taken, and in 178 Wendi decreed that three members of any family sending a horse to the government would be exempted from conscription. Not until political stability and economic prosperity were established in the last years of the reign of Jingdi (156–141 B.C.) could the government equip itself with a cavalry. Thirty-six grazing grounds, where horses were also broken in and trained, were created in the frontier regions of the north and west.

So the main body of the army under the Qin and the early Han was composed of foot soldiers, who constituted the majority of the conscripts. Those in Shi Huangdi's mausoleum were armed with spears, knives and longbows or crossbows. They wore knee-length gowns, puttees, square-toed sandals and armour covering the chest and upper arms. Archers and crossbowmen were similarly dressed, except that they wore trousers instead of puttees.

Apart from their size, the officers of this army are distinguished by the way in which their hair is dressed, the finer quality of their armour and the ornaments on their uniform rather than by any real difference in costume. Their double gown, worn over trousers, is knee-length. Their armour has shoulder-pieces, reaches to the waist at the back and is extended in front into a sort of apron.

From the end of the third century B.C. armour was already being made of a combination of metal (most probably iron) and leather. It was composed of overlapping plates. The square or rectangular plates were rigid on the chest and back but flexible on the shoulders, stomach, loins and round the neck. The plates were secured by rivets which were more numerous on the fixed plates than on the flexible ones; these were laced with cords. The plates on the chest were probably made of iron, those on the shoulders of leather.

Most of the weapons were still made of bronze; very few were of iron. Most of the arrows, spears, war axes and the mechanisms of the crossbows in the trenches around Shi Huangdi's mausoleum were made of bronze. Swords appear to have been fairly uncommon, and only officers, fighting charioteers and cavalrymen carried them.

The many statues of infantrymen and cavalry[9] found at Yangjiawan[2] and dating from the period 179 to 141 confirm the more realistic and precise information provided by the army of Shi Huangdi's mausoleum. These statuettes also show that the importance of the cavalry increased in relation to the infantry.

The Distribution of Wealth

Following upon the disorganization of production and the migrations caused by the rebellion against the Qin and by civil war, the period 179 to 141 saw a resumption of economic activity and a further increase in population. Agriculture gradually became prosperous again. At the same time, freedom to mint and the relaxation of restrictions on the development of secondary activities benefited the merchant and industrial classes.

Coinage

The monopoly of coining imposed by the Qin dynasty was abolished in 205 B.C. and replaced by a policy of free coinage. The coinage issued by the government was made of a standard alloy of copper and tin. In commercial transactions and government reckonings this legal cash stood as the norm against which heavier or lighter cash were weighed.

At the accession of the Han dynasty the Qin copper coin *(banliang)* weighing 12 *shu* or 7.60 grams was replaced by a lighter cash weighing 3 *shu* (1.92 g), in 186 by a *banliang* cash weighing 8 *shu* (5.12 g), in 182 again by a cash of 3 *shu,* and finally by a *banliang* cash weighing 8 *shu.*

A roll of cash was made up of a thousand pieces *(qian);* ten rolls, i.e. 10,000 cash, were worth a gold ingot of 1 *jin.* The Han monetary system was in fact based on the gold standard. The unit of reference, the gold *jin* (an ingot of about 244 g) was square-shaped with rounded corners, thicker in the centre than at the edges and called *bing,* for the shape suggested that of a cake.

In 205 B.C. a *shi* (20 l) of hulled grain was worth 10,000 cash (weighing 3 *shu*), a horse was worth 100 gold *jin* (or 1,000,000 cash). In the second century B.C. a very large fortune was reckoned at 10,000 gold *jin* or the equivalent of 100 million cash.

Counterfeit money, consisting of alloys of poor quality or coins that weighed light, continued to be made as long as coining was free, i.e. until 112 B.C. Furthermore, government apathy provided some with the opportunity to make considerable sums by melting down coins.

Wealth and political power—the two were usually closely linked—determined social status at the beginning of the Han era. At this period officials were recruited on grounds of wealth; money was used to buy not only land to lease, but also promotion and titles in the hierarchy of official functions. Although in the second half of the century the enrichment of the merchant and industrial classes was slowed down to a considerable extent, Counsellor Chao Cuo's words reflect the situation during the years 170 to 140 with some clarity: 'The merchants, whom laws and regulations disparage, are rich and honoured; while the peasantry, which the same laws honour, is poor and despised.'

In Han texts the 'people' *(shuren, min)* included farmers, craftsmen, shopkeepers and merchants, in contrast to the officials and the aristocracy.

The Peasantry

The peasant family of the Han period corresponded almost exactly to our conjugal family of four or five, though naturally with regional variations. The group, i.e. parents and two or three children, worked a plot of land of about 100 *mu* (approximately 4.5 ha) producing grain, with, in all probability, a garden, a walled farmyard and mulberry trees—all on a very small scale.

In a petition addressed to Wendi in 178, Chao Cuo described the life of the peasants thus:

Today, of a peasant family of five members, two are forced to perform corvées. The area of the fields that the family is capable of cultivating does not exceed 100 *mu,* and the harvest from a field of 100 *mu* is rarely more than 100 *shi* [20 hl] of seed.

In spring they plough, in summer they weed, in autumn they reap, in winter they gather in. They also have to cut wood for the winter, repair public buildings and engage in many other public works as part of their corvées. In spring they are exposed to the biting wind and dust; in summer they are subjected to the burning sun; numbed by the autumn rains, they shiver in winter. They have not a single day of rest in the whole year. And in this life of toil they must also find time for their family duties: accompanying departing members, receiving those who arrive, going to funerals, visiting the sick, caring for orphans and bringing up their children. They are harassed by a thousand chores, and further overwhelmed by natural disasters—drought or floods. They must submit to the injunctions of a too-hurried government, unseasonable collection of taxes, orders given in the morning and countermanded in the evening. So those who have some property sell it at half its value; those who own nothing borrow and undertake to repay twice the amount, so that finally the peasant is often obliged to sell all his property, his fields, his house and sometimes even his children and grandchildren to settle his debts.[3]

In his desire to draw the attention of the emperor to the danger represented by the newly rich merchants who were monopolizing the peasants' land,

Chao Cuo may have painted a rather blacker picture in order to make his point. In any case, the family owning 100 *mu* of land in 178, as cited by Chao Cuo, was not the worst off. As we have seen, the land tax was relatively low, and there were few natural disasters during the period. The fate of a peasant owning a plot of less than 100 *mu* was more precarious, and worse still was that of a farmer who cultivated the land of a landlord to whom he had to surrender half the harvest, or that of an agricultural labourer who was hired for the season.

The Merchant Class

Throughout the dynasty the possession of land spelt at least a minimum of security. This was of course true of the peasant class, but applied also to all who were in a position to invest. And during the first half of the second century B.C. merchants were still legally entitled to buy land and so to become landowners.

During the Han period the merchant class included not only shopkeepers and all those who

10
Landscape of south central China, Hubei province.

lived directly by commerce, but also the entrepreneurs who developed the mines (especially iron and cinnabar), salt merchants, cattle-breeders and usurers.

Traditionally disparaged in the hierarchy of social standing, crafts and trade were regarded by the educated of the early Han period as secondary or unproductive activities in contrast to agriculture, the essential activity on which the survival of the country depended. Furthermore, because of the wealth that they accumulated, the techniques that they mastered, the transactions that they negotiated, the contacts that they made, craftsmen and merchants, symbols of luxury and unnecessary expenditure—the first steps on the road to depravity and ruin—constituted a potential power that had to be controlled.

There were many families of great merchants and newly rich entrepreneurs at the beginning of the Han dynasty, among them the Zhuo and Cheng of Linqiong in south-west Sichuan province, who were famous for their iron foundries. The Zhuo owned nearly one thousand domestic slaves, land under cultivation, fish-ponds and hunting parks. As Chao Cuo bitterly remarks, this merchant class bought up land, dressed in silk, ate nothing but meat and the best cereals, rode sleek horses, drove fine carriages and consorted with princes and marquises. Fortunes such as these were a threat to the small operator, who was duped when he sold the produce of his land, paid expensively for essentials such as salt and iron tools, and ran into debt until a disaster or an accumulation of debts compelled him to sell his land and become a tenant-farmer to his creditors.

The fortunes of the merchants also threatened those other notables, the officials, who from this period onwards endeavoured to keep the monopoly of leased land and public office for themselves.

11
Bi disc.
Green jade, D. 30,2 cm, decoration of interlacing dragons forming four masks on the outer ring and circles in low relief, heightened with incised spirals, on the inner ring, end of the second century or first century B.C.
Metropolitan Museum of Art: Rogers Fund, 1917, New York.

The Officials and the Aristocracy

At the beginning of the dynasty, entry into a career in government depended on three things: a fortune, connections and recommendation. A fortune represented the commonest means of selection, since a minimum sum of 100,000 cash was required of a candidate for an official post, even, it would appear, for the post of a petty official in the central administration. The second means of selection was birth: to those with a father or close relative who was a high official the door was open. The third and straitest gate was recommendation. In an edict of 196, probably at the instigation of his prime minister, Xiao He, Gaozu requested his provincial officials to send all the meritorious and virtuous men known to them to the prime minister so that their talents might be used and they might be given a post. This practice, continued by Wendi and, after him by Wudi, may be considered the forerunner of the examination system.

The aristocracy of the empire—at the beginning of the second century B.C. it was essentially an aristocracy of the newly rich—included members of the imperial clan of the Liu, Gaozu's former companions in arms, the bravest generals and the highest dignitaries, as well as some members of the

families of the empresses and imperial favourites.

The emperor would normally choose one of his sons to succeed him and create the others vassal kings *(wang)*. To these he granted a fief, i.e. land and those living on it. These kings lived in their kingdoms, held court there, collected taxes and raised troops. They were obliged to return to Chang'an annually in the tenth month to pay homage to the emperor and to pay into the imperial treasury a tax of 4 gold *jin* (40,000 cash) for each thousand inhabitants of the fief. This court reception coincided with the New Year, celebrated until 104 B.C. on the first day of the tenth month. Their stay at Chang'an did not exceed twenty days and included audiences and banquets. They presented the emperor with jade rings *(bi)* and skins as tokens of good wishes for the New Year and as symbols of allegiance. In return they received gold, cash and various lavish gifts.

At the beginning of the Han dynasty, at the death of a king, his eldest son alone inherited the kingdom while the others merely received separate marquisates. Later, although the title of king remained the privilege of one of the sons only, the others received marquisates carved out of the kingdom, a measure which had the effect of reducing the size and power of the kingdoms.

Forced to live in their fiefs and thus excluded from public duties, the kings had no influence on the affairs of state except through the rebellions that they fomented up to 154 B.C. After 145 they had little political power in their own kingdoms, since from then onwards even their counsellors were appointed for them by the imperial court. Condemned to idleness, some kept brilliant courts, like Liu An (179–122 B.C.), prince of Huainan, who surrounded himself with Taoists and commissioned a collection of philosophical writings known as the *Huainanzi*.

The first Han marquises had been Gaozu's companions in arms; later, besides kings' sons, victorious generals, high dignitaries and relatives of empresses and favourites received marquisates. The power of the marquises in their fiefs was minimal. Justice, finance and administration were taken out of their hands and given to government officials; almost their only privilege, therefore, was the fiscal revenue (capitation and land tax) that they received, and this was often considerable. A mar-

quisate might contain between several hundred and over ten thousand homesteads. The marquises had the advantage over the kings that they were not bound to live in their marquisates, so that court appointments were open to them. Like all the members of the aristocracy and the high officials, they enjoyed a degree of protection before the law. The emperor's permission was required before severe punishment could be imposed upon them. However, this did not ensure total immunity; the law remained harsh for all, but the high dignitaries of the empire, if condemned to capital punishment, were permitted by special favour to commit suicide.

In addition to those with ties of blood and merits, the emperor's relatives by marriage—the families of the empresses and favourites—could be ennobled. Since from the beginning of the Han dynasty the emperor's blood relations were systematically excluded, the history of the dynasty was marked by blood rivalries between the clans that were related to the emperor by marriage.

There were many women of high rank in an emperor's palace and even more of lower degree. Similarly with the palace of the crown prince and, to a lesser extent, those of the kings and marquises. Powerful families sought positions for their daughters in the palace; young women of lower rank were chosen at beauty contests and were submitted from all parts of the empire. Some would have been noticed and chosen by the emperor during one of his journeys. When one of the emperor's women bore a child, especially if it were a boy, her male realtives received court appointments.

The crown prince was chosen by the emperor himself. In theory he should have been his eldest son, but the choice might fall upon the most brilliant, the one of whom he was fondest or indeed the son of the wife who belonged to the most powerful clan. Once the emperor had chosen, the mother of the crown prince automatically became empress and her family began to rise in the world. The first step was a title and a marquis's fief, which were usually bestowed on her father and often on her brothers. Little by little the close relatives of the empress managed to place members of their clan in government. As sons of the emperor by other wives grew up, they were sent to fiefs remote from the capital, so that their maternal family was deprived of its main access to the court.

Intrigue was not confined to this simple system. Sometimes an empress was repudiated, sometimes a crown prince was deposed before he ascended the throne and was replaced; sometimes too an emperor died without male issue and was compelled to choose a successor from the collateral line.

At the death of an emperor the crown prince ascended the throne. His mother became dowager empress; the new emperor's maternal grandfather, his uncles or cousins received new privileges. If the new emperor were young, his mother and uncles exercised real control over him and, through him, over the government. If he were an adult, already possessing several wives and many sons, the struggle over the choice of a crown prince began all over again. Thus different families related to the throne by marriage might simultaneously occupy important offices in the government and carry on intrigues to maintain or increase their power. The families in question would be those of the dowager empress, of the empress and of the wives of the crown prince. The empress was often considerably younger than her husband the emperor and might sometimes survive her son—in which case she was able to protect the interests of her clan for several decades.

In fact it was mainly from the time of Jingdi (156–141 B.C.) that the intrigues of the empresses' families began to besmirch Han domestic policy. However, the reign of Huidi (194–188), who ascended the throne at the age of sixteen and died when he was twenty-three, and the regency of his mother, the Dowager Empress Lü (who died in 180), was one succession of assassinations perpetrated by Lü. Her victims were the favourites of Gaozu and Huidi, as well as most of Gaozu's surviving sons. Reaction came swiftly at the death of Lü: in two months her clan was exterminated. The high officials and the heads of the Liu clan chose as Emperor Gaozu's eldest surviving son, the future Wendi (179–157).

Considerable space has been devoted to this somewhat fluid class, the aristocracy of the empire composed of the imperial families, because the mechanism of their rise and fall and their intrigues played a crucial part in the history of the period and strongly influenced the attitudes of those close to the throne. Moreover, the system was not wholly bad, for it was a continuing source of new blood for the aristocracy and of talent for the top ranks of government. The rivalries in themselves prevented a single family from monopolizing power for too long, and those families that owed their rise to the sovereign alone had no cause to harm him.

At all events, social fluidity, with its rises and dizzy falls, was one of the main features of the period of the Former Han. A man and his whole family might rise rapidly to the top of the social scale, while others fell headlong from the pinnacle to find themselves slaves or convicts again. Thus the aristocratic families of the leaders of the rebellion of the Seven Kingdoms in 154 B.C. were reduced to slavery.

The foundation of the Han dynasty had in itself been a total revolution and an unprecedented event, for it had brought men of the people, even convicted criminals, to power and had finally submerged what remained of the feudal aristocracy. Leaving aside Gaozu, the uneducated head of a posting station, his main companions, who later became marquises, were all men of the people and often natives of the same region (the north of Jiangsu province) as himself. They owed their rise to neither birth nor fortune, but to their talents.

One of the characteristics of the aristocracy of the empire was its impermanence. By 86 B.C., i.e. a little over a century later, none of the direct or collateral descendants of the marquises elevated by Gaozu, that is, the men who helped to found the dynasty, had retained his title of nobility.

It was not only the upper classes that were fluid. Any individual could find himself a convict or slave again from one day to the next; inversely, descendants of slaves or convicted criminals could become free men and even be ennobled later. Imperial amnesties were frequent, and in theory all convicted criminals were freed and their characters cleared after five years. In the same way slaves could regain their liberty and return to the mass of the people. We shall return to the question of this fluidity, to the feeling of instability and fragility that it implies, and to the atmosphere of rivalry, suspicion and violence that coloured it, at least in court circles.

Chapter IV

A Period of Consolidation of Power (206–141 B.C.)

A violent wind had risen
  Clouds towered and raced...
I have imposed my prestige on the world,
  And return to my native place.
Where shall I find heroes
  To guard the four horizons?[1]

Gaozu improvised this 'Song of the Great Wind' in the heat of a banquet at which wine flowed freely during a visit to his native region in 196. The poem, which was to become one of the ritual songs used in certain ceremonies in the ancestral temples, reflects the founder's career and aims: five years of civil war (206–202), the establishment of institutions and men for the protection of the empire from without and within, followed rapidly by mistrust of those whose loyalty seemed doubtful, a degree of inaction in the government of the people, an attitude of compromise in foreign policy and, behind all this, anxiety about the cultural unification of the country.

For sixty years Gaozu's successors (see table, p. 10) faced the same problems and tried with varying degrees of success to solve them, thus preparing the way for the political changes of the reign of Wudi (140–87 B.C.).

The Aristocracy of the Empire Reduced to Obedience

There was endless conflict throughout the period between the kings and the central government. The kings sought to maintain their independence and increase their power, while the government, conscious of the danger that this latent power might explode, endeavoured to reduce the size of the kingdoms and to control their administration. The crisis came to a head under Jingdi (156–141) with the rebellion of the Seven Kingdoms, a coalition set up in 154 by the Prince of Wu (modern Jiangsu province), lord of the richest of the vassal kingdoms. The revolt was put down in a few months, and thereafter the central power hastened the dismantling and control of the kingdoms.

A Policy of Appeasement

At the end of the third century B.C., after years of blinkered absolutism, extortion and warfare, the one desire of the Chinese people was for a truce and for security. While preserving the essential character of the Qin structures, the first Han emperors managed to make them more flexible and to promote a policy of non-interference in the administration that restored a measure of freedom and allowed the economy to revive. The ban on books was lifted in 191; in 167 penal mutilation was abolished; land tax and charges that weighed on the population were reduced; the coining of money was freed. At the same time, the emperors, and Wendi (179–157) in particular, insisted on a rough and frugal simplicity at court that contrasted with the megalomania of Qin Shi Huangdi.

However, the policy of appeasement and non-interference was not without its dangers. Wherever control was relaxed, rich landowners and merchants sought to dispossess the peasants of their land, and the end of the period saw a renewal of banditry and the activity of desperadoes *(youxia)*.

Towards Cultural Unification

Together with political separatism, local independence posed another threat of disruption to the new dynasty. Following the brief period of unification imposed by the Qin, China remained a confederation of states that had until recently been independent and of regional cultures that were very much alive. But political centralization needed cultural foundations. Gradually the ethical standards and ritual practices of the old state of Lu (in the west of modern Shandong province), home of Confucius and 'repository' of ancient traditions, came to predominate. As early as the reign of Gaozu, court ceremonial was created by invoking the aid of the scholars of Lu and combining Confucian ceremonial with that of the Qin court. In its eclecticism the process heralds what was to be the triumph of Confucianism as the official ideology in the reign of Wudi (140–87).

12
Landscape of Mongolia, region of the Northern Xiongnu, in the centre of the present central *aimag* of the People's Republic of Mongolia, near the capital, Ulan Bator.

The Xiongnu Peril and
the Chinese Compromise

The Xiongnu were not the first nomadic horsemen to attack northern China. As early as the end of the ninth century B.C. in Shaanxi, the Zhou were compelled to repulse attacks made by the Xianyun, who probably came from the Altai Mountains. These invasions were followed by others by the Bei Rong and the Di, who repeatedly attacked the small Chinese states in Shanxi province and neighbouring regions.

By the ninth century a pastoral nomadic culture based mainly on vast herds of horses—but also including agriculture of a kind—had spread over the whole area of the steppes. Although they failed to form a united political entity, these different groups of pastoral nomads shared certain cultural characteristics and a complex social structure dominated by a class of mounted warriors trained as archers. The technique of shooting in which the horseman turns in his saddle and shoots back over his shoulder was already familiar to the nomads of the ninth century. It was the only possible means of defence against warriors from the agricultural communities who were better armed and possessed war-chariots. Another characteristic of the nomadic peoples from the Caucasus to eastern Mongolia was their animal-style art. The mounted archers decked and adorned their horses with a whole panoply of ornaments—most made of bronze, but some of other materials—evoking their life and enjoyments: war and hunting.

12 By the end of the third century B.C., starting out from central Mongolia, the Xiongnu had brought all the ethnic groups of nomadic habits into what amounted to an empire extending from the Amur basin to that of the Irtysh in the west, and from Lake Baikal in the north to the loop of the Yellow River in the south (map, p. 223). To what ethnic and linguistic group the Xiongnu belonged is a matter of controversy. Some regard them as proto-Mongols, some as proto-Turks, while others would ally them to the palaeo-Siberian family.

The Xiongnu expansion coincided with the unrest that followed the death of Qin Shi Huangdi. Maodun (209–174), the Xiongnu chief, now subjugated the Donghu, nomadic cattle-raisers in western Manchuria and eastern Mongolia, and turned again to fight the Yuezhi. In the second century B.C., the Yuezhi, who are described as having light-coloured skin and speaking an Indo-European language, occupied western Gansu province and the region between the Altai and Tianshan mountains. In 175 or 174 B.C., ousted by the Xiongnu, the Yuezhi began their westward migration. A branch of the group, the Great Yuezhi, were to play a part in the destruction of the Greek kingdom of Bactria and the foundation of the Kushan empire.

Other peoples—the Wusun, nomads to the north of the Yuezhi, who also spoke an Indo-European language; the Qiang of Gansu, the Wuhuan of southern Manchuria—were subjugated by the Xiongnu, whose chief could boast in a reply to Wendi of the Han that he had 'made a single family of all the nations of archers'.[2]

The Xiongnu economy in the first half of the second century B.C. was based mainly on cattle-rearing (horses, bovids and sheep). There is evidence that agriculture existed, although it was of secondary importance. Tribute exacted from the conquered peoples, gifts and payments from 'friendly' states, and trade with foreign countries represented a not inconsiderable source of revenue.

Certain practices were borrowed from China, in particular the use of the title *shanyu* by Maodun and his successors, a term adapted from *huangdi* ('august emperor'), the pompous title assumed by the first Qin emperor. Thus, copying Qin Shi Huang-di, Maodun called himself the First *Shanyu*.

Also under Chinese influence, they built fortified towns, although they still retained their traditional yurts. Their love of luxury was reflected in their clothing, which was made mainly of leather, furs and silk imported from China, and in the jewels and ornaments with which they adorned themselves. Their bronze, gold or silver plaques and belt buckles continued to follow the animal style. The favourite theme was animal combat, which depicts a wild beast or a bird of prey attack-

13
Belt-buckle.
Gold. Mongolia: Xiongnu art, second century B.C.
Metropolitan Museum of Art, New York.

14
Plaque.
Bronze, H. 8.4 cm, L. 11 cm, Mongolia: Xiongnu art, second century B.C.
British Museum, London.

ing an ibex or a deer. But it was now treated in a more stylized and abstract manner than had been the case in the steppe art of earlier centuries. Bodies might be elongated, compressed or distorted to the point at which they become unidentifiable. Horns and manes took on a fantastic appearance, and certain ancient conventions were used fairly regularly; these included circular hollows at the articulation of the paws and almond-shaped hollows in the 13–14 borders of the plaques (which were originally encrusted with stones) and to suggest hooves and ears.

The formation of this great nomadic empire on her northern marches was to constitute a formidable threat to China; for the first time in her history she was faced with a rival worthy of the name.

Hostilities between the Han and the Xiongnu opened with the Xiongnu invasion of Shanxi in 201. At the end of that year Gaozu was defeated at Pingcheng (east of modern Datong). Raids continued and Gaozu was forced to conclude a pact with the Xiongnu. Without the means to maintain and equip the earth fortifications he had inherited from the Qin, occupied in consolidating his power in the interior of the empire, Gaozu adopted a policy of appeasement towards the Xiongnu, which was known as *heqin,* 'peace and friendship'. Relations between the Chinese court and the nomads continued in this vein until 135 B.C. The Han court was compelled to send an annual tribute to the Xiongnu (which, in order to save face the Chinese described as 'gifts'); this consisted of an agreed quantity of silks, alcohol, rice and other foodstuffs, and a princess of the imperial family was given in marriage to the *shanyu*. This was a peace for which the Chinese court paid dearly, receiving in return nothing but a hollow promise of non-aggression from the Xiongnu. The Great Wall was to be considered the frontier between the two empires.

China profited little from the policy. The Xiongnu resumed their raids in Shanxi and Shaanxi provinces in 182, 181, 177 and 169. In 166, during the reign of Wendi, 140,000 horsemen crossed the passes of eastern Gansu and rode down the Wei valley to reach Ganquan, less than 150 kilometres (300 *li*) from the capital. Wendi mustered 100,000 horsemen and 1,000 chariots to defend Chang'an. Peace was concluded in 162, but did not prevent further raids in 158, 144 and 142. Thus the initiative remained with the Xiongnu throughout this period, while China adopted a defensive stance. At the same time, the demands of the Xiongnu for 'gifts' were growing, and by the reign of Wendi the Chinese court was obliged to add specie to a steeply rising volume of tribute.

40

Chapter V

Life in This World and the Next: The Mawangdui Tombs

Chinese culture in the first half of the second century B.C. was transitional in character; it would in fact be more correct to speak of Chinese cultures, for local nuances were still conspicuous.

The provincial region of Changsha in Hunan has been chosen for two good reasons as the point from which to approach certain aspects of material, intellectual and artistic life. The first and most obvious reason is that the wealth of information that the three burials discovered at Mawangdui provide make them some of the most important known burial complexes of Han China. The second reason stems from their actual location, for the legacy of the old kingdom of Chu was crucial for Han civilization.

map, p. 221   The three Mawangdui tombs lie in the eastern suburb of Changsha. The first (tomb No. 1), excavated in 1974, disclosed the body of a dead woman in a perfect state of preservation, a wealth of grave goods (over one thousand objects) and one of the masterpieces of Chinese painting. The second and third tombs were discovered a year later and enabled scholars to identify and date the three burials; in addition, tomb No. 3 contained a remarkable group of ancient texts on wooden and bamboo slips and on silk.[1]

The occupant of tomb No. 2 has been identified from the seals. He was Li Cang, appointed prime minister to the king of Changsha in 193, enfeoffed marquis of Dai, and who died in 186 B.C.—which dates the tomb.

From a votive inscription to the 'master of the tomb' written on one of the wooden slips found in tomb No. 3, the tomb has been dated to 168 B.C. Inscriptions on lacquers indicate clearly that the dead man belonged to the house of Dai. He was aged about thirty and is believed to have been a younger son of the marquis of Dai.

Tomb No. 1 is slightly later than Nos. 2 and 3, for these were damaged when it was constructed. The dead woman, aged about fifty, was probably Li Cang's wife and mother of the occupant of tomb No. 3.

Here, then, are three burials belonging to the same family: that of Li Cang, marquis of Dai, who died in 186 (tomb No. 2), his wife, whom we shall call the Marchioness of Dai, who died soon after 168 (tomb No. 1), and one of their sons, who died in 168 (tomb No. 3). The fief of Dai granted to Li Cang contained 700 homesteads. This means that the marquisate was comparatively modest and that revenue alone would not account for the fortune to which the three tombs at Mawangdui testify. Li Cang appears to have been the last prime minister appointed by the king of Changsha; his successor was nominated by the central government. Yet the kingdom of Changsha was the only one to have retained until 157 B.C. kings who were not members of the imperial clan of Liu. The kingdom occupied the greater part of the modern province of Hunan, the north-east of Guangxi and the north of Guangdong provinces, with Linxiang (modern Changsha) as its capital.

Structure of the Tombs

The three tombs are similar in structure; the following description is of tomb No. 1, which is the largest and most carefully laid out.

p. 226 The tomb consists of a vertical shaft hollowed out of the earth to a depth of some 16 metres and surmounted by a truncated cone-shaped mound measuring from 50 to 60 metres in diameter.

The rectangular shaft lies on a north-south axis and measures 19.50 metres (N-S) by 17.90 metres (E-W) at the top. For the first 4 metres below the base of the mound, the space between the walls narrows in four steps; below that the narrowing becomes funnel-shaped. An access ramp runs from the north side to the bottom of the shaft. The outer coffin (guo), containing four inner nested coffins (guan), was placed in this sort of burial chamber (7.60 m [N-S] by 6.70 m [E-W]).

The wooden outer coffin stood on struts and was completely surrounded by a 40-centimetre layer of charcoal followed by a layer of white clay measuring between 100 and 130 centimetres. These two layers completely insulated the coffins and ensured that they were protected from air and humidity—hence, undoubtedly, the admirable state of preservation of the coffins, the body and the burial goods. On top of these layers the shaft was filled in with rammed earth.

The outer coffin is built of 70 beams and planks of cypress with mortice and tenon jointing and wooden pegs. It forms what amounts to a chamber measuring 6.73 metres long by 4.81 metres wide by 2.80 metres high. Planks divide the interior into compartments: a chamber for the coffins at the centre and four lateral compartments, which con-

24 tained the burial goods. The central area contained four nested coffins: the first inner coffin (2.95 m by 1.50 m by 1.44 m high) consists of a kind of crate and is painted black; the second inner coffin (2.56 m by 1.18 m by 1.14 m high) is decorated with paintings of mythological figures and animals

27, 30 on a black lacquer ground; the third inner coffin (2.30 m by 0.92 m by 0.89 m high) is decorated in various colours on a ground of red lacquer with

28 symbols of good augury; the fourth and last inner coffin (2.02 m by 0.69 m by 0.63 m high) contained the body of the dead woman. The surfaces were covered with embroidered silk framing a central field of satin decorated with an appliqué of feathers stuck to the ground. On the lid of this coffin a painted banner had been laid face downwards towards the body.

The body lay stretched out on its back, its head to the north, and wrapped in some twenty garments one on top of the other, the whole tied with silk ribbons. The body (height 1.54 m) was intact; the skin, muscles and organs had retained some of their elasticity. Since this extraordinary discovery, another tomb, of the same date and construction—tomb No. 168 at Fenghuangshan (Jiangling district, Hubei province) from 167 B.C.—has revealed a well-preserved body of a man, Sui Shaoyuan, a *ling* sub-prefect.

The mode of burial adopted at Mawangdui—a vertical-shaft tomb containing several nested coffins—was the old traditional mode of burial of the Zhou and, more particularly in the case of Mawangdui, of the kingdom of Chu. In fact, another type of construction had made its appearance in northern China as early as the fourth century B.C. This was the chambered tomb. These tombs consist of a vertical shaft as before, but a cavity forming a chamber is hollowed out of one of the lateral walls of the shaft, and the coffin placed there instead of at the bottom of the shaft. The chamber was gradually enlarged to hold both the body and the burial goods, while the shaft was reduced in size and importance to become simply a means of access. This type of burial, combined with the use of hollow bricks, which in a sense replaced the outer wooden coffin, became the commonest in northern China during the period of the Former Han.

The old tradition—that of Mawangdui—persisted to the end of the Former Han in the densely wooded areas of the south and in some northern regions that had not been deforested.

15
Bei bowls and lacquered box to hold them.
Wood, lacquered and painted, H. (box) 12.2 cm, L. 19 cm, W. 16.5 cm, inscription on inside of bowls: 'lord please drink the alcohol', from tomb No. 1 at Mawangdui, Changsha, Hunan, soon after 168 B.C.

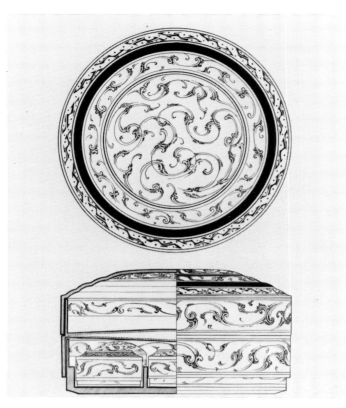

17
The nine small boxes inside the lower compartment of the toilet box in Pl. 16.

16
Drawing of toilet box *(lian)* with two compartments.
Lacquer on wood, D. 35.2 cm, H. 20.8 cm, decoration painted in red, gold and silver on a black ground, from tomb No. 1 at Mawangdui, Changsha, Hunan, soon after 168 B.C. (See Hunan sheng ..., vol. I, figs. 84–5).

Burial Goods

Mawangdui tomb No. 1 contained a unique group of everyday articles that had belonged to the dead woman, replicas *(mingqi)* made at her death and provisions, all intended to accompany her to the next world: the group comprised silk clothing and accessories, furniture, toilet boxes, lacquer dishes, pottery and bamboo food containers, provisions, medicinal herbs, wooden figurines to ward off evil spirits, statuettes in painted wood or wearing real clothes representing the dead woman's ladies and musicians, musical instruments and burial money made of earthenware in imitation of real cash.

18
Bamboo basket.
Sealed with characters for 'steward of the House of the Marquis of Dai' impressed in the clay, H. 15 cm, L. 53 cm, W. 29 cm, from tomb No. 1 at Mawangdui, Changsha, Hunan, soon after 168 B.C.

19   ▷
Tomb statuettes *(mingqi)*.
Wood, painted, H. (left) 46.5 cm, (right) 49 cm, from tomb No. 1 at Mawangdui, Changsha, Hunan, soon after 168 B.C. (See Hunan sheng ..., vol. II, p. 202).

Most of the lacquers carry painted inscriptions naming their owner, 'house of the marquis of Dai', or their use or capacity (1 *shi,* 4 *dou,* etc.). The food containers are often sealed with characters impressed in clay reading 'steward of the house of the marquis of Dai'. The tomb also contained an inventory of the burial goods drawn up on 312 bamboo slips tied in rolls with hempen string.

As we shall see, the painted silk banner that lay at the top of the innermost coffin and the paintings on two of the coffins were intended to guide one of the souls of the dead woman and to protect it on its journey to the next world, while the other soul would remain in the tomb surrounded by all these earthly goods.

The contents of Li Cang's tomb (tomb No. 2) are much less well preserved and include lacquerware, ceramics, a few bronzes, many inlaid with gold, also earthenware imitations of cash, gold ingots and pearls, as in tomb No. 1.

As in the case of tomb No. 2, water had seeped into tomb No. 3. Nevertheless, the tomb disclosed over 1,000 articles, including 316 lacquers, similar in style and bearing the same inscriptions as those

18

21, 23

20

Dress made of plain-coloured silk gauze, edged with silk braid.
Max. L. 1.60 m, max. W. 2.28 m, from tomb No. 1 at Mawangdui, Changsha, Hunan, soon after 168 B.C. (See *Hunan sheng ...*, vol. II, p. 78).

21 ▷

Detail of the vertical field of the banner in Pl. 23 from tomb No. 1 at Mawangdui.
Paint on silk, soon after 168 B.C. (See *Xi Han bohua,* Pl. VI).

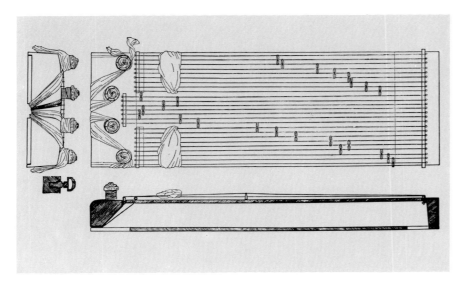

22
Drawing of a wooden *se* zither.
L. 1.16 m, W. 39.5 cm, from tomb No. 1 at Mawangdui, Changsha, Hunan, soon after 168 B.C. (See Hunan sheng ..., vol. I, fig. 94).

in tomb No. 1, wooden figurines and statuettes, many bamboo baskets containing provisions, clothing and pieces of silk, a game resembling backgammon, with its board, a lacquered wooden stand on which to rest weapons, lacquered crossbows and musical instruments. The tomb also contained four paintings on silk, including a banner similar to the one in tomb No. 1, an inventory on wooden slips and, most importantly, a highly significant group of texts on bamboo, wood and silk. The manuscripts on silk are the earliest texts on silk to have been found in China, apart from a manuscript of the Period of the Warring States, also found at Changsha. They were in a lacquer box which also contained three maps, the earliest known examples of Chinese cartography.

23
Drawing of a banner from tomb No. 1 at Mawangdui. Silk, H. 2.05 m, from Changsha, Hunan, soon after 168 B.C. (See Hunan sheng ..., vol. I, fig. 38).

48

Comfort and the Pleasures of the Table

Chinese houses of the Han period contained no seats; the family lived, worked and slept on floor-level or on low daises. Furniture included mats, low daises, arm-rests, chests and baskets, tables and low screens.

The mats found in the Mawangdui tombs are made of rushes or bamboo, mostly edged with braid, similar to the Japanese *tatami*. As is still the case with the latter, the mat of the Han period served as the unit of length for rooms, and the commonest measurements seem to have been fairly close to those of the modern *tatami*. Rules of etiquette required one to sit kneeling on one's heels on the mats, a posture that was transmitted from China to Japan via Korea.

Such mats, used as seating by all classes of society until the end of the dynasty, were also used for sleeping, at least by people in modest circumstances in central and southern China. The *kang* was already in use in northern China; this was an earthen platform faced with bricks and covered with mats, carpets, blankets or skins. A system of piping under the *kang* diffused an even heat from a hearth either inside or outside the house.

A wooden couch or low, movable platform, usually for a single person and with a canopy *(zhang)*, was already in use as a seat or bed in upper-class homes by the period of the Former Han. It became more common under the Latter Han.

To lessen the discomfort of kneeling on the heels a sort of combined arm and back-rest *(ji)* was used; it was a longish piece of furniture made of lacquered wood, comprising a flat top, sometimes curved inwards at the centre, and a stand. The high dignitary to whom prisoners of war are being presented on an engraved stone slab from Shandong province (middle register, left) leans on his elbow on a arm-rest of this type. He is seated on a dais, and a servant behind him holds a fly-whisk.

The screen, fixed and folding, was another piece of furniture represented at Mawangdui that was to be much used during the Han period. The example at Mawangdui is an almost square screen of painted wood (height 62 cm, length 72 cm, thickness 2.5 cm). In addition to their honorific and decorative purposes, these screens and, later, folding

24
Tomb No. 1 at Mawangdui, Changsha, Hunan.
View of the western half of the northern compartment of the outer coffin with burial goods—at the moment of discovery.

screens were certainly used as protection against draughts and perhaps sometimes as partitions in a bedroom.

In the homes of the rich the walls might be covered with hangings and paintings on silk. Two examples, unfortunately in very poor condition, were preserved in Mawangdui tomb No. 3. They are rectangular paintings (length 2.12 m, width 0.94 m) and were hung on the east and west walls of the chamber containing the coffins.

The Mawangdui tombs also contained a number of lacquered wooden boxes and baskets which at the time contained folded clothing, writing implements, manuscripts, toilet articles and some provisions.

Meals were taken at low tables, rather like individual rectangular or circular trays *(an)*, usually with feet; they were carried from the kitchens already laid with dishes, chopsticks, a spoon, cups with handles *(bei)* for gruel *(geng)* and for drinking alcohol, and a goblet for water. In the homes of the rich at least, all the tableware was made of lacquered wood, usually black outside and red within, enhanced with painted motifs. The same usually applies to trays. Metal (gilt bronze, silver and gold) or jade might replace lacquer in princely houses. Large wine jars and vessels for mulling wine were usually made of bronze and were sometimes gilt or inlaid. Ceramic vessels (earthenware and stoneware) were used largely for cooking and for preparing and storing solid food and liquids. Together with wood and bamboo, pottery dishes were also used by the poor and by all those who could not afford the luxury of lacquered tableware. Indeed, lacquer was more expensive even than bronze.

The variety and specialization of Han food containers is undoubtedly due to the variety of foods and of ways of preparing it already employed by Chinese cooks. In this latter sphere, the foods, methods of preparation and names of dishes found in the tombs of the Marchioness of Dai and her son confirm what is learnt from the chapter *'Neize'* ('Guide to the Domestic Virtues') of the *Liji* (first century B.C.), which had previously been our main source of information about Han food. They also enable us to study ingredients, preparation and presentation more closely and vividly.

Tomb No. 1 contained forty-eight bamboo baskets of prepared meats, fruit, etc., fifty-one ceramic containers (most of them full of food), hempen sacks of cereals, vegetables, cakes of sticky rice with honey or jujube jelly, a meal served in lacquer dishes, and bamboo slips that identify and provide valuable information on the methods of preparation and composition of the dishes. Tomb No. 3 contained a comparable selection.

Using evidence from these two tombs, some material from northern China—e.g. certain tombs at Shaogou to the north-west of Luoyang—and the chapter *'Neize'* of the *Liji,* an attempt has been made to list the main foods consumed during the second century B.C. Those which do not appear at Mawangdui are marked with a star:

cereals: rice, wheat, barley, millets and glutinous millet ('Job's tears'★);

vegetables (including tubers and roots): hemp-seed (often classed as a cereal in China), soya, kidney beans, mustard-seed, rape, bamboo shoots, lotus roots, taro, chives, lentils, ginger, melon, gourd★, mallow, shallot★, garlic★, knot-grass★, sow-thistle★;

fruit: pears, jujubes, plums, peaches, arbutus berries, oranges, persimmons, water-chestnuts;

meat (including poultry and game): beef, mutton, pork, sucking-pig, dog, horse★, hare, venison, boar★, chicken, pheasant, wild goose, duck, quail, sparrow (eggs were eaten);

fish: various kinds of carp, bream, perch;

seasoning and condiments: salt, sugar, honey, soya sauce *(jiang),* sauce made from salt beans *(shi),* leaven, vinegar, cinnamon, galingale, ginger;

beverages: various alcohols made from cereals (especially rice, wheat and millet), various fruit juices.

Methods of cooking included roasting, blanching, boiling, frying, braising and steaming. Foods were preserved by salting, sun-drying, smoking and pickling in vinegar. Many jars at Mawangdui contained meat and fish in brine, fish sauces, meat sauces and finely sliced or minced meat in a marinade.

The basic dish—and one with an already ancient tradition at the period of the Former Han—was *geng,* a kind of gruel or rather liquid stew that might contain cereals, pieces of meat and vegetables. Some *geng* were made of cereals and meat only, or meat and vegetables, or of vegetables only—recipes were limitless, depending on occasion and availability. The Mawangdui slips list some of these gruels in *ding* (tripod vessels in which food was cooked and served): venison and taro *geng,* fresh sturgeon *geng,* salt fish and lotus root *geng, geng* made of beef, rice, etc. The slips often

25
Toilet box *(lian).*
Lacquer, painted in red on a black ground and inlaid with silver leaf, D. 21 cm, first century B.C.
British Museum, London.

give particulars of the part of the animal that has been prepared (shoulder, tongue, liver, etc.).

Apart from the basic foods eaten by a rich family, the food buried at Mawangdui undoubtedly consisted mainly of refined dishes and foods of which the marchioness and her son were particularly fond. Also, our list takes little account of regional variations and social differences in eating. As a general rule the various kinds of millet and rice were the favourites, millets predominating in northern China and rice in the old kingdom of Chu and in Sichuan province. So rice was less common outside southern China and was still a luxury. It should be noted that cereals were eaten cooked, in the grain *(fan)*. Rice flour was the only milled grain and was used to make cakes; the use of wheat flour did not become widespread until the end of the Former Han.

The principal nourishment of the poor of northern China was wheat and soya; millet and meat gruel *(geng)* were dishes for feast days.

Cereals, meat, fish, fruit and vegetables might also be dried. The staple diet of travellers and soldiers on campaign, dried foods were also an important element in building up reserves of food and were ingredients in many recipes.

Chinese food in the second century B.C. remained unchanged from earlier centuries. Innovations appeared gradually in the wake of expansion from the reign of Wudi (140–87 B.C.) onwards. They took the form of imports or naturalization of new foods; and, especially from the first century B.C., the Chinese began to make noodles, steamed bread and wheat-flour cakes.

Personal Adornment

Two toilet or cosmetic boxes *(lian)* were found in tomb No. 1 at Mawangdui. They are circular, made of thin wood, the outsides covered in black lacquer, the insides in red. The more important of 16–17 the two consists of two inner compartments, one above the other, the outside decorated with painted geometric motifs in red, gold and silver. The upper compartment contained a towel, a belt, a case for a mirror and three pairs of silk mittens.

The lower compartment contained nine boxes of different shapes decorated in the same style as the lid of the large box. These boxes contained a long hairpiece, wooden combs, head ornaments and cosmetics. We reproduce two combs, identical with those from the tomb of the Marchioness of Dai, belonging to the Linden-Museum, Stuttgart, 26 and another toilet box, which, though a little later, 25 is decorated in the same style.

Both in number and in their exceptional quality the silks were another revelation from the tomb of the Marchioness of Dai. In addition to forty-six rolls of silk and the hangings of the northern compartment of the outer coffin, there were dresses, 24 skirts, mittens, shoes, socks, a pillow, scent sachets, mirror cases and many silk wrappings for burial goods.

All the weaving techniques known to the Han are represented here, most being plain silk taffetas, embroidered silks and gauzes. Those gauzes that 20 are not embroidered are painted or printed and are earlier than any previously known example of either technique. The tomb also contained figured silks, with woven designs in self colours, the most complicated of which is a double-sided taffeta pat-

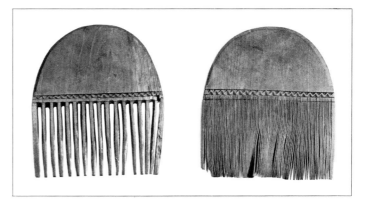

26
Fine and coarse-toothed combs.
Wood, 6.7 × 5.5 cm, Han, perhaps second century B.C.
Linden-Museum, Stuttgart.

27   ▷
Narrow end, rear, of second inner coffin.
Wood, lacquered and painted on a black ground, H. 1.14 m, W. 1.18 m, from tomb No. 1 at Mawangdui, Changsha, Hunan, soon after 168 B.C.

terned on one weft in relief, also a few figured silks with polychrome woven design. Mastery of dyeing techniques seems to have been complete, and there is a great variety of colours, including brown, grey, vermilion, dark red, purple, yellow, blue, green, black, gold and silver (on the painted silks).

The patterning of these silks combines two geometric repertoires inherited from the art of the kingdom of Chu and from the inlaid bronzes of the end of the Period of the Warring States. The first group of motifs, predominantly curvilinear, consists of reversed spirals, scrolling bands suggesting a cloud pattern and evolved from a stylization of dragon and bird motifs, fine scrolls heightened by short 'beards', and pointed Xs or quatrefoils alter- 19 (left) nating with undulating verticals. These motifs ap- 16–17 pear at Mawangdui on lacquered boxes, embroidered silks and in the decoration of the second in- 27, 30 ner coffin. They are, in the main, painterly motifs characterized by a sort of endless movement, by suppleness and fluidity of line. The other repertoire is more angular, combining the cloud scrolls with T-shaped diagonal meanders, scrolls that become meanders, and lozenge-trellises. At Ma- 19 (right) wangdui these motifs are found on figured silks with woven patterns, on the satin with appliqué 28 feathers that covers the innermost coffin, on the borders of some lacquerware and on the border of the third inner coffin.

Thus all the articles from the Mawangdui tombs —painted coffins, lacquers and textiles—are uniform in style as regards not merely the choice of decorative vocabulary but also the ways in which the motifs are combined and treated. This must give a fairly true picture of the nature of ornament in the lives of rich families in the kingdom of Changsha in the first half of the second century B.C. This picture confirms other discoveries, for example, the painted coffin from Shazitang in Changsha.[2]

Spiritual Nourishment and Beliefs in the Next World

It is clear from the models of instruments buried with them, even more than from the figurines of musicians, which are fairly common in Han tombs, that the Marchioness of Dai and her son were fond of music. Although little is yet known about Han music, the texts make clear that the Chu musical tradition, which was highly appreciated, occupied an important place at the court of the Former Han.

With the Marchioness of Dai in her tomb was a *se* zither with 4 pegs, 25 strings and the same 22 number of movable bridges. The musician usually sat on his heels with the instrument on the ground in front of him. The tomb also contained a bamboo *yu* mouth-organ (height 78 cm), with 22 tubes in two rows and a diapason consisting of 12 pipes of different lengths producing the 12 notes of the Chinese scale. The name of the note is written in ink at the base of each tube. A musician playing a mouth-organ is shown with other musicians in the bottom right-hand corner of an engraved slab dated A.D. 114. 119

Mawangdui tomb No. 3 also contained a *se* and a *yu*, as well as a seven-stringed *qin* zither. No example of a *qin* of the Han period had been known before, only representations on brick or stone dating from the Latter Han, like the figure playing a *qin* from a scene of music and dance on a brick from 143 Sichuan province.

It is impossible here to discuss in detail the texts buried with the Marquis of Dai's son. It was not unusual during the Han period to bury a part of a man's library or archives with him—presumably those books or documents that meant most to him; however, it is unusual for the documents to have survived. There have been more discoveries of ancient texts since 1972: the tombs of Fenghuangshan in Hubei province, of Linyi in Shandong province (4,942 slips unearthed from two tombs), and Mawangdui in Hunan province, to cite only the burials of the Former Han. Most of the texts that have been found are written on wooden or bamboo slips; Mawangdui tomb No. 3 alone contained manuscripts on silk. Some of these are copies of

28 ▷
Narrow end, front, of third inner coffin.
Wood, lacquered and painted on a red ground, H. 89 cm, W. 92 cm, from tomb No. 1 at Mawangdui, Changsha, Hunan, soon after 168 B.C.

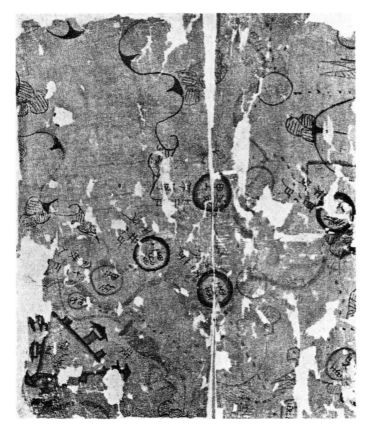

29

Detail (central section) of a military map of the south of the kingdom of Changsha. Paint on silk, (map) 78 × 98 cm, from tomb No. 3 at Mawangdui, Changsha, Hunan, 168 B.C. (See *Wenwu*, no. 1 [1976]: Pl. I [left]).

well-known works; some are fragments of lost works and are occasionally difficult to identify. The main texts discovered at Mawangdui are:
– the *Yijing* or *Book of Changes*, a very ancient work on divination;
– two copies of the *Laozi (Daodejing)*, preceded by Taoist writtings of a school which would seem to stand half-way between the classical Taoism of the *Laozi* and the Legalist tradition;
– a version of the *Zhanguoce* or *Intrigues of the Warring States*;
– texts concerning punishments and virtues *(Xingde)*;
– two medical treatises with a painting illustrating Taoist breathing exercises;

– a treatise on astronomy, meteorology and divination;
– two texts on *Yin-Yang* and the Five Phases or Elements;
– a treatise on physiognomy as applied to horses.
There were also three maps: a topographical map of the southern region of the kingdom of Changsha, a military map of the same region indi- 29 cating garrisons, and a town-plan.

The silk strips on which these texts are copied measure either 24 or 48 centimetres in height, roughly the same lengths as the two types of wooden slips: long ones were used for laws and the Classics, short ones for administrative texts.

The texts are written in vertical columns of between sixty and seventy characters, sometimes within a red border. Some of the manuscripts written in a combination of *xiaozhuan* (small-seal script) and *lishu* (the scribal hand) may date from the reign of Gaozu; those entirely in *lishu* probably date from the reign of Wendi (179–157). Some texts are on rolls, but most were folded and preserved in lacquer boxes.

Silk was an expensive material, but is easier to handle, lighter, and easier to put away and transport than slips, and it rapidly became widely used for writing during the Han period, although it did not replace wooden slips. These were used for cor- 77 respondence, for example, for definitive editions, illustrations and documents used in ceremonies.

Apart from the manuscripts on silk, tomb No. 3 contained an inventory of the burial goods and a medical treatise on wooden and bamboo slips.

The chapter on the history of science will discuss what can be gleaned from these texts about Han medicine, astronomy and cartography. Does the choice reveal a point in time, an environment or the taste of an individual? Presumably the latter. The presence of geographical maps in the tomb has led certain scholars to conclude that Li Cang's son was one of the staff officers detailed to defend the southern frontiers of the kingdom of Changsha against the attacks of the Nan Yue. The hypothesis is attractive but no less risky than the one that would like to see Li Cang's son as an adept of the philosophy of the *Laozi* solely on the basis of the texts buried with him. We shall be on safer ground if we say simply that, like many of his contemporaries, the dead man was interested in Taoism, medicine and various forms of divination and that he possessed extremely accurate documents on the topography and the military situation in the south of the kingdom. We should also remember that Taoism was in high favour at this period and that the *Daodejing* was read not only as a philosophical text but also as a manual of conduct and a handbook on an art of governing, which was closely connected with the quest for sanctity and longevity on the part of the sovereign or his delegate at the local level.

Such beliefs in the next world as can be glimpsed from the painted coffins and banners from the Mawangdui tombs belong to the ancient stock of cosmological and shamanist traditions of the kingdom of Chu. Works of art of great perfection—not only are these among the earliest known examples of Chinese painting, they are also among its masterpieces—these works are complex, difficult to read and remain obscure in many respects. Nevertheless, the various interpretations agree on the broad themes, which are the only ones that concern us here, i.e. the journey of the deceased to the next world, the ascent of his soul *(hun)* to immortality, the protection it required on the ascent, and the implied contact between the divine and human worlds.

These themes are evoked by two banners (tombs Nos. 1 and 3) and two painted coffins (tomb No. 1). Since the broad outlines of the iconography of the two banners are fairly similar, only that of the Marchioness of Dai will be discussed. The banner that was placed on the lid of the innermost coffin is made up of three pieces of silk sewn together to form a letter T. The whole measures 2.05 metres in length by 92 centimetres in width at the top and 47.7 centimetres at the bottom. It is de- 23 scribed as *feiyi* ('flying garment') in the inventory of the burial goods, and it could in fact be taken for a closed kimono in silhouette. The top edge of the banner was rolled onto a bamboo cane and had a cord by which it could be hung and perhaps carried in procession in the funeral procession before being buried. A similar custom of parading a banner carrying the name of the dead person at the funeral is securely attested in the Han period and has persisted until today.

The technical and stylistic qualities of the banner will be discussed in the chapter on painting; here we shall deal only with its iconography, which centres on the soul's journey to the next world. A living man possesses two groups of souls: the three *hun,* or superior souls and the seven *po,* or inferior, ones; however, each group is considered to be an entity, so that in practice it is as though men had only two souls. These separate at death: the *hun* begins the perilous journey that will take it to heaven and the abode of the Immortals; the *po* remains for a while in the tomb before becoming a ghost *(gui)* or descending to the Yellow Springs in the bowels of the earth. The destiny of the *po* varies according to different traditions, but all insist on the necessity of providing it with sufficient offerings to ensure that it remains with the body for as long as possible and does not come to seek revenge on the survivors. These offerings are made up largely of the burial goods and the sacrifices offered by the descendants. This is a greatly simplified outline; but is does explain the concepts that underlay the burial ritual and the aspirations of the men of the period, especially in the region of Chu, where life was rooted in a mythical universe and was part of a cosmogony to which many of the keys have been lost. Love of legend, the hidden presence of spirits everywhere, the need to communicate with them through the shamans are characteristic features of Chu civilization. They are expressed in the *Shanhaijing* (the *Classic of Mountains and Lakes*), parts of which may date to the fourth century B.C., and especially in the *Chuci (Songs of Chu),* an anthology of poems by Qu Yuan (340–278 B.C.) and other Chu poets. The descriptions and suggestions in these poems have been the main sources for the study and interpretation of the Mawangdui banner and the extraction of its major themes.

The painting is divided into three sections: the 21, 23 subterranean world surrounding the two fish in the lower part, the earth (the upper two-thirds of the vertical section), and the celestical world (the horizontal member of the T).

The subterranean world, the realm of water and darkness, is represented by two large interlacing fish. Two dragons—one red and the other whitish-blue— issue from the lower part. They ascend in a perfectly symmetrical movement, pass into a jade ring *(bi),* interlace and continue upwards. Dragons mounted or harnessed by divinities play the same part in regard to the *hun* souls

of the dead, which they carry on their ascent towards immortality.

An atlante stands on the back of the fish; a snake
passes between his legs, its head and tail interlacing
with the tails of the dragons. The atlante supports
the first platform, which belongs to the terrestrial
world. Six men are seated on the platform on
either side of what is believed to represent the dead
woman's body wrapped in silk and lying on a dais.

30
Tomb No. 1 at Mawangdui (shortly after 168 B.C.): second
inner coffin, as discovered.
Lacquered wood, H. 1.14 m, L. 2.56 m, W. 1.18 m,
Changsha, Hunan.

There is a seventh standing figure at the left. In the
foreground are sacrifical vessels: three large *ding*
and two jars *(hu)*. In the background cups with
handles *(bei)* and jars stand on a table. There can be
no doubt that the scene represents the sacrifice offered to the dead woman by her family.

A large jade pendant *(heng)* is suspended above
the scene from the *bi* ring, by ribbons with free
ends floating on either side. The jade *bi* and *heng* are
precious objects that, when combined to form a
pendant, are linked with ideas of alliance, of communication between heaven and mankind, between the living and the dead. They protect the
dead woman's *hun* soul on its perilous journey to
heaven.

Above the *bi,* a sloping plane flanked by two red
leopards leads to a second white platform. In the
centre of the platform stands an old woman leaning
on a stick; two men kneel in front of her, while behind her stand three women. Although the authorities are divided in their interpretation of the
scene, which is the climax and nub of the design, all
regard the central figure as the dead women. It is
noteworthy that her dress is decorated with the
same cloud motifs as the material on the couch of
the lower platform. Some see the scene as depicting the heavenly messengers arriving to receive the
deceased; others believe that it represents the rite of
recalling the soul. During this rite the family call
the *hun* soul of the recently deceased person and in-
vite it to return to its former home; in this context
the scene would depict the welcoming back of the
soul. A third reading has it that the platform is that
of a chariot drawn by the two dragons on which
the dead woman makes her ascent to heaven, accompanied by attendants.

An owl and a dais, symbolizing dignity, surmount the scene. The two birds perched on the
dais may be phoenixes, birds of good augury that
escort the soul on its journey to heaven. The
leopards below the platform are probably also protectors of the soul on its journey.

Above the dais and the scene that in all probability depicts the soul's ascent to immortality, a kind
of door leads to the upper part, which is heaven.
Here again leopards defend the door. Inside are
two seated men regarded by some as divinities responsible for human destiny and by others as messengers of the Celestial Emperor who have come
to receive the soul. Above them a bell is suspended
by two cords held by two Immortals mounted on
fantastic horses.

The upper part of the painting depicts, on the
left, the crescent moon with its inhabitants the hare
and the toad. Below it the young woman carried
on the wings of a dragon may be Chang'e, wife of
the archer Yi, who having robbed him of the herb
of immortality, ascended into the sky and alighted
on the moon. To the right, symmetrical with the
moon, is the disc of the sun, with the crow, its
emblem and essence. Below the sun, a tree with
branches interlacing with the dragon probably represents the mulberry-tree *(fusang)* in which the
sun stands each morning before ascending into the

sky. The eight small red discs among the branches
of the tree may symbolize the different positions of
the sun in its path.

Seated at the top centre of the painting is a female
divinity whose human body, dressed in a bluish-
green robe, terminates in a coiling dragon's tail.
This is probably Nügua, creator and ancestress of
mankind, here representing the Celestial Emperor.

Painted symbols on two of the inner coffins of
tomb No. 1 complete the iconographic programme of the Marchioness of Dai's banner,
which is repeated with minor variations on that of
her son (Mawangdui tomb No. 3). Many of the
motifs on the banner reappear there: dragons
whose bodies pass through a *bi* ring suspended by
a ribbon, leopards, Immortals on horseback, etc.
Other mythological and fantastic figures, many of
them hybrids (e.g. a lion's head with the antlers of
a stag, human bodies with animals' feet) seem to
possess an apotropaic quality and, especially on the
second inner coffin with the black background, to
be meant to ward off the evil spirits, serpents and
demons who might enter the coffin and attack the
body of the dead woman. The four beasts of good
augury—the stag, tiger, phoenix and dragon—depicted several times over on the third inner coffin
with a red ground probably served to transport and
assist the soul to surmount the dangers of its ascent
to heaven, a journey that might almost be called an
initiation.

The motif of the mountain that appears on this
coffin with a red ground developed significantly in
Han iconography. In this case it is treated in a fairly
stylized manner as a pointed triangle with two lateral projections. Sofukawa Hiroshi believes that it
represents Mount Kunlun, a sacred mountain in
north-west China, round which many mythological stories have crystalized. During the Han period
Mount Kunlun came to be regarded as the abode of
the Immortals, like the three islands of the East
Sea, the residence of Xiwangmu (the Queen
Mother of the West), and the goal of the ascending
souls of the dead. Does this already depict the ascent of a soul to Mount Kunlun? It is hard to say,
just as it is still hard to date the development of
concepts connected with immortality between the
beginning and end of the Former Han. However,
the coffins of tomb No. 1 and the banners at
Mawangdui are not entirely isolated works. There

21

27, 30

59

are other paintings that are close to them, and all belong to the cultural area of Chu:

- two banners dating from the Period of the Warring States that have been found in the vicinity of Changsha (banners of Chenjiadashan and Zidanku) depict the ascent of the deceased to immortality in what is still a very simple style;
- a painted coffin, the iconography of which is extremely close to the Mawangdui coffin with a red background, was discovered in 1961 at Shazitang, the southern suburb of Changsha.[3] The tomb, which had been robbed, contained burial goods of the same type as those at Mawangdui and is probably contemporary. It consists of an outer and three inner coffins, of which the second (painted) coffin is exactly similar in position, size, symbolism and style to the Mawangdui coffin with a red background;
- a banner discovered in 1976 in tomb No. 9 at Jinqueshan (district of Linyi) in Shandong province illustrates the evolution of the theme of the ascent (*Wenwu,* no. 11 [1977]).[4] The banner comes from the south of Shandong, a region which was strongly influenced by Chu at the beginning of the third century B.C. and at the beginning of the Han. Datable from the burial goods in the tomb, the banner belongs to the reign of Wudi (140–87 B.C.) and so is later than the Mawangdui banners. The sun and moon, the two dragons and a portrait of the dead woman appear here, as at Mawangdui. But the rest of the iconographic programme has changed considerably: the different registers of the painting depict the life of the dead woman after her ascent to immortality, in scenes borrowed from the real world—the world of the blest was thought of as a replica of the world here below. Three sugarloaf mountains appear at the top of the painting below the sun and moon. Seen by some scholars as the mountains of the Immortals in the East Sea and by others as Mount Kunlun, they must certainly depict the dwelling-place to which the soul of the dead woman has ascended.

Comparing this banner with those of Mawangdui, one is struck by the fact that the mythological elements have been eliminated in favour of realistic scenes. From now on, interest was to lie in life after death as an endless prolongation of all that had been best in the earthly life.

Desire for immortality, belief in the ascent of the *hun* soul to a paradise of the Immortals, which was soon assimilated to Mount Kunlun, constitute one of the major themes of the Han period. In burial art the ascent itself, which was still being depicted at the time of Wudi—e.g. on the painted ceiling of the tomb of Bu Qianqiu and his wife at Luoyang[5]—was to give way increasingly to evocations of the pleasures of the next world, to representations of Xiwangmu, who reigns over this paradise, and of protective beasts and emblems.

Part II

The Reign of Wudi (140–87 B.C.)

Chapter I

Reinforcement of Central Power and the Recruitment of Officials

In 140 B.C. a youth of fifteen ascended the throne; history was to know him as Wudi (the 'warrior emperor'), and he has remained the most renowned if not the greatest of the Han emperors. His policy and the radical solutions that he imposed were characterized by their dynamism, appreciation of efficiency, a sense of grandeur, even despotism and ran counter to the laissez-faire of his predecessors. His long reign (140–87) of over fifty years of absolute power inaugurated a new era in the history of China. Under his impetus precedents were introduced, institutions evolved and an official ideology established—all of which were to shape Chinese policy and thought for over a thousand years, while some of the ideals by which society had lived at the end of the Zhou and beginning of the Han dynasties were relegated to the background and sometimes forgotten.

The first emperors of the Han dynasty had delegated their power to the court dignitaries, particularly to the Grand Counsellor or prime minister, and were usually content to approve or reject the suggestions and initiatives of their ministers. Legalist and Taoist in inspiration, this style of government by non-intervention found its way into the administration of the empire, and many high officials practised the laissez-faire policy advocated in the *Daodejing*.

Wudi saw the rôle of monarch in a different light, and in 131 at the death of Tian Fen, his uncle and prime minister, he took the reins of government into his own hands. Thenceforth none of his Grand Counsellors was permitted to gain sufficient prestige to thwart his own policy or to control affairs in any real sense.

By making himself an absolute monarch and ruling in person, Wudi stifled all possibility of criticism of the government's policy, since the slightest protest became a crime of lèse-majesté. This situation accounts for the gravest economic and political errors of his reign.

Refusing to allow the power of his prime minister to curtail his own, Wudi surrounded himself with new men whom he made his privy counsellors and ennobled. He gave appointments and fiefs to his relatives by marriage and governed increasingly through his secretariat *(shangshu)*. Every document and all reports passed through the hands of that parallel administration—'the inner court'—where the dossiers deemed fit for the emperor's eye were selected and which thus in large measure determined his decisions. Being the instrument of imperial authority, the secretariat opposed the old administrative structure—'the outer court'—and especially the prime minister. And later, during the first century B.C., this new political force gained so great a measure of autonomy that it became the *de facto* government whenever an emperor was under age, incapable or inactive. The prime minister became a mere figurehead.

With the same forcefulness Wudi dealt the death blow to the old imperial aristocracy by systematically breaking up the fiefs. Thenceforth, when a king died, his dependencies ceased to pass to his eldest heir, but were divided among all the sons (127 B.C.). The only privilege remaining to the kings, now that they were stripped of political power, was the fortune they derived from the fief. The task of internal consolidation that had begun at the beginning of the century was thus completed, and the final bids for separatism, such as that of Liu An, prince of Huainan in Anhui province, driven to suicide in 122, ended in failure.

At the same time, certain unnecessarily large administrative units were reduced in order to prevent excessive local power becoming concentrated in the hands of a single high official. Thus in 135 the region of the capital was split into two parts, one of which was again subdivided in 104 B.C. The body of inspectors (cishi) was created as part of the same thinking.

Wudi was as well aware as his predecessors of the potential threat posed by the rich and powerful clans composed of widely ramified families whose members intermarried and exercised extensive patronage. Measures were taken to break them up; for instance, they were ordered to move close to the capital to a town that had been created near the mausoleum of one of the emperors; all the members of a clan were forbidden to live together, etc. When these measures proved insufficient or ineffective, Wudi authorized his administrators to ruin and even to exterminate these great, over-powerful families.

Wudi's assertion of personal power and his desire to centralize were accompanied by a wish to strengthen the dynastic idea. In 104 B.C. a new calendar was adopted to replace the one inherited by the Han from the Qin. It was announced that the year would in future begin on the first day of the first spring moon instead of on the first day of the tenth lunar month. The first spring moon corresponds roughly with our month of February, and the new calendar has remained in force up to the present. The Reform of the calendar was underlined by the adoption of a name for the era (nianhao) that was full of promise: Taichu, 'the great beginning'. Another innovation was this giving of special names to periods of varying length within a reign; the custom persisted up to the accession of the Ming (A.D. 1368), after which a single nianhao corresponded to the reign of each emperor.

In the year in which it abandoned the Qin calendar, the Han dynasty also abandoned the Water phase and its colour, black, which had been the Qin emblem, in favour of the Earth phase and its colour, yellow. Because in one of the cycles of the theory of the Five Phases Earth conquers Water,

the Han thus confirmed their position as the dynasty that subjugated and succeeded the Qin.

The authoritarian measures taken by Wudi in many fields reflected the worst methods of the Legalists. Nevertheless, it was Confucianism that received his official patronage and round which he tried to promote cultural unity. Indeed, it was impossible for him to go back to Legalism, for this was the doctrine that had been espoused by the dynasty which his own clan had swept out of power some sixty years before; while Taoism, which had been favoured by his father and his grandmother, Dowager Empress Dou, advocated a mode of government that conflicted with Wudi's ideas. The third way, to which there was no real alternative and which was to become the official ideology, was an updated Confucianism, fed, as we shall see, from a variety of sources, in particular borrowings from Legalism and from the theory of the Five Phases.

In 124 B.C., at the instigation of some of his Confucian counsellors, Wudi created the imperial university, designed to provide the administration with capable officials. The university, the Grand School (taixue) was established 3 kilometres northwest of the capital. The five Classics were taught there: *The Book of Changes (Yijing), The Book of Documents (Shujing), The Book of Odes (Shijing), The Book of Rites (Liji)* and the *Spring and Autumn Annals (Chunqiu)*. Several chairs were created for each of these ancient texts, and each was entrusted to a teacher known as a 'scholar of great knowledge' (boshi), who taught his own philosophical interpretation of the Classic or that of the school to which he belonged. However, the 'scholars of great knowledge' favoured only their own disciples (dizi) with their teaching; these became their assistants, and it was the latter who transmitted the teaching from master to pupils.

At the same time an official school was opened in the chief town of each commandery; the director, who had studied at the Grand School, taught one or more of the Classics. His pupils usually entered local government; the cleverest might be sent to the capital, where they attended the university courses side by side with the sons of high officials. The number of students at the imperial university was restricted to fifty under Wudi, but increased steadily until it reached three thousand for a time at the end of the Former Han, ten thousand under Wang Mang, and yet more at the period of the Latter Han.

The Grand School and the commandery schools were a breeding ground for officials. Furthermore, by training Confucian state officials they encouraged Chinese cultural unification—as well as sameness—since non-Confucians were naturally debarred from the bureaucracy.

However, the establishment of an imperial university did not wholly replace the old methods of recruitment—money, nepotism and recommendation—especially for court appointments. It was by recommendation, 'calling upon the aid of the wise' as established under Gaozu, that Wudi was able to summon up new men, such as Gongsun Hong, to whom he entrusted the reorganization of finances and education, and Dong Zhongshu (c. 175–105 B.C.), who was his counsellor for fifteen years. Other scholars tried their luck by addressing memoranda to the throne. Dongfang Shuo, Wudi's fool, for example, owed his admission to the court to a letter through which one glimpses his ebullience and a temperament that does not appear to have been cowed by humility:

> When still a child I lost my parents and was brought up by my elder brother and his wife. At thirteen years old [twelve by western reckoning] I began to learn to write; after three winters I could master the ordinary texts and annals. At fifteen I learned to fence. At sixteen I studied the *Book of Odes* and the *Book of Documents,* and I could soon recite 220,000 words. At nineteen I studied works on military science by Masters Sun and Wu .... I could memorize a further 220,000 words, so that in all I could recite 440,000 words. Besides, I have always borne in mind the formula of Zilu [Zilu had told the Master: '...give me a kingdom possessing one thousand warchariots to govern... in three years I will have the people performing feats of gallantry and will make them understand the direction they ought to take.' *Analects of Confucius,* XI:25]. I am twenty-two years old, measure 9 *chi* 3 *cun* [about 2.13 m], have eyes like pendent pearls and teeth like strings of cowries. I am as brave as Meng Ben, as swift as Qingji, as scrupulous as Bao Shu, as loyal as Wei Sheng.... Thus I am capable of becoming a great minister of the Son of Heaven. Risking death and prostrating myself many times, I submit this report.[1]

The letter is extremely interesting not only on account of the anecdote but also for what it reveals of the qualifications of a young scholar and of teaching methods that were based largely on learning by rote.

Chapter II

Technological Progress and a Planned Economy

Hydraulic Engineering and Agricultural Techniques

The great enterprises of the reign of Wudi to improve agricultural production were undertaken in response to the need to control the waterways in order to maintain the courses of the rivers, protect the land against floods and drought, irrigate the fields and transport the grain received as tax. The first concern of the reign was in the domain of transport. As agricultural production increased in Guandong (southern Shanxi, northern Henan and western Shandong provinces), which was the second cereal granary of the capital, it became essential to improve transportation by water on the Yellow and the Wei rivers. Between 134 and 131 B.C., 125 kilometres of canal were dug to link Chang'an with the Yellow River. The canal reduced the distance by two-thirds and the duration of the journey by half (three months instead of six); it also served to irrigate 45,000 hectares. These great enterprises, which employed tens of thousands of soldiers, were not always successful. A canal constructed in Hedong (Shanxi province) at the same period became unusable a few years after its completion when the course of the Yellow River became deflected.

The main aim of these two vast operations of the beginning of the reign had been to facilitate transport. Soon the increasingly urgent need for grain, the poor yield of the ground and the seizure of land that drove the peasants to abandon their fields determined government to increase production and

consequently to enter upon a programme of irrigation. For the major problem facing the farmer in northern China seeking to develop land was that of conservation of moisture. There is little rain in that part of the country, and much of the precipitation falls as snow. It was therefore essential to prevent water from evaporating from the soil and to make the best possible use of the spring rains, which alone fostered growth. This emerges clearly from the earliest surviving Chinese manual on agronomy—in fact only part has survived—by Fan Shengzhi (second half of the first century B.C.). Several times the author recommends working the ground after rain; in order to conserve moisture until spring he also advocates: 'in winter, after each fall of snow, roll the ground to bury the snow deeply, so that the wind cannot scatter the snow'.

An irrigation system was the only means of reducing the threat of permanent aridity. The kings of Qin had understood this clearly, and the opening in 246 B.C. of the Zhengguo canal (named after Zheng Guo, the engineer in charge of the enterprise) had transformed the valley of the Jing, near the Qin capital, into a flourishing agricultural region. In 111 B.C. Wudi resumed the policy of promoting irrigation. Six more canals were constructed. The Zhengguo canal itself had become silted up and unusable and had to be rebuilt in 95 B.C. The new canal, renamed Bo after the contractor, joined the Jing farther upstream than the Zhengguo; sloping more steeply, it flowed into the Wei after a course of some 83 kilometres and irrigated over 21,000 hectares.

Other canals were dug to cross the newly developed land of the prefectures flanking the northern loop of the Yellow River, as well as in Shandong province and further south round the Huai River.

Besides drought the authorities faced a ceaseless struggle against flooding. The years of famine during the reign of Wudi (*c.* 130, 120, 115 and 90 B.C.) were partly the result of floods, especially those of the Yellow River. In 132 the river broke its banks at Huzi (the Gourd Dike) in Hebei province, flowed southwards and poured into the Huai River. The Huzi breach was repaired, but the dike burst again and was not properly sealed until 109 B.C. The catastrophe of 132 and the repair works that Wudi visited in 109 inspired him to write a poem; a few passages are quoted below:

> The Gourd Dike has burst;
> What to do in this ordeal?
> Immensely, wave has piled upon wave;
> Villages are now mere River water.
>
> Mere River water! The country
> Knows neither rest nor quiet.
> These works, they never end;
> Mount Yü is being stripped!
>
> ...
>
> The water will rejoin its former bed,
> So well the gods protect us!
> Had I not performed the Double Cult★,
> What would I know of the outside?
>
> The waters of the River, seething,
> Flood in with rapid flow;
> To deflect their course to the North,
> To hold it here, what an arduous task!★★
>
> ...
>
> Cut the bamboos in the parks,★★★
> Drive in piles and rocks!
> At Xuanfang the breach is stopped
> All good fortune draws near![1]

[★ The double cult refers to the two sacrifices: *Feng* (to Heaven) and *Shan* (to the Earth).
★★ The problem was to redirect the river into its old bed and to ensure that it remained there.
★★★ To make brushwood faggots.]

The repairing of the Gourd Dike was not Wudi's only piece of hydraulic engineering; he also ordered vast schemes to harness water-courses (dikes, canals and reservoirs) with the two-fold aim of flood-prevention and irrigation of the fields.

Besides drought and flooding, a third danger of a very different order was a perennial threat to the peasantry and consequently to the State, whose resources depended largely on the production of cereals. This scourge was the seizure of the peasants' land by the ruling class. There had been no reduction in the formation of great landed estates since the beginning of the second century B.C., especially in the densely populated, well-irrigated areas surrounding the capital and large towns. Dong Zhongshu proposed to Wudi measures to limit the area of private estates, but these first measures, taken in 119 and 113 and primarily intended to fill the empty coffers of the Treasury, only affected the merchants, whereas the real danger came from the high officials who were investing in land.

While Wudi's reign was a period of vast achievements in irrigation, conservation of water and transportation of grain, the period is also characterized by advances in agricultural techniques, which, though less spectacular, were of capital importance in the long term. Agricultural techniques were assisted by new inventions, improvements to old ones and by the fact that more and more varied iron tools were produced after 119 B.C., when foundries were nationalized.

The swing-plough drawn by oxen and driven by hand had made its appearance before the Period of the Warring States and had become widespread between the fourth and second centuries B.C. At the end of the second century ploughs usually had a single shaft (or beam) yoked to two oxen and were

31–2

31 ▷
The two sections of an iron mould for casting the ploughshare of a swing-plough.
H. 25.5 cm, W. 28.2 cm, provenance: district of Laiwu, Shandong, second century B.C. (See *Xin Zhongguo chutu wenwu,* p. 102; *Wenwu,* no. 7 [1977]: 68).

32 ▷
The two sections of an iron mould for casting a hoe.
H. 20 cm, W. 11.8 cm, provenance: district of Laiwu, Shandong, second century B.C. (See *Xin Zhongguo chutu wenwu,* p. 103; *Wenwu,* no. 7 [1977]: 70).

◁ 33
Ploughing and sowing.
Paint on brick. H. 17 cm, W. 36 cm, from tomb No. 1 at Jiayuguan, Gansu, A.D. 220–316. (See *Chūka Jimmin Kyōwakoku Kan Tō,* p. 34).

◁ 34
Pounder and rotary mill for grain.
Tomb model: earthenware with iridescent green glaze, H. 14.3 cm, first century B.C. to second century A.D.
Seattle Art Museum: Eugene Fuller Memorial Collection.

35
Lever pounder and rotary winnower worked by a crank.
Tomb model: earthenware, found in a tomb in the district of Jiyuan, Henan, end of the period of the Former Han. (See *Wenwu,* no. 2 [1973]: 46–53).

driven and guided by three men. But there were also swing-ploughs drawn by two oxen and guided by a single man, as well as a kind of plough drawn by a single ox between two shafts.

The Han swing-plough consisted of a long, straight shaft, a strut joining the shaft to the stock, a single handle and no coulter. The plough-share had an iron cutting edge. The earliest iron shares were short, almost forming an equilateral triangle, but after the beginning of the first century B.C. they became longer to form an isosceles triangle, which enabled them to plough a wider and deeper furrow. Mould-boards—and thus the classic plough—seem to have made their appearance during the reign of Wudi or during the first century B.C.

Both types of Han plough were better suited to working flat than uneven ground because of the length and shape of the shaft. They had been conceived for soils that were fairly easy to till and persisted unchanged through the first and second centuries A.D., and even longer in certain regions.

At the end of Wudi's reign a mechanical seeder was perfected; it had three feet, seeded three furrows at a time and is said to have been invented by Zhao Guo. Also at Zhao Guo's instigation experi-

ments were made with a type of rotation by bands of ground in which crops were alternated *(daitian).* Zhao Guo also called for more attentive cultivation of the soil, especially weeding and earthing up young plants as soon as they appeared.

Considerable advances were made in the preparation of grain (hulling, winnowing, polishing and grinding). Besides hand-operated rotary millstones and pounders worked with levers, which seem to have been common under the Former Han, a winnower with rotary wings worked by a crank made its appearance, probably in the second half of the second century B.C. Earthenware models of the machine are found in the tombs of northern China by the end of the Former Han, which would seem to indicate that it was fairly common by that time. This is the earliest known example of the use of the crank, predating by several centuries the first attested form in Europe.

Besides the simple winnowing basket and the rotary winnower, Han farmers used a third method of winnowing: beating the grain with two vertical stakes. This technique is often depicted on burial bricks dating from the Latter Han.

The earliest hydraulic mills appeared at the end of the Former Han. They were first used in agricul-

36
Hulling (left) and winnowing grain (right) in front of a barn on stilts.
Rubbing from a brick decorated in low relief, H. 25 cm, W. 39 cm, period of the Latter Han. (See Liu Zhiyuan, *Sichuan Han*, no. 7).
Sichuan Provincial Museum.

tural developments to power the levered pounders and later, in the first century A.D., in the bellows of foundries.

Industry and Craftsmanship

The main regions in which industry and craftsmanship flourished during the reign of Wudi were Guanzhong, Guandong and modern Sichuan province, all densely populated zones in which agriculture prospered.

37
Steel sword in lacquered bamboo scabbard.
(Guard and tip of scabbard) lacquer on wood, L. 85 cm, second century B.C.
British Museum, London.

38
Jade sword guard, decorated with a dragon in high relief, mounted on a fragment of a tanged iron sword.
The tang of the sword was encased in wood. Max. H. 1.7 cm, L. 5.8 cm, second or first century B.C.
Fogg Art Museum (Grenville L. Winthrop Bequest) Harvard University, Cambridge, MA.

1 *Iron*. Iron remained the most important of these industries. The experience gained in bronze casting made it easy for the Chinese to proceed at an early date to the casting of iron. The art of casting had been mastered by the sixth century B.C. and developed considerably in the fourth century B.C. as is testified by many agricultural tools made of cast iron that have been found in the tombs of the period. More breakable and less sharp than bronze, which remained the favourite precious metal for weapons during the Period of the Warring States, cast iron had the great advantage that it could be produced in quantity and consequently more cheaply: 'The effect of iron casting was to accustom the Chinese world at a very early date to the idea of a model and mass reproduction of the same tool, which has only become really familiar to us since the development of modern industry .... The moulds used for casting iron were employed for mass production, and they were often designed to produce several examples of the same article in a single operation'.[2]

China's advances in iron and steel metallurgy were not confined to cast iron, for by the Period of the Warring States the Chinese were already able to produce steel by heating and alloying irons of different carbon content. Gradually, as iron metallurgy progressed, steel weapons replaced those of bronze.

In 119 B.C., when the State monopoly of iron and salt was instituted, forty-nine foundries were brought under State control and run by the government; each employed between a few hundred and one thousand workers, most of them conscripts or convicts. Many of these foundries, thenceforth the only ones authorized to manufacture articles made of iron, lay in the modern provinces of Shandong, Henan (especially the regions of Gongxian, Nanyang and Zhengzhou), Sichuan and in the north-west of Jiangsu province. Blast-furnaces, larger than those of the Period of the Warring States, made greatly increased production possible. They were built of heat-resistant bricks and fuelled with coal; limestone was used as the flux. The Han period also saw the appearance of the twin-action piston bellows, which uses a system of valves to create continuous air-pressure resulting in higher temperatures.

The foundries were often comparatively specialized and produced agricultural implements, 31–2 components for carts, cooking pots, various everyday articles (scissors, etc.), and also weapons 37–8 of extremely high quality.

2 *Salt*. Salt was the second industry to be brought under government monopoly in 119 B.C.

The main salt-producing regions in Wudi's reign were Shandong and Sichuan provinces. The south of Sichuan contains reserves of salt and natural gas that were already exploited by the Han. Thus there are ornamental impressed bricks from the walls of tombs in the region of Chengdu dating from the 7 second century A.D. that depict salt being extracted and treated. Very deep wells were sunk, and the saline liquid was hoisted up in bamboo receptacles by means of a pulley attached to the winding-gear. The liquid was then left to evaporate in cauldrons above a large furnace fuelled by natural gas conducted in bamboo pipes.

3 *Copper and Bronze Metallurgy*. This appears to have been widely scattered despite its dependence on the presence of copper mines. Casting and dec-
41, 63 oration of ritual vessels and tableware, lamps,
39–40 mirrors, clasps, various ornaments, and certain metals, not to mention money, must have occupied innumerable craftsmen in the foundries and workshops of every important Chinese town of the day. At the beginning of Wudi's reign every

fief and almost every commandery struck its own coinage. Between 119 and 112, the central government gradually prohibited these different currencies; in 112 it imposed a State monopoly on the casting of coins and issued a cash *(wushu)* weighing 1 (no. 3) 3.2 grams, which remained the only cash in circulation until A.D. 7.

4 *Alcoholic Beverages*. This was another monopoly created in 98 B.C. What is called for convenience alcohol or wine *(jiu)* was in fact in the Han period a fermented beverage made from grain. Distilled alcohols were not produced until later. The standard recipe for fermented beverages as it appears in the *Hanshu* consisted in taking 2 *hu* (about 40 l) of poor-quality hulled grain and 1 *hu* of malt to make 6 *hu* 6 *dou* (132 l) of alcohol. The monopoly of 98, which was cancelled in 80 B.C., covered both manufacture and sale. The State made and supplied fermented beverages to official drinking establishments at a fixed price. The revenue was considerable, for the price was set very high.[3]

5 *Silk and Lacquer*. The other branches of craftsmanship, which did not become State monopolies, expanded rapidly during the second half of the second century; government workshops were set up for some which catered for the luxury trade and were exported. Foremost among these were the crafts of silk and lacquer.

Apart from the capital, Shandong and Henan provinces remained the principal centres of silk manufacture throughout the dynasty, even though they did not possess exclusive rights to weave silk. Most agricultural concerns in Han China raised silkworms, and this work, which was done by the women of the house, was carried right through to the woven material, to be used by the family or sold. The old kingdoms of Qi and Lu were renowned especially for the excellence of their silk and the skill of their women weavers and embroiderers. Wang Chong (A.D. 27–c. 100) was to

39
Mirror back.
Bronze, D. 10.5 cm, decorated with four dragons coiled round four bosses, second or first century B.C.
Museum für Ostasiatische Kunst, Cologne.

40   ▷
Mirror back.
Bronze, D. 18.4 cm, main decoration: four almost identical groups of human figures and animals in a stylized landscape of hills and trees, second century B.C.
Freer Gallery of Art, Washington, D.C.

celebrate their art in his *Lunheng* ('Critical Essays'): 'The people of Qi [western Shandong] have been embroiderers for generations, and there is not a single woman who cannot embroider. The inhabitants of Xiangyi [modern Suixian in Henan] weave polychrome silks [*jin*], and even idiot girls are proficient in this art'.[4]

Together with Linzi in Shandong, Xiangyi in Henan was one of the capitals of the silk trade in the Han period; private and government workshops worked there for the State, the court and all who could afford to buy this luxury product and, if possible, build up reserves. Many payments were in fact made in rolls of silk.

Besides silk and, at a later date, porcelain, lacquer, made from the natural sap of the lacquer tree *(Rhus vernicifera),* represents one of China's major contributions to the world's art of living. Being extraordinarily resistant to water, heat and acids, lacquer not only forms a perfect protective coating (for wood, bamboo and cloth), but also an admirable means of decorating a surface. It was used for these purposes during the Han period on a whole series of everyday articles, including tableware, furniture (daises, screens, pillows, toilet boxes, baskets) wearing-apparel (bonnets, shoes), weapons and their accessories (sword scabbards, bows and shields), and coffins.

As has been seen in the description of the Mawangdui tombs, these articles were lacquered in black on the outside and in red on the inside. The decoration, which was usually on the outside, was painted in black, red, white, blue, brown, green and yellow, occasionally with the addition of gold and silver. Han lacquers were often heightened with precious metals (gold, silver, bronze) or tortoise-shell on handles, hilts, feet or stands, or inlaid into the decoration. All these were luxury articles, highly priced because of the long hours and fine workmanship involved in making them.

The main centres of lacquer manufacture during the Han period were in Henan province and especially the commanderies of Shu and Guanghan in Sichuan province. Government factories had been set up here and produced some of the most refined pieces. In contrast to the private workshops, these factories always marked their wares with inscriptions of varying length, some of which list the principal craftsmen who made the piece, the date of execution and the officials responsible. Therefore, we possess a certain number of signed lacquers, in particular cups *(bei)* that date to around the first years A.D. The cup preserved in the Musée Guimet, found in Korea, where it must have belonged to a high official of the Lelang commandery, is one such. The inscription is finely incised on the lower rim, round the foot: 'The third year of the Yuanshi era [A.D. 3]. Made at the western factory of the commandery of Shu. Imperial model. Lacquered wooden cup [*bei*], engraved and painted with gilt [bronze] handles. Capacity 1 *sheng* 16 *yue*. Sized by Jin; lacquered by Ji; final coat by Qin [?]; handles gilt by Mao [?]; painted by Li; [inscription] engraved by Yi; cleaned and polished by Zheng; checked by Yi; officer commanding the factory guard, Zhang; director, Liang; deputy director, Feng; assistant, Long; scribe, Bao'.

Two important points emerge from this inscription and others like it, in which only the names of the craftsmen differ. The first concerns the division of labour: each craftsman appears to have been very much a specialist, and articles therefore passed from hand to hand until they were finished. Given the many successive operations necessary to the making of a piece of lacquer, this was undoubtedly the best way of making the work profitable. The second striking point about these inscriptions is the large number of officials who are mentioned (five), almost as many as the craftsmen (eight).

Communications

Such rapid expansion of industry and craftsmanship would have been unthinkable without a good communications network (rivers, canals, roads). The drive initiated under Qin Shi Huangdi for purposes of strategy and unification was continued

41
Vessel *(bianhu)*.
Bronze, H. 22.1 cm, W. 26.3 cm, incised decoration of birds and geometric motifs, second or first century B.C., probably from Guangxi province.
Art Institute of Chicago.

74

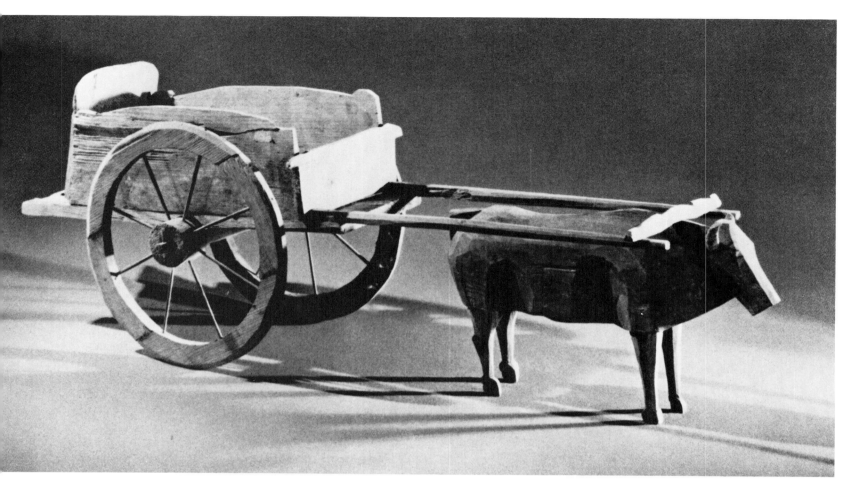

42
Ox-drawn cart.
Tomb model: wood, provenance: district of Wuwei, Gansu, first century B.C. or first century A.D. (See Zhongguo ke-xueyuan ..., *Xin Zhongguo*, p. 84).

by Wudi as required by his policy of expansion, until finally the Han road system was equalled only by that of the Romans.

One of the most important and difficult achievements of the Han engineers was the construction of passes over the Qinling Mountains on the road linking Shaanxi with Sichuan. New roads from Sichuan to the south were opened, one through Guizhou to Guangxi and Guangdong, and one to Yunnan (map, p. 221).

Han roads were avenues 100 feet wide (about 23 m), divided into three lanes: a paved central lane was reserved for the imperial posts, inspectors on assignment and local officials moving round their district; the two verges were for the use of carts, merchants' barrows and pedestrians. Traffic using this road included horse-drawn carts, waggons drawn by oxen and—from the first century 42 B.C.—by donkeys.

The way of harnessing draught-horses was revolutionized at the Period of the Warring States. Thus, as early as the fourth century B.C., the Chinese substituted breast-harnesses for the type of collar that encircled the horse's neck and impeded its breathing, the only form of harness known in the west until the fifth or sixth century A.D. The strain of pulling was taken by the shoulders, and the breast-harness therefore remained the best form of harness until the shoulder-collar was invented—again in China—around the fifth century A.D.

Another Chinese invention, dating from the end of the Period of the Warring States at latest, consisted in setting spokes at a slight angle to the plane of a wheel, wheels dished in this way having greater resistance to lateral shocks. The practice was not introduced into Europe until the sixteenth century.

56, 82, 96 Han carts, as depicted on impressed bricks, wall paintings and incised slabs in tombs and as imitated in earthenware or bronze models included among burial goods, were most commonly drawn by one horse. They had two curved shafts, which were attached to the breast-harness half-way along their length. Wheels were large, with a diameter about equal to the length of the body. Carts could accommodate several passengers, and those belonging to officials had a circular canopy on top.

There were small posting stations for mail every 5 *li* (about 2 km), a postal relay *(ting)* every 10 *li* and a larger posting station every 30 *li* along the Han roads. Distances were kept short so that signals and calls could be easily received from one relay to the next. Postal relays were provided with stabling for horses, an inn for officials and for travellers authorized to use them, as well as gaols for prisoners in transit from one town to another. Relays often also had a private hostel for those not permitted to use the government inn. The Han road network, with the accompanying system of postal relays and the fatigue parties that helped to maintain them, was not only the backbone of the economic system, but also and above all the key factor in Han military expansion and cultural penetration.

Financial Difficulties and the Planned Economy

The private enterprise that had flourished during the first half of the second century B.C. and Wudi's dynamic policy both inside the empire and in his external conquests favoured not only the rapid expansion of craftsmanship and trade, but also the formation of huge fortunes in the merchant class, among the high officials and the aristocracy. Ironmasters, masters of salt-mines as well as speculators in grain and usurers amassed fortunes of up to 100 million cash. At the other end of the social scale, the condition of the peasants, forcibly conscripted into the army and liable to the corvée in

any of the great enterprises, worsened year by year.

From 127 B.C. when the first military campaigns had exhausted the reserves of the imperial treasury, the government exploited every means of setting its army, finances and potential work-force back on their feet. It sold titles of nobility and appointments; it granted the title of *lang* ('gentleman of the court') to those who offered slaves to the state when it did not purely and simply confiscate slaves. It set up a monopoly on the striking of money (112 B.C.), and required businessmen, like Dongguo Xianyang of Qi, master of a salt-mine, and Kong Jin, ironmaster of Nanyang, to organize and apply monopolies of salt and iron (119 B.C.) under the direction of the competent minister, in order to refill the state coffers. At this time too Sang Hongyang (152–80 B.C.), son of a Luoyang merchant, made a reputation for business acumen and became financial counsellor to the emperor. In 115–110 B.C. he created state transport offices *(junshu)* to provide fresh supplies to the frontiers and to disaster areas in times of famine or flood. By transporting foodstuffs from regions in which they were plentiful and cheap to those where they were rare and costly, this organization ensured that the State kept control of the traffic in merchandise. At the same time, in 110, Sang tried to fix and equalize prices throughout the empire. The office of 'standardization' *(pingzhun)* bought foodstuffs on the market when prices were low and sold them at a fixed price when they had risen. The aim of this measure was to limit fluctuations in prices and to prevent speculation by the great merchants. This attempt at State commerce and redistribution of wealth was of short duration; nevertheless, together with other measures, it helped to bring individual initiative increasingly closely under official control and to ruin private trade and industry. In 119 merchants were forbidden to own land. Although this prohibition was never rigorously enforced, it none the less proved decisive since there was no other way of investing capital.

When all these measures proved insufficient, Wudi raised trading dues and taxes, created new ones—on businesses, carts, livestock, boats, etc.— taxed private fortunes, exercised a policy of confiscation and imposed a monopoly on fermented beverages. When regular conscription for military

43
Landscape of western Gansu, Jiayuguan, west of Jiuquan.

service was exhausted, the prisons were thrown open and an amnesty granted to all who agreed to join the army.

Fifty years of war and territorial expansion, extravagant diplomacy and a magnificent court had consumed all the human and economic resources of the Han empire. In 87 Wudi left China drained of its life-blood, just as Louis XIV was to leave France eighteen centuries later.

Chapter III

Wars against the Xiongnu and Chinese Expansionism

The policy of concession towards the Xiongnu pursued by the first Han emperors bore little fruit. With the consolidation of the power of the centre, a change of outlook became possible and, surer of its rear, the Chinese government could engage in active diplomacy, in an offensive and, finally, in an expansionist policy. Wars against the Xiongnu and the pursuit of new alliances were the great concerns of Wudi's reign. During the fifty years from 138 to 90 B.C. Han strategy led to a number of operations, all of which—at least at the outset—were part and parcel of the struggle against the Xiongnu:

- solid defensive positions were established in northern and north-western China;
- Central Asia was penetrated in order to secure the aid of allies on the western flank of the Xiongnu and to open a safe line of communication to the allies;
- offensives were mounted to thwart Xiongnu concentration along the Chinese borders;
- penetration to the south and north-east was effected to free the empire from encirclement, to gain allies and to ensure that the government kept control of lines of communication and trade.

The Missions of Zhang Qian and the Offensive against the Xiongnu

The first move of the Chinese court was to seek allies. Among the possible partners none could have been more hostile to the Xiongnu than the Yuezhi.

As we have seen, the Yuezhi—who spoke an Indo-European language—had been crushed by the Xiongnu and driven back westwards some twenty-five years previously. A part of this ethnic group, the Da Yuezhi or 'Great Yuezhi', had finally established themselves in Bactria, on the north-western edge of the Indian world, where they gave rise to the state of Kushan. Wudi believed that the Da Yuezhi were established in the Ili valley. In 138, therefore, he sent an embassy in that direction consisting of about one hundred men headed by Zhang Qian. The embassy was to form an alliance with the Da Yuezhi against the common enemy. In the event, Zhang Qian was seized almost immediately by the Xiongnu and was held prisoner for ten years. He managed to escape at last, reached Ferghana (Dayuan) in the high valley of the Syr-Darya and finally Bactria (Daxia), which lay north and south of the Amu-Darya, i.e. in the north of modern Afghanistan and in what is now Soviet territory. But the Da Yuezhi, who were now settled and satisfied with their new country, cared little about an alliance with distant China. So Zhang Qian retraced his steps and arrived in Chang'an in 126 B.C. map, p. 223

In 115 Zhang Qian set out again for what were then known as the 'western countries' *(Xiyu)* on a new diplomatic mission, this time to the land of the Wusun, who were horse-breeders in the Ili valley, south-west of Lake Balkhash; he revisited Ferghana and afterwards Sogdiana and the oases of Central Asia.

The epic of Zhang Qian is one of the most extraordinary expeditions of exploration in antiquity,

not only for the length of time he took and the distance he covered—to the eastern confines of the Greek world—but also for the great variety of plants and natural produce that he brought back and, last and most important, for the cultural and political consequences of his missions. They opened unsuspected horizons to the Chinese court, and his descriptions of the countries through which he had passed and of the commercial links that existed were of capital importance to the westward expansion of the Chinese empire and to the future of what is commonly called the Silk Road, a natural line of communication between the Iranian and Chinese worlds.

While Zhang Qian was being held prisoner by the Xiongnu, there was a reversal of policy in Chang'an that was to be of the greatest consequences for them. In 133 the party in favour of war gained the upper hand, and the Han government decided to discontinue the traditional policy of *heqin*.

Steps were at first confined to Chinese territory. Frontiers were consolidated; then in 129 four generals, each commanding 10,000 horsemen, launched offensives against the Xiongnu on the frontier marches. In 128 and 127 counter-attacks against Xiongnu raids culminated in the reconquest of the Ordos, south of the loop of the Yellow River, in the establishment of the commanderies of Shuofang and Wuyuan and the forcible transfer of 100,000 people to populate the region.

From 127 the initiative remained with the Chinese, and the famous campaigns of Wei Qing and Huo Qubing in 119 B.C. gave them western Gansu; the prestige gained at these battles long outlived subsequent reverses. By the end of the century they had conquered the whole Gansu corridor as far as the edge of the desert, separated the Qiang from the Xiongnu, who had subjugated them, and set up an administration in the newly established commanderies of Jiuquan, Dunhuang, Zhangye and Wuwei (map, p. 222). At the same time the Great Wall was extended westwards to Yumenguan and a line of frontier posts and small forts built between Jiuquan and Yumenguan.

Although unconquered, the Xiongnu sustained heavy losses. In 119 they were forced to move their headquarters further north to the vicinity of Lake Baikal, and the grip in which they had held the whole of eastern Turkestan for over seventy years slackened. Some of their clans even went over to the enemy, like the king who surrendered to China with his vassals in 121; five dependent states *(shuguo)* were created for the Xiongnu who had 'come over', where they were expected to settle under Han authority.

45
Cowrie container in the shape of a bronze drum. Bronze, overall H. 39.5 cm, Circum. (convex part) 1.27 m, (on the cover) a procession of tributaries to the king of Dian. A second drum once fitted onto the centre of the cover, but only a fragment of the base survives. From tomb No. 13 at Shizhaishan, Jinning, Yunnan: kingdom of Dian, second half of the second or beginning of the first century B.C.

Expansion to the South and North-East

From the Chunqiu period (722–453 B.C.) onwards, various clearly interrelated cultures that had been influenced in differing degrees by the kingdom of

46
Bronze drum known as the Sōng Da or Moulié drum.
D. (flat top) 78 cm, H. 61 cm, incised decoration of geometric motifs, plumed warriors, people in ritual scenes and birds, from Thanh Hoa province, Vietnam, second or first century B.C.
Musée Guimet, Paris.

47
Detail of Pl. 46: flat top of drum.

Chu developed in the south of China and the north of Vietnam. Remarkable work by Chinese and Vietnamese archaeologists over the past thirty years has provided glimpses of the origins, interaction and evolution of these different centres, although a number of major problems persist.

The best known, and possibly the richest, of these civilizations was the kingdom of Dian, which reached its height shortly before it was colonized by China and was centred on the region of Lake Dian in eastern Yunnan province (map, p. 222). The discovery of the royal cemetery of Shizhaishan in 1955 was followed by that of three contemporary cemeteries (second-first century B.C.) situated within a radius of 40 kilometres of Jinning: Taijishan was excavated in 1964, Lijiashan in 1972 and Chenggong in 1974. Two earlier sites, reflecting a phase before Yunnan's bronze age, have also been excavated; they are Dapona to the south-west of Dali (1964) and Wanjiaba in Chuxiong district (1975). The tombs unearthed on these sites date from between *c.* 600 and *c.* 300 B.C. and have yielded the earliest bronze drums to have been found in China so far.[1]

The kingdom of Dian was not alone in this vast region of the south-west. Its principal neighbours to the east and north were the Yelang, who inhabited the western part of Guizhou province, and the Qiong, in the south-west of the province of Sichuan, whom some archaeologists believe to have been responsible for the large ossuary-tombs constructed of stone slabs and blocks that have been discovered in recent years.[2] To the west of these groups of settled agriculturists who farmed by the burn-baiting method—Yelang, Dian and Qiong—two ethnic groups of nomadic cattle breeders, the Sui and the Kunming, dominated western Yunnan.

The kingdom of Dian would appear to have been the richest of these regions, with a very varied

48   ▷
Cowrie container.
Bronze, max. D. 25.3 cm, H. 50 cm. Four oxen process round a horse and rider in gilt bronze; the two handles are in the shape of tigers. From tomb No. 10 at Shizhaishan, Jinning, Yunnan: kingdom of Dian, second half of the second or beginning of the first century B.C. (See *Chūka Jimmin Kyōwakoku shutsudo*, p. 81).

terrain in which salt marshes and forests lay side by side with cultivated fields, pastures and fishponds. Not only had it produce from the land, and horses, oxen and sheep, but its mineral resources were also abundant (gold, silver, copper, tin and lead) which accounts for the development of bronze metallurgy in Dian, as well as the sumptuous quality of the gold and silver ornaments found in the royal tombs. Trade, to which the leading clan owed at least part of its prosperity, was transacted in merchandise, in Chinese cash and very often in cowries, which have been found in their thousands preserved in drum-shaped vessels in the rich tombs 45, 48 of Shizhaishan. Dian society, as revealed by the excavations at the four known cemeteries, consisted of clearly differentiated classes, dominated by a royal clan and a warrior-aristocracy. Together with the organization of religious festivals, hunting and warfare on horseback seem to have constituted the major occupations of the aristocracy. In this society of warriors, which employed many prisoners of war and would seem to have practised a form of head-hunting, women appear to have played a major rôle—which suggests that here was a survival of matriarchal law.

The social and religious life of Dian was centred and crystallized round the bronze drums. They appear to have played a part at every level of the social structure and mythical thinking. An emblem of power and prestige designed for the chiefs alone, a musical instrument endowed with magic power and marking events in the life of the group (festivals, ceremonies, gatherings), the bronze drum, at 46–7 Dian, as in the Yue civilizations of Guangxi and North Vietnam, symbolized the fertilizing power of the rains, maintaining fruitfulness and endless renewal. It was also the only article and the only totally non-Chinese symbol that the non-Han ethnic groups of southern China and northern Indochina have continued to make, preserve and venerate up to modern times.

Dian civilization reached its height in the second and first centuries B.C. and appears to have been exceptionally rich and complex. Of the very large number of objects unearthed, the great majority were made of bronze; in addition to many tools, they comprised weapons and everyday utensils, decorated drums, receptacles for cowries, musical 45, 48 instruments, ritual weapons with inlaid animals as 49

49
Figure of a parasol carrier.
Bronze, H. 56.5 cm, Wt. 12.29 kg, from tomb No. 13 at Shizhaishan, Jinning, Yunnan: kingdom of Dian, second half of the second or beginning of the first century B.C. (See *Chūka Jimmin Kyōwakoku shutsudo*, p. 89).

ornament, statues, figurines and anthropomorphic and zoomorphic ornaments, many pieces of jewellery and harness, not to mention mirrors and coins imported from China. Iron seems also to have been imported, but was used only for a few weapons and tools. By contrast, the luxury and refinement of the gold, silver, jade, agate and turquoise jewellery is astonishing for a people regarded by the Han as barbarians. Although probably not the actual seal presented by Wudi in 109 B.C., the gold seal found in Shizhaishan tomb No. 6 is certainly one that was granted by the Han to a king of Dian after the Chinese conquest.

One is immediately struck by the astonishing variety of metallurgical techniques, as well as by the forms and means of expression used in Dian art. While the major themes may centre round hunting, warfare and sacrificial rites accompanied by music and dance, the realism of the representations and their evocative power, fondness for movement, relief and detail are combined, sometimes in the same piece, with symbolic or decorative motifs treated in a much more stylized and hieratic manner.

At first glance this narrative art in bronze—dashing, complex, with perfect mastery of its artistic

51
Bronze ornament representing two tigers attacking a boar: a snake bites the tail of one of the tigers as it sinks its claws into the boar's back.
H. 17.1 cm, from tomb No. 3 at Shizhaishan, Jinning, Yunnan: kingdom of Dian, second or first century B.C.

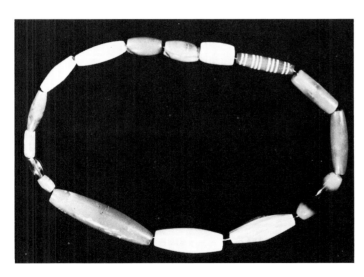

50
Necklace of 16 spindle-shaped agate beads.
L. (of beads) varies between 1.1 cm and 7.3 cm, from tomb No. 13 at Shizhaishan, Jinning, Yunnan: kingdom of Dian, second half of the second or beginning of the first century B.C.

means—owes little to the pre-Han Chinese world. Yet it does reflect the meeting of many cultural strands, despite the fact that the borrowings have been totally assimilated and freely adapted. For example, Dian bronzes contain features of Sichuan origin that had already undergone Chinese influence and others that originated in the kingdom of Chu, as well as influences from the animal style of the steppes. These last borrowings are obvious in the representations of animal combats and in the shape and ornament of some weapons.

The kingdom of Dian had close contacts with the Yue cultures of Guangxi, Guangdong and North Vietnam too. These Yue, the Nan Yue ('Yue kingdom of the south'), whose sovereign was of Chinese origin, had regrouped to form an independent kingdom as early as 207 B.C.; they lived by agriculture and fishing, together with some trade with ports such as Canton and Hepu. They sold pearls, rhinoceros horns, tortoise-shells, fruit, including lichees (lizhi), and cloth to Chinese merchants, receiving weapons and iron tools in exchange. Roads and waterways linked their main

centres to the kingdoms of Yelang (Guizhou) and Dian (eastern Yunnan), as well as to Sichuan across Yelang and to the region of Changsha in Hunan.

Despite recent excavations in China and North Vietnam, present knowledge of Nan Yue culture is still fragmentary. Excavations have confirmed the fact, mentioned in the historical documents, that at an early date they already had close, sometimes warlike, connections with the south of the old kingdom of Chu; Chu culture certainly played a large part in the genesis of the Nan Yue cultures. These southern peoples showed other distinctive characteristics; for example, their dwellings were built on piles, they had special burial practices— 54 their coffins were shaped like dugout canoes, bronze situlae and drums were used as burial urns. But most important was the use, as in Dian, of bronze drums that were part of the chief's protective insignia and were decorated, here again, with ritual scenes and symbolic motifs. In the field of 46–7 decorative techniques, some bronzes discovered mainly in Guangxi province are characterized by 41, 55 finely engraved ornament; the same engraved ornament, though at times scarcely visible, is also found as background decoration on Dian bronzes. 45, 53

These different Yue and Dian centres, together with others as yet undiscovered, probably constituted in the second half of the first millennium B.C. a kind of mosaic that was also a cultural confederation, within which a whole network of influences were active. For example, it seems clear that southwestern China received influences from the steppes and passed some elements of these to the centres of North Vietnam.

Relatively untouched by the Qin campaigns of the third century B.C., in the following century these various civilizations found themselves under pressure from the Han civilization. The kingdom of Nan Yue was destroyed, incorporated into the

52 a/b
Gold seal of the king of Dian.
H. 2 cm, L. (sides) 2.4 cm, seal surmounted by a boss representing a snake, incised inscription in *zhuan* script: 'seal of the king of Dian', from tomb No. 6 at Shizhaishan, Jinning, Yunnan, end of the second or beginning of the first century B.C.

53
Detail of the cowrie container in Pl. 45 from tomb No. 13 at Shizhaishan.

54
Model of a house on stilts, with veranda.
Bronze, H. 37 cm, L. 79.4 cm, from a tomb at Hepu, Guangxi, second half of the first century B.C.

Han empire and divided into commanderies in 111 B.C.; this was followed by the surrender of the king of Yelang, and that of the king of Dian in 109 B.C.

The merchants of Sichuan province had prepared the way for Chinese colonization. The main commodities traded with the Nan Yue have been mentioned. From the 'barbarians' of the south-west Shu merchants bought horses, yaks, long-haired oxen and young slaves; they sold them tools, weapons, iron vessels and probably silks, lacquers and bronze mirrors.

The Sichuan merchants seem also to have traded with more westerly countries. For in Bactria Zhang Qian found Shu cloth and bamboo from the country of the Qiong in the south-west of Sichuan, which Shu traders hoped to sell in India. On his return to China Zhang Qian held out to the emperor bright prospects of a road through Sichuan and Yunnan provinces—in all probability the Burma road—that would have provided the empire with links to India and Bactria. The road was not found,

but the embassy despatched to find it provided the Han with their first opportunity of making official contact with the kingdom of Dian.

The conquest of the south-west in 109 B.C., prepared by the merchants and inspired by the desire to take more important adversaries—the Nan Yue and the Xiongnu—from the rear, was not a major episode of Wudi's policy. Yet it was to have tremendous repercussions in the regions concerned which soon (86, 83 B.C.) made efforts to shake off the Han yoke. Caught in the stranglehold of Chinese colonization, some of the peoples of Yunnan and other southern provinces probably scattered, extending earlier contacts in south-east Asia and spreading some of the elements of their civilization, such as bronze drums, over a wider area. Those peoples who stayed where they were soon saw their traditions submerged beneath the rising tide of Han civilization.

While the colonization of the south was being organized, Chinese forces were simultaneously establishing colonies and administrative outposts in the north-east (Manchuria) and Korea. Here again the aim of Chinese strategy was to separate the Xiongnu from their tributaries—in this case the horse-breeders of Wuhuan and Donghu—and to safeguard their lines of communication. For that matter, the Chinese presence in Manchuria had been of long standing, and the population of the modern provinces of Liaoning and Jilin must have

55
Pair of lamps in the shape of birds.
Bronze, H. 33 cm, L. 42 cm, incised decoration representing the birds' plumage. The necks are in two parts and are movable; the 'lampshades' that the birds spew from their beaks connect with the necks and bodies to form flues through which the smoke and ash can escape. From a tomb at Hepu, Guangxi, second half of the first century B.C.

been of somewhat mixed ancestry; similarly, links with Korea had always been easy—by sea from Shandong and overland through southern Manchuria. Between 109 and 106 B.C. the Chinese occupied the whole northern part of the Korean peninsula and founded four commanderies: Lelang in the north-west, Zhenfan on the west coast, Lintun in the east and Xuantu in the north, straddling the Yalu River. From these outposts, especially Lelang near modern Pyongyang, the influence of Han civilization spread to the south of the peninsula and thence to Japan.

map, p. 222

Embassies and Campaigns in Central Asia

Since 125 B.C. Zhang Qian and other travellers had been praising the merits of Central Asia, the power and wealth of the different regions, the horses of Ferghana (Dayuan) and the country of the Wusun. These fine, large chargers of the Ili valley, and especially of Ferghana, were swift and tireless at the gallop; the Chinese called them 'celestial horses' (tianma) or 'horses that sweat blood', and both Han and Xiongnu thought them superior to the ponies of the steppes.

map, p. 223

In 110 B.C. the Wusun chief asked for the hand of a Chinese princess and sent a thousand horses as a betrothal present. He was given Liu Xijun, a princess of the blood, who set off for the Ili valley in great state, accompanied by an escort of servants. The princess remained in that distant land and tradition has kept alive the echoes of her homesickness, the earliest expression of the theme of a Chinese princess married to a 'barbarian' chief, which was to inspire literature and painting throughout Chinese history:

> The round tent is my palace,
> Its walls are made of felt,
> Dried meat is my only food,
> Koumiss is my drink.
>
> Endlessly I dream of my country,
> And my heart is all bruised.
> Oh to be the yellow swan
> That returns to its homeland!...[3]

In 109 the state of Loulan, at the entrance of the north and south routes of the future Silk Road, sur-

rendered to China. Loulan's power stemmed from its position on the route to the 'western countries' (Xiyu). For it could either grant or refuse provisions, water, guides and escorts, thus assisting or impeding Chinese diplomatic missions and military campaigns. Depending on the alliance of the moment, it could spy for the Chinese or the Xiongnu on the other's movements, a service it was not slow to perform.

Once past the Gansu corridor, which had been recently conquered and fortified, and past the state of Loulan, Chinese embassies, travellers and troops entered the Tarim Basin (modern Xinjiang province), along routes bordering the desert, where provisions were sparse and where men and animals depended entirely on the goodwill of the local people. The agricultural communities that inhabited the oases surrounding the Taklamakan Desert were in a strong position, for they had sole control of the watering places and were able to act as local guides. At the same time, situated as they were between two enemy powers, the Xiongnu—whose suzerainty they had recognized since the beginning of the second century—and the Han, they could not hope to remain neutral.

map, p. 223

In 101 B.C., after a long journey and three years of endeavour, the Chinese general Li Guangli succeeded in conquering Dayuan (Ferghana), beyond the Pamir Mountains, subjugating the capital of the kingdom and capturing its horses. In the mind of Wudi this campaign and other operations in Central Asia at the end of his reign had a threefold aim: to put a stop to Xiongnu invasions, to cut the Xiongnu off from their western bases—which were valuable sources of fresh supplies—and to provide his stud-farms and the army with riding horses.

The embassies and campaigns of the second century did not achieve a stable and definitive conquest of the region; the city-states of the oases retained some of their independence and vacillated between the Xiongnu and the Han according to which side pressed them. But to China's advantage the campaigns disturbed the old balance of power in Central Asia, and this in itself weakened the Xiongnu, but also, and most importantly, now that the Tarim Basin had been crossed, commodities, ideas and influences could get through.

As a result of the opening of these routes to the

western regions, garrisons were established to protect the roads and those who used them. Garrisons surrounding their watch-towers were set up as far as Yumenguan, near Dunhuang, and extended northwards towards the lakes of Juyan. Hundreds of military settlers were sent to Xinjiang itself; an imperial commissioner of ambassadors kept a watchful eye on the settlers and the land they cultivated, since it was they who provisioned ambassadors on foreign missions.

Han Successes: Reasons and Cost

Han power, as exercised during the reign of Wudi against the 'barbarians', was partly due to the régime's capacity for organization. Having got into its stride, the governmental machine could enlist conscripts not only to go on campaign, but also to secure fresh supplies and construct roads; similarly, the system of lines of defence, which we call the Great Wall, was well maintained and was extended at this period.

China had another crucial advantage over her enemies. She could rely on her agricultural economy and to an even greater degree on the products 37–8 of her industry and craftsmanship—iron and steel weapons, luxury articles like silk—which the surrounding peoples wished to buy. These products of state-controlled factories (after 119 B.C.) constituted a means of exerting pressure, a trading asset, a major trump card in the game of Chinese diplomacy, the economic basis on which the system of tribute was to be founded. The government also kept strict control of the export of goods (weapons, iron tools and domestic animals) that might strengthen the military power or increase the economic resources of the barbarians.

Another cause of success was the fact that Chinese fighting methods had changed radically since the beginning of the century, having adapted to those of her enemies. The use of the chariot in battle was virtually abandoned. In their encounters with the Xiongnu the Han showed a technical virtuosity and a mobility that they had learnt from the nomads. The commonest tactic on both sides consisted in rapid raids employing few men, mostly horsemen, designed to dislodge the enemy, seize his cattle and horses, and induce his chiefs to surrender. Clearly such a form of battle did not result in decisive victory for either camp; Wudi never finally defeated the Xiongnu. Fighting methods were very different in Central Asia; they required troops who were less highly trained but could endure long marches and lay siege to towns.

Conscripts—mounted bowmen of the northern and north-western provinces, crossbowmen on foot and other infantrymen of the central and eastern provinces—made up but a small part of the army at the end of the second century; the core of the troops consisted of mercenaries, true professionals, and convicts.

A further source of Han superiority was its weaponry, which was increasingly made of iron 37 and steel, especially in the case of the long swords used by the cavalry; instead of leather armour, armour made of iron plaques was improved as the plaques became smaller and were used in conjunction with scale-like plates. This coat of mail now also covered a larger area of the chest and shoulders. The crossbow, which had been invented during the Period of the Warring States and had a bronze mechanism of extraordinary precision which the Han kept secret—remained one of the weapons that China's neighbours feared most. Improved models like the repeating crossbow may 56, 82 have come into common use at this time.

Yet another cause of the Han victories, especially those of the years 129 to 119, lay in the valour of their generals, who included Wei Qing and Huo Qubing (died 117, aged twenty-four), Li Guangli and Li Guang. Not all received equal reward for their merits. Li Guang, who was an extraordinary bowman, committed suicide when he was over sixty rather than suffer sentence for having lost his way in the desert with his men; Li Ling, his grandson and another ill-starred officer, surrendered to the Xiongnu in 99 B.C. after defeat in unequal combat. It should be remembered that a Chinese general returning after a setback risked beheading and that an officer who surrendered to the Xiongnu and was taken prisoner endangered his whole family. Li Ling's mother, wife and son were executed when the government heard of his defection. Sima Qian, the historian, who had defended him before the emperor, was accused of wishing to deceive the

56
Battle on a bridge.
Incised stone slab from the offering chambers of the Wu family *(Wuliang ci),* Shandong, H. 50 cm, L. 1.98 m, *c.* A.D. 150. (See Chavannes, *Mission archéologique,* vol. I, Pl. LIII, no. 109). Note (top right) two partly damaged seated figures drawing crossbows and pushing against them with their feet; in front of them stands a soldier leaning on his crossbow.

latter and was sentenced to castration. Thus the last campaigns of Wudi's reign cost China many brave officers, including Li Guangli, who went over to the enemy in 90, and Li Ling, who died among the Xiongnu in 74.

Every Han victory depended not only on good organization, on the bravery and endurance of the men and on rapid conveyance of provisions, but also on an adequate supply of horses. Wudi's wars emptied all the stud-farms of the empire; the campaigns of 119 B.C. alone resulted in the loss of 100,000 horses. We touch here on a vital point and one of the major difficulties encountered by the Han: an insufficient supply of fresh horses. In 118 the government fixed the price of a stallion at 200,000 cash (or 20 gold *jin*). In this way it encouraged the breeding of horses. Moreover, the introduction of new breeds from the western lands, the planting of lucerne from seeds brought back by Zhang Qian, had enabled the government to reconstitute a cavalry. The fact remains that Wudi's campaigns were extremely expensive in horses, equipment and above all in human lives. To cite a single example: Li Guangli returned from the Ferghana campaign with 10,000 of the 60,000 soldiers with whom he had set out. These wars were also costly in terms of the defensive systems involved, the need to maintain garrisons and provide them with grain. Yet in the long term the implementation of the government's policy of colonization proved an asset. Conquered commanderies, especially those of the north-west, were occupied immediately by Chinese colonists, despatched (usually forcibly) to develop the new territories. The main transfers of population took place in 127 (100,000 persons in Shuofang commandery), 120 (725,000 persons), 118, 111, 100, 99 and 92 B.C. It has been calculated that over two million persons were directed to the northern frontiers in this way during Wudi's reign.

Chapter IV

Urban Civilization and Court Life

The Capital Chang'an
(map, p. 224)

Virtually nothing—except a few sections of wall and some rammed earth terraces—survives of the town that from 202 B.C. until A.D. 24 was the capital of the Former Han dynasty and one of the largest cities in the known world. Though feeble testimony to vanished splendours, these remains have given archaeologists a fairly accurate idea of the city and some of its palaces. As for the texts, they are more prolix, and one could sometimes wish that they were less given to hyperbole. Thus we have to seek an approach to Chang'an of the Han that lies somewhere between secure but meagre archaeological data and eulogies that are fuller of poetical, often rather conventional, evocations than of concrete information. Fortunately, the excavations carried out since 1959 at the site of Xianyang of the Qin dynasty and the ensuing attempts at reconstruction[1] provide a better understanding of the architecture of the palaces of Chang'an. Here, as in so many other spheres, the first Han sovereigns followed in the footsteps of the Qin.

The site selected in 202 was that of an old Qin imperial residence to the south of Xianyang in an extremely fertile plain watered by three rivers—the Yellow River, the Wei and the Jing—and sheltered by mountains. Gaozu settled at Chang'an in 200 in the two palaces of Changle and Weiyang, which were gradually enlarged and embellished. The walls were built between 194 and 190 B.C. in the

reign of Huidi. But the city did not assume its definitive appearance until the reign of Wudi, by which time many improvements had been made and new buildings constructed. These included the three palace complexes of the North, Gui and Mingguang in the city itself, Jianzhang Palace and Shanglin Park, with its pleasure palaces and Kunming Lake, to the west and south-west of the city

Thus Chang'an was not built to a predetermined plan but rather grew as the palaces were enlarged—which explains its somewhat irregular plan. However, tradition links the line of the northern wall with the Great Bear constellation *(Beidou)* and that of the southern part with Sagittarius *(Nandou)*, the Weiyang Palace, the sovereign's residence, occupying the position of the Polar Star. It is hard to say whether the tradition is based on any real intention of the Han emperors. It seems more likely to have been recognized later as an apposite idea. Nevertheless, it proves the existence of a system of symbols, of the magic integration of the emperor into the cosmic order, expressed in this privileged place, the capital, where imperial power and virtue were exalted. For, with two-thirds of the land inside the walls occupied by palaces, Chang'an was primarily the seat of political authority and of the court, the centre of the world and, as it were, the fabulous display-case for the riches and power of the empire.

The city of Wudi's day was surrounded by a wall of rammed earth 16 metres wide at the base and some 25 kilometres in perimeter. There were twelve gates in the wall, three on each side, the whole surrounded by a moat. Each gateway comprised three lanes 8 metres wide, allowing twelve vehicles abreast to pass through. Vast three-lane avenues—the central lane was reserved for the emperor—led from the gates to the palace and other districts.

The southern part of the city, which stood higher than the northern part, was occupied by the vast complexes of the Weiyang and Changle palaces and the arsenal. The Weiyang *gong,* which alone covered one fifth of the city, consisted of some forty buildings, one of them, the outer hall to the south, measuring 340 metres long by 150 metres wide. Like all the palaces of the period, this impressive audience chamber stood on a terrace with steps leading up to it; here there was also a ramp for the emperor's carriage. The Weiyang Palace also contained the private apartments of the emperor, empress and court ladies, libraries and the temple of the ancestors. The various buildings were linked by raised, roofed passage-ways. The Changle *gong* ('Palace of Eternal Joy') was used largely as the residence of the dowager empresses. Here, in front of the Daxia hall, stood the twelve bronze colossi that Qin Shi Huangdi had ordered to be set up before the Ebang Palace to celebrate the unification of the empire, and which the Han had moved to Chang'an. Other bronze figures, as well as bells, stood at the entrances of the principal palace buildings in the Han period. At the fall of the dynasty they shared the fate of Qin's colossi and were melted down for coinage. However, if we imagine the earthenware warriors unearthed near Qin Shi Huangdi's mausoleum transposed into bronze we shall have some idea of the majesty of these palace entrances.

Some of the palaces in the northern part of the city were reserved for government offices. Two markets (the east and the west) occupied the north-western corner of Chang'an, near the river.

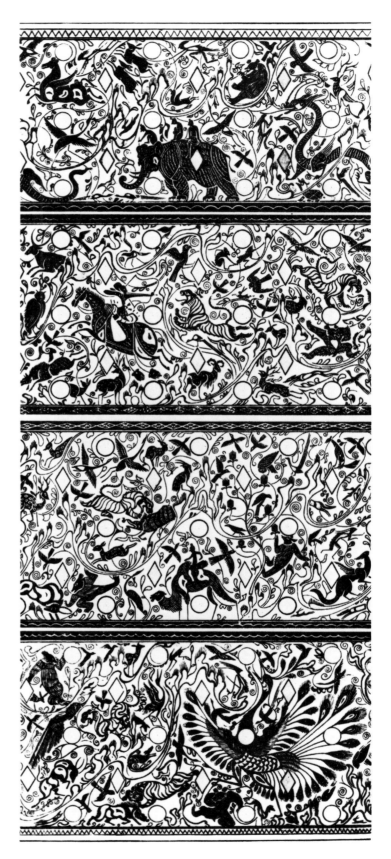

57
Drawing of decoration on a chariot ornament.
Bronze, inlaid with gold, silver and turquoises, D. 3.6 cm, L. 26.5 cm, hunting scenes and fabulous and exotic beasts (elephant and camel) surrounded by cloud-mountains, unearthed in 1965 at Dingxian, Hebei, end of the second or first century B.C. (See *Zhonghua Remin,* p. 66).

Commerce of all kinds flourished there, including the luxury trade. It was also a meeting-place for strollers, public entertainers and scholars in search of work. The north-eastern section of the city was residential. The whole of the city, apart from the areas occupied by the five palace complexes, was divided into districts *(li)* separated from one another by streets or avenues. Each district contained about 100 houses and was surrounded by a wall in which there was only one gate. Lanes led from the single entrance to every house. The gateway to each district was guarded and might be closed at night or when danger threatened.

A complex system of earthenware drains, laid parallel to the avenues, streets and lanes, crisscrossed the city and carried waste water to the canals that linked the city to the rivers.

The residential and commercial districts extended into the north-western and north-eastern suburbs, where rich merchants and aristocrats had settled to escape the congested streets of the Former Han capital.

The west and south-west of the city was occupied by the Shanglin *yuan*, the immense park and hunting reserve, that had existed under the Qin but which Wudi enlarged and altered. A pleasure park and a nature reserve, the Shanglin *yuan* was also, and most importantly, a kind of microcosm, a quintessence of the empire, where every species of plant and animal of the known world was gathered; it was a magical image of wild nature, exotic but subject to the Power of the one man who was emperor. The flora and fauna collected from every province, the recently imported plants confirmed and secured the power of the Son of Heaven over his universal kingdom, of which they formed a microcosmic image. In the wooded mountains and at the lakesides so often celebrated by Han poets the emperor had his pleasure pavilions. Here were held the great imperial hunts, which were both military and political parades and aristocratic sports. As we shall see, the fondness of Han high society for these hunts or carnages, outlets as they were for violence and brutality and counterbalances to social constraints, makes itself felt throughout the literature and art of the period. It occurs in the rhyme-prose *(fu)* of Sima Xiangru (*c.* 179–117 B.C.), Yang Xiong (53 B.C.–A.D. 18) and Ban Gu (32–927), and in the hymn *(song)* of

Ma Rong (79–166), in the decoration of dwelling places, tombs and precious articles. 57–9

The projected enlargement under Wudi of the Shanglin *yuan*, which already extended over more than 100 kilometres, aroused protest. Although it had no effect, the memorandum addressed to the emperor by Dongfang Shuo is worth quoting: 'Jade, gold, silver, copper, iron, camphor, *tan* wood, the *zhi* mulberry and exotic things come

58
Wine warmer *(wen jiu zun)*.
Gilt bronze, D. 23.4 cm, H. 24.5 cm, dated 26 B.C., from Youyu in the north of Shanxi. (See *Wenwu*, no. 11 [1963]: 4–12), relief decoration of animals in a mountainous landscape, inscription bordering the lip: 'vessel [*zun*] for warming wine weighs 24 *jin*, made by Hu Fu of Zhongling [modern Youyu], third year Heping [26 B.C.]'.

59   ▷
Censer *(boshanlu)*.
Bronze inlaid with gold, silver, turquoises and cornelians, H. 17.9 cm, second century B.C.
Freer Gallery of Art, Washington, D.C.

94

from the mountains [of the region]; these innumerable plants and minerals give the craftsmen their raw materials and provide for the needs of the people. The region is rich in millet, rice, pear-trees, chestnut-trees, mulberry-trees, hemp and bamboo too. The soil suits ginger and taro; the rivers abound in fish and frogs. Poor people gather enough to satisfy the needs of their families and do not suffer from hunger or cold. This is why the region between the Feng and Hao rivers is called "fat land" and is reckoned to be worth a gold ingot, a *mu*. If now the order is given to make this region a park, if [the people's] catches from the lakes and ponds are cut, if their fertile ground is taken away, the State will be deprived of its resources, and agriculture and the silk industry will be impoverished....' Such is Dongfang Shuo's first objection; the second, which is in a similar vein, insists even more strongly on the protection of the people and on the resentment that would result if they were dispossessed in this way. He observes that to monopolize this land and use it for breeding deer, to enlarge a park for foxes and hares, a den of tigers and wolves, and, in so doing, to destroy the people's tombs and raze their houses to the ground, would be to provoke nostalgia for the lost land in the young and weak, and tears of anguish in the old.[2] The text is interesting on more than one count. It reminds us of the fertility of Guanzhong and the problem that the creation and enlargement of reserves would pose for part at least of its population; it also shows just how far criticism could go in opposing the emperor's will—though admittedly this critic was the emperor's fool.

Han texts often describe the splendour of the palaces of Wudi and his successors, but this wood-framed architecture was eminently perishable. Moreover, although the many burial models and tomb decorations give an impression, albeit a stylized one, of how a house, farm buildings, pleasure pavilions belonging to certain land-owners (especially from the first century B.C. onwards) may have looked, it is much more difficult to visualize the princely and imperial residences. Surveys and digs on the site of the Qin capital have revealed a vast palace complex that may be regarded as one of the prototypes of the palaces of the second century B.C. The reconstruction proposed by Chinese archaeologists[3] shows a vast three-storeyed building with two symmetrical wings built on different levels of a high rammed-earth terrace. Wooden columns and framework have naturally disappeared, but sections of wall in fired and unfired brick have survived. In some of the rooms these inner walls, faced with several layers of cob and fine clay, followed by a thin layer of whitewash, were decorated with painted geometric motifs in brownish-red, yellow, blue and black. Rooms were connected by galleries and staircases paved with engraved or impressed hollow bricks. Some of the rooms were heated by a kind of brick stove related to the *kang*. Roofs were covered with grey pantiles with geometric or zoomorphic decoration on the eaves tiles. Eaves tiles, of which often only the circular fronton remains, have also been found in large numbers on the Han palace sites. The frontons are frequently inscribed with the name of the palace, the roof of which they had adorned; some were also decorated with geometric motifs of animals of the four directions or votive formulae. 60

The surviving fragments at Xianyang give some small idea of the construction and elevation of the Chang'an buildings. Thus the storeyed buildings so highly esteemed by the Han aristocracy were not a new invention; it was simply that the vogue for tall pavilions intensified after the tours de force built at Wudi's command. These included the Boliang pavilion, the Shenming tower, and there were many others. The tallest pavilion of the Jianzhang Palace in the western suburb of Chang'an is reputed to have measured 115 metres in height. At once symbols of world domination and open gateways to Heaven, these towers and terraces were lines of communication with the world of the Immortals;[4] their function and the fact that they were built at all is very much in keeping with the preoccupations of the imperial circle.

Wudi's megalomania did not stop at these breathtakingly tall towers. It was reflected also in the wealth of decoration and the comfort of his palaces: beams, capitals and columns were made of scented or painted woods, heightened with ornament made of metal or semi-precious stones; column bases were made of jade; inner walls were faced with wood or covered with paintings or hung with silk. While the imperial palaces set the tone, they were not alone in their luxury, and

60

Four frontons from eaves tiles.
Grey earthenware: (1) D. 18 cm, decorated with the red bird, the symbol of the South, (2) decorated with wishes for good fortune: '*Yong shou jia fu*', (3) decorated with the two characters '*zuo ge*', (4) D. 19.5 cm, decorated with good wishes: '*Chang sheng wei yang*' ('long life without calamities'), period of the Former Han (106 B.C.–A.D. 9).
Musée Guimet, Paris.

princely residences of the period would seem to have rivalled them in sumptuousness and extravagance.

At the heart of the Chang'an palaces, that city within a city, was the emperor. Except for solemn audiences, councils, receptions and ceremonies, he lived withdrawn from the world, in the midst of his ladies, his 'faithful' and his eunuchs, 'in the splendour of a majesty that cut him off from the commerce of men'.[5] Only some few courtiers, the relations of the empress, a few rare favourites, personal friends, the 'faithful' or catamites were admitted to his intimacy. The Han emperors were bisexual and almost all of them—like most of the Roman emperors—were active or passive pederasts; and throughout the dynasty the court seems to have sacrificed widely to Uranian love.

A man without peer, whose personal name was taboo, only the emperor could wear certain kinds of clothing or jewellery, or ride in certain kinds of carriages, all of which were specially designed for him. The official ideology, the magico-religious practices that developed during the reign of Wudi only accentuated the aura of uniqueness, mystery and sanctity that surrounded the imperial personage.

The Official Ideology

During the reign of Wudi certain beliefs, cosmological ideas and ancient philosophical trends were collected, rethought, combined with Confucian teaching and codified to form a new, extremely eclectic ideology: Han Confucianism, initiated by Dong Zhongshu (*c.* 175–105 B.C.). The ideas arranged by Dong Zhongshu to form an organic whole comprised the ancient conceptions of the schools of *Yin-Yang* and of the Five Phases (or Elements), with the addition of numerological speculations.

This is not the place to discuss the well known theories of *Yin-Yang*, which stand for the antithetical and concrete aspects of time and space: *Yin* meaning repose, darkness, the female principle, interior, etc.; *Yang* meaning movement, light, the masculine principle, exterior, etc. The infinite alternation of the two aspects constitutes and governs the physical and moral world. A relative, complementary and rhythmic opposition, *Yin-Yang* also suggests the idea of a concrete distribution and classification at the heart of the universe as a whole.

The idea of the Five Phases *(wuxing)*, like that of *Yin-Yang* a legacy of soothsayers and derived from a very ancient repertoire of mythological classifications, was revived, combined with *Yin-Yang* and systematized by Zou Yan (*c.* 305–240 B.C.) in the kingdom of Qi. Through the *fangshi* ('scholars of method') the doctrine thus elaborated by Zou Yan was to leave its mark on all Qin and Han cosmological and political thought.

In his synthesis Zou Yan proposed what might be called a philosophy of history based on a balance between political drives and cosmic rhythm. Each historical period was thought of as governed by one of the Five Phases (earth, wood, metal, fire and water) that succeeded one another in a fixed and infinite cycle. Each Phase accomplished its cycle of growth and decline, to be vanquished and replaced by a young Phase. Thus, since each dynasty is governed by one of the Phases, it is temporary; it is destined to experience a period of ascent followed by one of decline before yielding to a new dynasty. The appearance of presages is a sign of heavenly investiture for the appointed individual or the dynasty, but only for a limited period. This new conception of the cycle of history differs from the old theory of the mandate of heaven *(ming)*, by virtue of which the Zhou dynasty ruled and which foresaw no temporal limitation; only moral faults committed by the dynasty could cause it to fall.

Zou Yan's philosophy of history seems to have had considerable success and was adopted by Qin Shi Huangdi. The Zhou dynasty was thought to have possessed the virtue of Fire; so the first Qin emperor adopted that of Water, since water conquers (i.e. extinguishes) fire. Water corresponds to the colour black and the number six, so black was used as the colour for clothing, flags, etc., and six as the basic number.

At the fall of the Qin, the founder of the Han dynasty considered himself heir to the power of the Qin phase of Water. But, as we have seen, in 104 B.C. Wudi adopted the Earth phase and the colour yellow.

In their reflections on antiquity the Confucian scholars of the beginning of the Han dynasty interested themselves in the legendary sovereigns. These sovereigns did not succeed one another by conquest: each ceded the throne to his successor. A cyclical theory, according to which power (and thus the Phase that governed it) asserted itself through conquest of its predecessor, scarcely fitted this period of antiquity. So Dong Zhongshu proposed a theory maintaining that each of the Five Phases gives rise to its successor: wood produces fire, which produces earth (ash), which produces metal (minerals), which produces water (as it liquefies), which produces (i. e. feeds) wood (vegetation). This new theory, according to which the Phases are generated by one another, gained wide acceptance and was revived by Liu Xiang (79–8

B.C.) a century later. At the end of the Former Han the dynasty was believed to be reigning by virtue of Fire, the colour of which is red. From this point of view the Qin represented an interpolated dynasty lacking the mandate of heaven, so that the Han succeeded the Zhou dynasty, to which the virtue of Wood (which generates Fire) was attributed.

Dong Zhongshu was a crucial influence in the development of this philosophy that was to dominate Han thought. In formulating a system of connections between the natural and human worlds, he was not merely following a trend that pervaded all the philosophical enquiries of his time, including those of the Confucians as well as the Taoism of the *Huainanzi*; through the coherence and political correlations of his system he also laid the foundations for all later pseudo-scientific attempts to explain the world. With his cosmological speculations he combined an interpretation of history based on the commentary of Gongyang to the *Spring and Autumn Annals (Chunqiu)*. This synthesis, which appeared in Dong's parent work, the *Chunqiu fanlu,* aroused the enthusiasm of the scholars of the time and could not fail to please Wudi since it justified the dynastic notion of the 'Great Han' who were to dominate the world.

The system of space-time connections, or the theory of *Yin* and *Yang* and the Five Phases *(Yinyang wuxing shuo)*, as adopted in the reign of Wudi, provided an explanation of the universe as a whole, gave the reigning power the magico-religious basis that it lacked and coloured every facet of Han social, political and cultural life. Although points of view of the various schools concerning the play of connections and the succession of the phases might differ, the principle of equivalences between the Phases, seasons, directions, colours, tastes, sounds, numbers, planets, entrails, etc. was accepted by all and shaped all ideas, including the idea that things were distributed between four zones arranged round a centre.

The idea underlying the whole system is that heaven and man are totally interdependent. Every disorder, every error perpetrated by man has its repercussions and endangers the order of the universe.

This is the usual table of equivalents:

98

Phase	Direction	Season	Beasts Symbolizing the Four Quarters of Heaven (sishen)	Household Deities	Planets	Yin-Yang
Wood	East	Spring	green dragon	inner doors	Jupiter	*Yang* ascending
Fire	South	Summer	red bird	stove	Mars	*Yang* at zenith
Earth	Centre	—	—	impluvium	Saturn	point of balance
Metal	West	Autumn	white tiger	outer door	Venus	*Yin* ascending
Water	North	Winter	'black warrior' (tortoise)	passages in the house	Mercury	*Yin* at zenith

Imperial Cults, Magic and Sorcery

Within the framework of the cosmological concepts of the official ideology and fostered by the throngs of wonder-workers at the court, imperial cults proliferated and a whole liturgy dominated by space-time correspondences evolved. Similarly, magico-religious rites, through which the emperor was believed to make contact with the world of the Immortals, assumed ever greater importance and were often closely linked with the sacrifices and ceremonies of the official cult.

In 130 B.C. on Wudi's orders an altar was set up in the south-eastern suburb of Chang'an to Taiyi, the Supreme Unity, who, according to the Taoist magician Miao Ji, was the most venerable of all the deities and the one who rules the universe. At the same time, at the ancient site of Yong, to the west of the capital and a sacred place for the Qin, Wudi continued to offer the *jiao* sacrifice to the Five Emperors, who, in the new pantheon, were relegated to the rank of assistants in the triad dominated by Taiyi and embracing also Heaven (Tianyi) and Earth (Diyi).

In 113 a new altar to Taiyi was set up at Ganquan, north of the Wei River. It was a three-storeyed structure and was surrounded at the base by the altars of the Five Emperors. Each of the officiating priests wore vestments of his emperor's colour, while those responsible for the sacrifice to Taiyi were dressed in purple, the colour symbolizing the Supreme Unity.

Another State cult devoted to the Earth was celebrated at Fenyin in Hedong. Finally, in 110, Wudi instituted two sacrifices, *Feng* to Heaven and *Shan* to the Earth, officially to celebrate the triumph of the dynasty and to perform an expiatory rite but also in the hope of gaining immortality for himself. We have already noted the reference to the *Feng* and *Shan* sacrifices on the Taishan Mountains in the poem about the Gourd Dike (p. 66), for it was during his journey in 110 B.C. that the sovereign was able to see for himself the disaster caused by the Yellow River in 132. The celebrations of 110, at which his subjects could observe the emperor in direct contact with Heaven, were accompanied by the construction at Fenggao, near the Taishan Mountains, of a *mingtang* or house of the calendar and small-scale model of the Universe. This *mingtang* was believed to be a replica of the one built in the reign of Huangdi, the Yellow Emperor. Sacrifices were offered to Taiyi and the Five Emperors on the upper floors and to the Earth on the lower.

All the ceremonies of the imperial cult were articulated by sung hymns mimed by dancers. The hymns have been preserved in the *Hanshu*. The first, a hymn to Heaven, greeted the descent of the divinity and his escort of gods:

The nine storeys of the skies have opened—see the standards of the divinity.
... The chariot of the divinity—is made of clouds;
It is drawn by winged dragons; innumerable are the feathered pennants.
The descent of the divinity—as though carried by the chargers of the wind!
To the left the Green Dragon,—to the right the White Tiger ...
Now the divinity has taken its place!—the music sounds well ordered harmonies.

The rejoicing lasts until dawn,—let us offer this pleasure to
    the divinity . . .
Beautiful dancers have gathered—all have a rare elegance;
Their faces are like the flowers of the milkweed,—their agile
    bodies whirl.[6]

Veneration of Heaven, Earth and the Five Emperors was not in itself new to Chinese thought;
the novelty lay rather in the hierarchy that had been
instituted, in the forms of the cult, the solemnity of
the ceremonies and above all in the active participa-
tion of the emperor. The Son of Heaven, the
earthly representative of the Supreme Unity
(Taiyi), the emperor was henceforth held to be the
only individual permitted to sacrifice to the supreme divinities from whom he held his mandate.
    We have seen how the *fangshi* (magicians and
those learned in esoteric methods) of Yan and Qi
flocked to the court. They included authorities on
the theory of the Five Phases, geomancers, seers
who could foretell the hours of good and bad luck,
authorities on the calendar, astrologers and alchemists seeking to transmute cinnabar into gold.
Each promised miracles to Wudi: one would harness the Yellow River, another would produce or
search for the elixir of life, yet another would
summon the Immortals from the islands of the
blessed. Many magicians thus had honours and
favours heaped upon them by Wudi—only to die
on the block when none of their prescriptions had
proved effective or their deceptions had been un-
covered. Despite everything, the emperor never
lost his credulity, but to the end of his life remained
avid for longevity and immortality.
    Black magic, so widespread at the princely
courts of the period, was in keeping with this climate of superstition. In 130 at Chang'an a palace
lady was accused of having used evil spells,
conjurations and sacrifices to restore Wudi's first
empress, née Chen, to the emperor's favour. The
crime was *dani budao* (impious). The empress was
dismissed; the guilty woman was executed, together with over 300 persons 'implicated' by the
system of collective responsibility. As the reign
neared its end, sorcery *(wugu)* flourished among
the ageing autocrat's women. Thus sombre practices cost two imperial princesses and a number of
high dignitaries their lives, while the crown prince
was driven to revolt and suicide.

Exegesis and Literature—
From Orthodoxy to Disguised Criticism

Although through his desire for physical immortality Wudi became a follower of magicians who
practised a form of Taoism, his concept of power,
policy of conquest, journeys of inspection, the
strictness of his laws and his espousal of the planned economy stem directly from Legalism and Qin
methods. In reality he was influenced by all the
doctrines that were current in his day. The new
imperial cult centred on the triad dominated by
Taiyi (the Supreme Unity) was profoundly influenced by Taoism; while the official ideology, as it
had evolved by the end of the second century,
seems to have been a mixture of naturalism and
morality. The naturalistic element is reflected in
the cosmological concept of *Yin-Yang* and the Five
Phases, which explains the multitude of phenomena by a network of classifications within a
harmonious whole. Moreover contact between
man and nature enables man to interpret strange
phenomena and to foretell the future, and forms
the basis of ethical behaviour, since bad conduct
has immediate repercussions on the natural order.
    This concept of the world, combining cosmol-
ogy, morality, history and a political aim was applied by Dong Zhongshu (*c.* 175–105) to interpretation of the Classics. Dong taught the *Spring and
Autumn Annals (Chunqiu)* with commentary by
Gongyang at the Grand School *(taixue)*. Gongyang's commentary attached an esoteric meaning
to the *Chunqiu*, which could henceforth be used as
a guide to understanding the present and predicting the future. Basing himself on the *Chunqiu*,
Dong interpreted calamities and marvels as ad-
monitions from Heaven to the master of the world
when his conduct became aberrant. Thus Dong
Zhongshu founded a tradition of exegesis directed
towards prophecy; under the name of school of
Modern Texts *(jinwen)*, because it was based on
texts that had been transmitted orally and were
written down in the writing of the period, this
tradition was to prevail until the end of the Former
Han.
    The adoption of the new Confucian ideology
under the aegis of the Grand School and concern
for cultural unification drove other lines of thought

to the fringes of orthodoxy, although they too were sustained by the naturalistic theory of the Five Phases. Taoism, the most important of these doctrines, maintained that the adept could achieve immortality by way of asceticism. Many Taoist thinkers of the beginning of Wudi's reign gathered at the court of Liu An (179–122 B.C.), king of Huainan. Their collected proceedings, the *Huainanzi,* revived the ideas of Laozi and Zhuangzi on simplicity and spontaneity, on the primacy of Nature over Culture, and on the relativity of institutions and customs; it also revived cosmogonic and cosmological theories that were close to those of Zou Yan. The concept of echo, which is central to the collection and according to which all phenomena and all beings in the universe are closely correlated and respond naturally to one another, also shows clear affinities with the schools of *Yin-Yang* and of the Five Phases.

Wudi did not proscribe the most dynamic of the Taoist philosophical trends of the second century, the Huanglao School (the doctrine of the Yellow Emperor [Huangdi]), but it was obliged to pursue its teaching more or less clandestinely, outside official circles.

The boundaries of free expression were narrow at court, and the historian Sima Qian (*c.* 145–86 B.C.) suffered tragically from the emperor's despotism. Nevertheless his *Records of the Historian (Shiji)* appear to be in many respects a polemic against Wudi's centralism and against the sycophantic spirit that prevailed at the time.

Sima Tan, father of Sima Qian, conceived the idea of the *Records of the Historian* and began to collect and work on the material. He was a specialist in astrology and divination and was Grand Astrologer *(Taishigong)* from 140 to 110 B.C. The title was in fact more imposing than the office: 'My father was a clerk concerned with the stars and the calendar; he was ranked next to the category of soothsayers and priors; the sovereign looked upon him as a plaything for his amusement and supported him like a singer or an actor; the common herd had little regard for him'.[7]

On his return from extensive travels in the south and east of the empire that gave him direct experience to compare with the written sources, Sima Qian was appointed gentleman of the court *(lang)* in one of the offices in the capital. In 111 he was sent to inspect the recently conquered south-western regions. He succeeded his father as Grand Astrologer and was involved in the reform of the calendar in 104.

In 99, he was condemned to castration for having spoken to the emperor in defence of General Li Ling (see pp. 90–1). Unable to redeem his penalty since he had no personal fortune or devoted and influential friends, he suffered this punishment in 98. He nevertheless continued to serve and later was even appointed *Zhongshuling* (Head of the Imperial Secretariat). The post was an important one since the incumbent attended to all contacts with the throne and all the imperial decrees. The last known document on the life of Sima Qian is his heart-rending letter of 91 to Ren An, who was involved in the tragedy that cost the crown prince his life. This letter and testament, in which Qian refuses to intercede on Ren An's behalf, reminding him that his condition as a eunuch had rendered him contemptible and robbed him of all authority, is a long series of confidences on his own sufferings: 'If I do anything I find that I have acted wrongly; if I wish to help, I am on the contrary harmful.... There is no greater shame than to undergo the punishment of castration. A eunuch is no longer counted among the number of men.... I have dishonoured my ancestors; how could I now face the tombs of my father and mother?'

His work is his only comfort: 'I have collected and collated all the old traditions that were scattered and as it were lost in the world; I have examined how affairs were conducted; I have looked for the explanation of their success or failure...; I have done 130 chapters in all. For my part I have wanted to examine everything that concerns heaven and man, to understand the evolution that has been proceeding from antiquity to our own day and make it the work of a single author. Before I had finished the draft this misfortune struck me; I would have been sorry not to finish my task; that is why I have suffered the most terrible of punishments without annoyance. When I have finished writing this book I shall place it on the "famous mountain" [the palace archives] so that it may be passed to men able to understand it and so that it may find its way into the towns and great cities. Then I shall have washed away the shame of my old disgrace'.[8]

Sima Qian has been censured for having written a satirical book. And certainly the *Shiji* is full of indirect attacks on Wudi; they include veiled criticism of the emperor's credulity, ironical criticism of the omnipotence of money, of the courtly mentality, of tyrannical officials. Having travelled and afterwards spent some twenty years at court, Sima Qian knew the true state of affairs and could assess the merits of the régime. The misfortune that darkened the last years of his life does not entirely explain his attitude. Qian was nostalgic for the past, for the vanished ideals responsible for the rough glories of the end of the Zhou and the beginning of the Han, when brave and distinguished actions could take a man to the top of the tree, when links of chivalry were forged between the chief and his men and when the sovereign was open to the candour of his counsellors. Qian found the qualities that he admired—courage, independence, determination, generosity—in the knights-errant who risked their own lives to defend the righteous against miscarriages of justice, in those who die as heroes out of patriotism and loyalty. He commends great devotion, bold decisions, ideals for which lives may worthily be sacrificed. He conceives his *Records* as a work of reparation to all men of merit who have gone unrecognized in their own time but for whom he, as a historian, will find a place in posterity. 'I have come to the aid of extraordinary virtues,' he wrote. This cult of the hero was new in history; a century and a half before Plutarch, Sima Qian considered that the biography of an exceptional individual merited the historian's attention.

When writing the *Shiji,* Sima Qian collected, assessed and used every available source. The unification of the empire and the literary renaissance of the second century B.C. did in fact make it possible for the first time to survey China's past as a whole. Besides the traditional sources (the *Shujing, Chunqiu* and *Guoyu,* etc.), Qian included many speeches, poems, official reports, and decrees from the imperial and princely archives. Moreover, in his biographies of poets and philosophers he quotes their writings instead of dwelling on the events of their lives. From this point of view the *Records of the Historian* forms a kind of anthology of early literature.

The one hundred and thirty chapters of the *Shiji* are divided into five sections: the annals *(ji),* chronological tables *(biao),* treatises *(shu),* Hereditary Houses *(shijia),* biographies and monographs on foreign peoples *(liezhuan).* In the treatises Sima Qian discusses the rites, music, the calendar, astrology as well as public works and the economy. His interest in foreign peoples is also new and typical of his period. But although he integrates these peoples into his history he does not consider them the equals of the Chinese on the cultural level.

Eclectic in learning, rational in method, Sima Qian regards the rôle of history as moral and didactic. He sees the past as the best source of education. Thus he often groups his biographies according to character or activity, mentioning in turn Confucian scholars, wandering knights-errant *(youxia),* patriotic assassins *(cike),* catamites, fine talkers and rich merchants.

The *Shiji,* a general history of China from its origins to *c.* 90 B.C., became the prototype for all subsequent dynastic histories, of which the first—the *Hanshu (History of the Former Han Dynasty)*—was compiled at the time of the Latter Han.

Court Verse

Literature and politics are rarely separable in the Han period, and poetry was no exception. The whole *oeuvre* of Sima Xiangru (*c.* 179–117 B.C.), the most illustrious Han poet, centred round court life and the affairs of State.

Born in Shu, in Sichuan province, Sima Xiangru came of a well-to-do family, through whom he had access to the post of gentleman of the court *(lang).* Although promotion came fast, in 150 he left the virtually unlettered court of Jingdi for that of Liu Wu (*c.* 186–144 B.C.), king of Liang, who had gathered a brilliant group of scholars and poets round him. Sima Xiangru composed the first of his known works, the *Zixu fu,* in the capital of Liang, in eastern Henan province. At the death of his patron in 114, Xiangru returned to Sichuan. His family was ruined. At Linqiong he fell in love with Zhao Wenjun, daughter of an extremely rich local contractor. He fascinated her, and she eloped with him. Lacking means of support the couple opened a drinking booth in the market-place of Linqiong, until finally Wenjun's father recognized the marriage and granted the young woman her share of the inheritance. Once more back on their feet, Xiangru and Wenjun settled in Chengdu. In *c.* 138 young Wudi, who had just discovered the *Zixu fu*, summoned the poet to Chang'an and gave him a position at court. Apart from a mission to the south-west, Sima Xiangru spent the rest of his life at court, becoming the official poet and a familiar of the emperor.

The *fu*, or rhyme-prose, brought to perfection by Sima Xiangru, made its appearance as a literary genre at the beginning of the Han and in less than one generation became the form of poetic expression par excellence. It was a kind of essay in a mixture of verse and prose, usually descriptive and concrete; on the formal level it was characterized by the use of parallelism and metaphor, literary quotations, catalogues, difficult, recondite language and a flowery vocabulary. Han rhyme-prose stems from both Chu verse and the Chinese rhetorical tradition. As regards form—rhymed lines of irregular length meant to be declaimed— the poetry of Qu Yuan (340–278 B.C.) and his imitators that constitutes the *Songs of Chu (Chuci)* was the origin of the prosody of the Han *fu*. The other source was the School of Politicians *(Zonghengjia)*, who devoted all their eloquence to persuasion or indirect criticism. These itinerant politicians *(youshui)* of the Period of the Warring States would offer their counsel and stratagems to the princes; their art of persuasion consisted not in attacking an interlocutor head-on, but in leading him by indirect argument to reach the desired decision spontaneously, as though by his own effort. To this end the good rhetorician used various techniques: he examined several alternatives and analysed their consequences, enumerated historical examples and recited synonyms to amplify and decorate his piece. Similarly the Han *fu* contains oratorical debates between imaginary persons, a fondness for historical reference, catalogues and synonyms, designed at once to convince, to generate a sense of grandeur and to embellish the piece.

The School of Politicians was not wholly dead at the beginning of the Han dynasty, and the poets of the beginning of the second century, Lu Jia

(228–*c.*140 B.C.) and Jia Yi (*c.* 200–168 B.C.), were both rhetoricians and poets. The *fu* flowered in the mid-century with Mei Sheng, Mei Gao and, especially, Sima Xiangru. From the beginning the genre embraced pieces of rather different types, in both tone and content; they included:

- entertaining pieces, the sole aim of which was to please the prince with the scenes they evoked, the richness of the descriptive language and the beauty of the style;
- pieces that were more didactic, moralizing or critical, deriving from the techniques of rhetoric;
- declamations that were more subjective and personal, in which, like Qu Yuan in his *Lisao*, the poet expresses his grief, resentment and lamentation in the face of an unseeing prince, a cruel fate or a corrupt society.

Of the work of Sima Xiangru only four *fu* of undoubted authenticity have survived; they are: two *fu* on hunting, i.e. the *Zixu fu* and the *Shanglin fu*, the *Ai Qin Ershi fu* (Lamentations on the Misfortunes of the Second Qin Emperor) and the *Daren fu* (Fu of the Great Man). The first two are the most famous and were the most influential. The *Zixu fu* describes the hunting parks of the kingdoms of Chu and Qi; this was followed by the *Shanglin fu*, which describes the imperial reserve and celebrates the greatness of the emperor who decides, at the height of his pleasure, to renounce these extravagances, open the Shanglin Park to the people, devote himself to affairs of State and let his virtue shine upon the world. Thus the *Shanglin fu* is a remarkable rhetorical exercise. The poet tries to persuade the emperor to abandon hunting as a pastime by putting all the arguments in favour of such a decision into his mouth. At the same time Sima Xiangru clothes his intention in the form of a panegyric; the whole description of the park, intended to glorify and exalt the imperial majesty, is thus a skilful accumulation of hyperboles, a catalogue of trees, flowers, animals, a torrent of impressive, descriptive passages, of inessential resonances designed to evoke the magnificence of the Han:

..., birch, balm, philodendron and smoke-tree,
Betel and coconut-palm,
Areca palm-tree, Chinese palm,
Dalbergia and obovate-leafed magnolia,

Camphor-tree and Japanese privet
Have grown to a thousand yards,
Are so thick that it takes several people to put their arms
round them.
Their flowers and branches spread out straight,
Fruit and leaves in luxuriant growth,
The trees grow close to stand erect, cluster to lean on one
another:
All is twisting, overlapping,
Entangling, crushing,
Struggling, clinching and sublimely soaring....[9]

In the description of the actual hunt, the real, the convincing and the supernatural are inextricably interwoven: the imperial team rises into the air in an apotheosis, a cavalcade worthy of the *Chuci*.

...it outrides the winds that make men tremble,
Gallops through the terrible whirlwinds;
It bestrides the void of the ether
And moves in convoy with the spirits.

It crushes the ash-grey crane,
Scatters the yellow cranes,
Drives the peacock and the argus,
Harries the golden pheasant,
Starts the five-coloured bird,
Snatches the *fenghuang* in flight....[10]

In this *fu*, as in the *Fu of the Great Man*, which is at once a paeon to Wudi and a satire on his quest for immortality, Sima Xiangru combines court entertainment and moralizing lecture, the two main currents of rhyme-prose. But form rather than the message is pre-eminent in Sima Xiangru's writing. He was a court poet and appears above all to have been fascinated by language, by the magic of words, the flow of images and resonances—which lends itself perfectly to declamation. Although some of his descriptions may seem forced and excessively contrived, there is a kind of intoxication

61
Plan of the tomb of Liu Sheng, king of Zhongshan.
Mancheng, Hebei (See Wen Fong [ed.], *Great Bronze Age*, fig. 112): (1) tomb passage, (2) entrance hall, (3) storage area, (4) stable for horses and carriages, (5) central chamber, (6) burial chamber, (7) bathroom, (8) encircling corridor.

62   ▷
Lamp known as the lamp of the Changxin Palace: young woman attendant holding an oil lamp.
Gilt bronze, H. 48 cm, Wt. 15.85 kg, first half of the second century B.C., from the tomb of Princess Dou Wan at Mancheng, Hebei.
Hebei Provincial Museum.

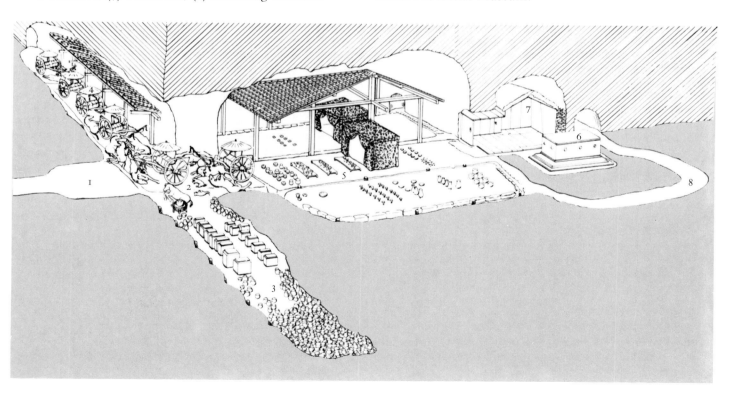

in the words and rhythms. Sima Xiangru is certainly one of the most extraordinary creators of descriptive vocabulary and was the uncontested master of the later *fu* poets, who did not always succeed in rediscovering the originality, audacity, exuberance and perfection of his language.

The Bureau of Music

Wudi wished to have the cults that he had instituted accompanied by music fit to charm the gods and men. The early music of the Zhou was to all intents and purposes dead by the end of the second century B.C. Wudi turned to the light music of the former principality of Zheng, which was anathema to the Confucians because it was aimed solely at giving pleasure, and he entrusted the creation of a new religious music based on secular airs to the musician Li Yannian, whom he appointed Chief of Harmony. Wudi brought this revolution about within the framework of the Bureau of Music *(Yuefu)* by reshaping it, changing its orien-

64
Bronze dagger.
L. 28.1 cm, from the tomb of Prince Liu Sheng (d. 113 B.C.), Mancheng, Hebei, second century B.C. (*c.* 140–113 B.C.).

63
Lamp in the shape of a ram.
Bronze, H. 18.5 cm, L. 23 cm. The ram's back is hinged to form a reservoir for the oil; the wick must have hung out of the dish so that the flame burned above the hollow body of the ram. From the tomb of Liu Sheng, king of Zhongshan, Mancheng, Hebei, before 113 B.C.

65 ▷
Detail of the jade shroud sewn with gold wire in which Princess Dou Wan was buried, and pillow of gilt bronze inlaid with jade.
H. (pillow) 41.3 cm, L. (shroud) 1.72 m, from the tomb of Princess Dou Wan at Mancheng, Hebei, end of the second century B.C.

66
Bowl *(pan)*.
Grey earthenware with painted decoration of fish and scroll-work in red, black and white, D. 55.5 cm, H. 14.7 cm, end of the second century B.C., from the tomb of Princess Dou Wan at Mancheng, Hebei.

67
Measure *(zhong)* in the shape of a *hu* vessel with cover.
Bronze, inlaid with gold and silver, H. 59.5 cm, inscription of 18 characters on the foot, before 113 B.C., from the tomb of Liu Sheng, king of Zhongshan, Mancheng, Hebei.

68   ▷
Vessel *(hu)* with cover and chain for suspending.
Gilt bronze, decoration incised and painted by the mercury process to simulate silver inlay, H. 48 cm, inscription under the foot: 'vessel [*hu*] plated in gold and silver holding 2 *dou* and weighing 11 *jin* 4 *liang* with the cover, property of the house of Guanyi', second or first century B.C.
Musée Guimet, Paris.

tation and encouraging collaboration between poets and musicians. Thus the Bureau of Music became an important State service responsible for both official ceremonies—for which orchestras, choirs and choreography were required—and the entertainments of a court that was becoming more and more luxury-loving and refined. One of the functions of the Bureau was to collect popular songs. The musicians of the *Yuefu* altered the songs, set them to music, or took well known melodies to which they set new words; the sacrificial hymns, of which an extract was quoted on page 99, were in all probability based on popular melodies in this way.

A good scholar himself, with a great interest in literature and a sensitive appreciation of music, Wudi thus inspired, or at least encouraged, a new trend in music and verse that was to be the basis of the lyric poetry of the early centuries of the Christian era. The verses composed by the court poets, minstrels and entertainers of the Bureau of Music were ephemeral accompaniments to banquets. Their favourite themes revolved round separation, the passage of time and fleeting pleasure. In contrast to the splendours and solemnities of the *fu*, they retained the simplicity and spontaneity of the

popular lament. This purely sentimental verse was sung to the accompaniment of the *qin* or the *zheng* zither, the melancholy and poignant tonality of which are often stressed in contemporary texts. As J.P.Diény remarks,[11] 'it would appear that the Han preferred music that made them weep to any other kind'. So, sad songs for court banquets: this may appear illogical, but was in fact no more than the expression of a haunting fear. In a period of profound change, in which new ways of life, relationships and thought were being introduced, in a period of wayward fortunes, nothing seemed more certain on this earth below than the imminence of death. A sense of the brevity of life, of the fragility of things, obsessed high society under the Han and left them prey to epicureanism, the habit of *carpe diem* and the search for longevity and immortality.

Court Art

Fear of death, epicureanism, the extreme luxury of the court—all are reflected in numerous contemporary objects and in many recently discovered princely tombs, especially those of Mancheng in Hebei province. The burials of Liu Sheng, king of Zhongshan and Princess Dou Wan, his wife, were excavated in 1968.[12]

map, p. 221

The tombs had been deeply hollowed out of rocky cliffs and both resembled subterranean palaces with their stables for horses and vehicles, their stores of food and alcohol, their vast central hall for banquets and audiences and, at the far end of each tomb, the burial chamber in which lay the body, clothed in its jade shroud, in a lacquered wooden coffin inlaid with jade. The two wings that formed the stables and the central chamber were constructed of a wooden framework roofed with tiles; the burial-chamber walls were faced with narrow stone slabs. The proportions of these underground palaces matched the stature of their occupants. Thus Liu Sheng's tomb was hollowed out to a length of 51.70 metres, a width of 37.50 metres and a height of 6.80 metres.

61

Nearly 3,000 articles were found stored in the various chambers of the two tombs; these included

62–3

69
Censer *(boshanlu)* with openwork cover in the shape of the Mountain of the Immortals; the censer is supported by the figure of a man seated on an animal's back.
Bronze, H. 24 cm, end of the second century B.C.
William Rockhill Nelson Gallery of Art–Atkins Museum of Fine Arts (Nelson Fund), Kansas City.

70   ▷
Leopard couchant, one of a pair.
Bronze, inlaid with gold, silver and garnets, H. 3.5 cm, L. 5.8 cm, from the tomb of Princess Dou Wan at Mancheng, Hebei, end of the second century B.C.

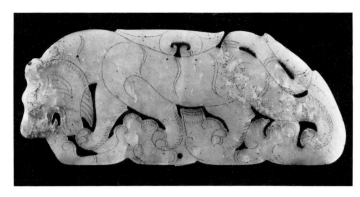

71

Flat pendant in the shape of a tiger passant.
White jade, H. 7.1 cm, L. 19 cm, second or first century B.C.
Musée Guimet, Paris.

64, 66 lamps, censers, bronze, iron and steel weapons, silks, ceramics, and gold and silver acupuncture needles. Most were personal objects that the owners of the tombs had used in their lifetime. Given the rank of the deceased, the whole may be regarded as representative of the taste of the imperial family and of the court in Wudi's time. Liu Sheng was in fact a son of Jingdi. He was king of Zhongshan from 154 until his death in 113 and had little interest in the arcana of politics, preferring wine, good food, music and women.

This epicurean and his wife had been clothed in shrouds consisting of over 2,000 jade tablets sewn 65 together with gold wire. These 'jade armours' *(yu-jia)*, as the Han texts call them, were used at the time as burial clothing for emperors, members of the imperial family and high officials, with variations depending on the rank of the deceased. They were supposed to be even more effective than the jades placed in the corpse's orifices in preserving the corpse and preventing the *po* soul from leaving it, an undecayed body being a sign of immortality. Despite all these precautions, the bodies of Liu Sheng and Dou Wan decomposed, but their shrouds, which have been remounted on dummies, testify to the extraordinary skill of the jade workers who cut this very hard stone into thin plates, pierced holes in them symmetrically to take the gold wire and slit them over the eye sockets.
62, 67 Many bronzes from these tombs bear engraved inscriptions recalling the name of the owner or his palace, the name of the object, its weight, capacity

and sometimes the date of execution and price. Such inscriptions are not confined to the Man-cheng bronzes; they are found on other precious 68 vessels of the period. They show how highly these objects were prized; they were collected and sometimes passed down through serveral generations. The Changxin lamp, possibly the most prestigious 62 piece to have been found in the tomb of Dou Wan, is an example of these princely treasures. The lamp is conceived in the form of a young woman sitting back on her heels and holding a vessel in her left hand. Two semi-circular shutters slide in a groove round the lamp, so that the direction of the beam can be varied. The young woman's right arm is hollow and forms a chimney through which the smoke of the lamp can escape, the soot being deposited in the body of the statuette. The various elements of the lamp, as well as the right arm and head of the statue are movable to facilitate cleaning. The piece must have been cast by the lost-wax 59, 69 method like many Han bronzes of highly elaborate, almost sculptural form. Many inscriptions recall successive owners and the history of the piece. Made for a royal family during the first half of the second century, perhaps in 173 B.C., the lamp must have entered the imperial palace through confiscation in 151. It seems to have pleased Dowager Empress Dou, Liu Sheng's grandmother and a relative of Dou Wan. Many inscriptions do in fact mention the Changxin Palace, which was the residence of Dowager Empress Dou. She probably gave the lamp to Dou Wan. The Changxin lamp is one of the masterpieces of Han sculpture. Although the realism and naturalness of the posture, the feeling for volume, the drapery with its rather rigid folds are still in the Qin tradition, the sensitive modelling of the face, the serenity of the expression behind the idealized features, and the supple lines of the body, which is partly revealed through the robe, testify to a far more subtle artistry.

72   ▷

Vessel *(hu)* for funerary use.
Earthenware, decoration painted in horizontal bands depicting fabulous beasts, clouds and spirals, H. 45.5 cm. The shape and decoration are designed to imitate contemporary bronzes and lacquerware. Second or first century B.C.
British Museum, London.

There can be no doubt that an unprecedented concentration of riches in the hands of the emperor and a few princes of the blood constituted an extraordinary stimulus to the arts and prompted an aesthetic quest for a new refinement. Chang'an and, to a lesser extent, a few provincial courts formed a crucible in which a court art was forged and flourished—and continued to flourish throughout the first century B.C.

The concentration of wealth, the importance and the means accorded the imperial workshops do not of themselves account for the flowering of art during the second and first centuries B.C.; cosmopolitanism undoubtedly played an important part, at a time when many regional artistic traditions, new produce and foreign fashions were becoming naturalized at court. Produce introduced in the wake of Chinese expansion included vines and lucerne seeds brought back by Zhang Qian, as well as koumiss (fermented mare's milk). Animals included the Bactrian camel, horses from Ferghana and donkeys; imported from the Xiongnu, these last were greatly appreciated in China for their low price, their ability to carry heavy loads and their patience over long and difficult journeys. But curiosity did not stop at the naturalization of plants and animals; from the end of the second century onwards the nobility craved luxury articles from abroad, including furs, woollen cloth, jade, coral, pearls, ivory and tropical fruits like the lichee (lizhi). At the same time court entertainments were revivified by foreign and regional traditions such as the dances of the Sichuan peoples, songs from Dian, music and dance from Chu and Qin, and the art of the strolling players of Central Asia. Finally, continued contact with the art of the steppes enriched the repertory of ornament. This last influence was revealed most clearly in a fondness for inlays of precious stones and in a style depicting animals tearing each other to pieces, pursuing one another or simply passant.

Feeling for the exotic and love of hunting combine in a remarkable way in the ornament of a chariot decoration found at Dingxian. As in Sima Xiangru's hunting *fu*, animals—real, rare (elephant and camel) and fabulous—combine in ornament in which, despite the fantasy, density, frenzied movement and even preciosity, there is a certain masterly strictness of composition. It has something of the same spirit, the same aspirations and is addressed to the same public as Sima Xiangru's verses.

The decorative art of the court of the Former Han is characterized by a love of gilding, of gold and silver damascening and of inlays of precious stones; and the techniques of mercury painting enabled the bronze worker to equal the fluidity, movement and sharpness of lacquer painting in his motifs. Thus the art of the period is dominated by a calligraphic play of curves and waves, an astonishing sense of movement and a love of precious materials and warm colours. This applies to bronzes, jades, lacquers and ceramics, which were often painted in imitation of lacquers.

Yet this art should not be dismissed as pure decoration; an artefact often had a religious significance, whether it were a jade *bi*—token of alliance and protector of the dead, placed beside the body in the coffin—or a mirror, the everyday use of which should not obscure its magical properties and power to ward off demons. The form of the object and its ornament came to echo the pleasures, tastes, preoccupations and beliefs of the time. Censers *(boshanlu)* represent but one example; their covers evoke the islands of the Immortals—the paradise which, like the emperor, every nobleman dreamed of attaining—or mountains where dialogues with the Immortals might be held. The form may have been new but, like the sweet-smelling smoke that escaped from the openings in the cover, appears in any case to have been closely connected with the quest for immortality that pervaded the aristocratic life of the period. The animals that inhabit the pointed cover of the *boshanlu* of the time are also the earliest examples of the depiction of wild nature in Chinese art. Mountains that are rather similar, although smaller and treated as simple scene-setting elements, decorate certain mirrors of the same date. Here too, undoubtedly, the theme has many meanings, both magical and profane.

Part III

A Century of Reforms (86 B.C.–A.D. 23)

Chapter I

First Questionings

By the end of the reign of Wudi an ardent desire for peace and an acute awareness of the losses and sacrifices they had endured developed among both the Han and their enemies, the Xiongnu. The reign of Zhaodi (86–74 B.C.) and especially that of Xuandi (73–49 B.C.) gave China a chance to recover and opened the way to a new tendency within the government. We shall follow Michael Loewe[1] and call it reformist in contrast to the modernist thinking that had prevailed under Wudi.

The first measures designed to ease the lot of the populace date from 86 B.C., when a commission was sent to the provinces to enquire into the sufferings of the people. Action was taken in the following year to assist the most sorely deprived. In 81 sixty Confucian scholars from different parts of the empire were recommended and sent to the capital to explain the needs of the people and suggest remedies. An impassioned dialogue then began at Chang'an between those in power, represented by Sang Hongyang, Grand Officer of Censorship, and the scholars, who demanded the suppression of the monopolies in iron, salt and alcohol and attacked the office of standardization, the unbridled expenditure of the court and the direction of foreign policy. A decade or two later Huan Kuan published a lengthy report of the dialogue under the title *Yantielun (Debates on Salt and Iron)*. This unique document, compiled by a supporter of the reformists, records the controversies of 81 B.C. between the modernists and reformists in the form of dialogues of remarkable clarity. The modernists, believers in *realpolitik*, not overburdened with moral scruples and heirs to Legalist methods, defended their own governmental policy, by which they hoped to solve the problems of the day; the reformists for their part denounced the abuses of this policy and advocated economies, disengagement and a return to the conditions they believed to have existed at the beginning of the Zhou dynasty. At the risk of greatly simplifying, one could say that the modernists advocated an economy of wide scope, planned by the State and supported by active trading with the outside world, which flowed from and was encouraged by the policy of expansion. At the opposite pole the reformists wanted to return to an agricultural economy of an introverted, self-sufficient and anti-mercantile type, in which craft industry was directed towards satisfying the needs of the community and no more.

The main points of the debate concerned monopolies, foreign policy and the aims and methods of government.

State Monopolies

The scholars believed that the monopolies had diverted the human resources of the country from agriculture, which had previously been the basic occupation and should remain so. With the introduction of monopolies the people had turned to commerce, the craft industries and transport.

The government party argued that it was absurd to think of contemporary society as purely agricultural, since it also depended on craft industry and trade. In both these domains controls had played an essential part: they had allowed proper development of non-agricultural resources and just and regular distribution, thanks to efficient means of transport. Thus, for Sang Hongyang, regulation of trade was a way of redistributing wealth, a sound measure to counter the monopolies of the rich. But the reformists attacked the operation of the monopolies as well as the principle. They maintained that the State foundries were more anxious to reach their production quota than to serve the public interest, and produced agricultural tools that were unsuitable and of poor quality, thus obliging the peasants to work even harder. Moreover, prices for both iron tools and salt were too high and beyond the reach of poor peasants.

Foreign Policy

The scholars protested against Wudi's wars of expansion, which they considered to be ruinous in terms of men and money. The whole weight of these wars (taxes and military service) had fallen upon the people. As for the trade which expansion had fostered, it was a luxury trade and benefited only the rich. The reformists therefore called for a policy of peace, isolationism and non-interference in the affairs of others—especially the Xiongnu. Such a policy, they held, would enable China to recover her economic health.

Sang Hongyang's reply to this somewhat utopian criticism was realistic; he recalled that the Xiongnu attacks had been continuing since the beginning of the century, that the northern frontiers had needed defending for centuries and that the inhabitants of the frontier zones required protection. He recalled that defensive operations and the establishment of garrisons had called for funds that could only be raised by State intervention in regard to basic products like salt and iron. Sang Hongyang also believed that a certain display of pomp and luxury at court had inspired loyalty in the non-Chinese communities and their leaders and that expansion had prompted a commercial movement which had benefited the country. The reformists retorted that the best weapon with which to subdue foreign peoples was virtue and that, like the State monopolies, monetary transactions had benefited only merchants and officials, who had grown rich at the expense of the peasants whom they had oppressed. As we shall see, this laudable concern for the interests of the peasantry championed by the reformists tended to be forgotten when they assumed the reins of government in the second half of the century.

Aims and Methods of Government

Thus in 81 B.C. the assembled Confucian scholars fiercely opposed the Legalist ideas of Sang Hongyang and Wudi. They rejected monopolies, controls and State intervention; they advocated a return to laissez-faire and to government by the influence of virtue; they called for a reduction in expenditure, easing of taxes, of military corvées and of hard labour, which were diverting the agricultural workers from the soil. In their estimation society was sick because it was based on profit-seeking. Since the 130s B.C., they said, public life had been characterized by oppressive government, economic imbalance, decadent morals, extortion by those in authority and impoverishment of the people, the logical consequence of all of which had been growing lawlessness and a weakening of civic sense.

The modernists emphasized in vain the prosperity of the principal cities of the empire: the reformists countered with the poverty of many agricultural regions, the over-population of the metropolitan zone and the dangers of an overmanned and unscrupulous bureaucracy. They maintained that the penal code inherited from the Legalists was iniquitous and contrary to the principles of Heaven. Morality needed to be restored to improve a situation that had been vitiated by crime and violence. Similarly, they demanded that officials be selected by a genuine application of the examination system; candidates should be assessed primarily on their moral qualities, for the task of government is to assist the sovereign, promote civilization, harmonize *Yin* and *Yang* and reduce the sufferings of the people.

Sang Hongyang pointed out that moralists and idealists like Confucius and his disciples had shown themselves to be incapable of dealing with the practical problems of government. Instead, he praised the successes of Shang Yang. Whereas the scholars insisted on the primacy of ideals, on a return to the 'golden age' of the early Zhou, Sang gave priority to practical considerations and to the need for a government to change with the times instead of clinging to tradition for its own sake. The Confucians replied that the strength of certain principles is immutable and that they are valid for all time. Although not a document of reformist propaganda, for it sets out to be impartial, the *Yantielun* often gives the advantage to the scholars and shows them never to have been short of arguments. In the long term they triumphed, and the reforms of the years 85–45 B.C. already bear the stamp of their ideas.

The monopolies of salt and iron were too lucrative to be abrogated, but a compromise was reached: State control of alcohol was abolished and the making of alcohol authorized against payment of a tax. Social measures were taken at the same time: taxes were waived in bad years; there were loans to the poor; many services required of the people were abolished, and the bureaucracy was reduced and cleaned up. The interest he took in the lot of the people, his economic measures, his advocacy of a sense of justice in government and the success of his foreign policy, all these made Xuandi, who implemented many of these reforms, undoubtedly one of the best emperors of the Former Han.

118

Chapter II

Fruits of Expansion: *Pax Sinica*

The Submission of the Xiongnu and the Tribute System

From the beginning of the rule of Huo Guang—whom Wudi had made executor of his last will and protector of his heir Zhaodi—there were signs of disengagement in foreign policy. Thus the Xiongnu raid of 87 B.C. was not followed by a vast punitive campaign, and Huo Guang merely defended the frontiers. The Xiongnu were in fact faced with serious economic and political difficulties. During Wudi's wars they had lost a great part of their herds and consequently their wealth, a situation from which their former vassals, the Wuhuan to the east and the Wusun to the west, sought to profit. Attacked from both sides, the Xiongnu concentrated their efforts against the Wusun. The battle ended in victory (71 B.C.) for the Wusun, who were supported by the Chinese. Soon afterwards, struggles for the succession broke out among the Xiongnu, and in 57 five claimants to the throne came face to face. Two rival confederations emerged from this clan struggle; one was led by Zhizhi, with whom the peoples of northern Mongolia sided, the other by Huhanxie, who controlled southern Mongolia. In 53 B.C. the *Shanyu* Huhanxie decided to surrender to the Han. For fifty years this allegiance relieved China of the Xiongnu menace, the vassal state of Huhanxie acting as buffer and shield on the northern frontiers of the empire. Before long, Zhizhi's confederation moved westwards towards Dzungaria and the upper Irtysh, north of the Tianshan Mountains.

In 48 B.C. Huhanxie reoccupied northern Mongolia. Huhanxie's surrender, resulting from the economic and political weakening of the Xiongnu, enabled the Chinese to bring them into the tribute system. Thus Xuandi's diplomacy finally accomplished what Wudi had begun by force of arms, succeeding where military superiority alone had failed to triumph.

In broad outline and with varying degrees of success, the tribute system as practised in the first century B.C. persisted until the twentieth century; it characterized the whole Chinese attitude towards foreign races. In this system the Son of Heaven assumed the status of a monarch dealing with vassals, a superior dealing with an inferior. In the case of Huhanxie the vassal received a seal granted by the emperor. Either in person or represented by one of his noblemen, he was expected to be present at court for the great annual reception on the first day of the New Year. He brought a tribute, in exchange for which he received gifts from the emperor. Distant states were permitted to visit at longer intervals but were obliged to present themselves at least once in the course of a reign.

The vassal king also undertook to send one of his sons as hostage. The young prince was brought up at court at the emperor's expense, learning respect for Chinese power and civilization.

The vassal was expected to keep the peace—the main duty of the Xiongnu was to put a stop to their own raids—and might receive a regular subsidy from the Chinese in exchange. When a military campaign was afoot he also had to send auxiliary troops with supplies and fodder. Like the governors of commanderies, he received the left-hand half of an inscribed bronze badge—which was usually in the form of a tiger—while the right-hand half was kept at the palace. When necessary, the right-hand half was given to an imperial envoy who conveyed the orders of the Son of Heaven to the vassal king. The authenticity of the imperial message was tested by fitting the two halves of the *fu* badge together.

China did not intervene in the domestic policy of the vassal states, but imperial envoys were for ever passing backwards and forwards between the two 'allies'. They kept the Han court informed of events in the subject state, maintained a semblance of Chinese suzerainty and took advantage of it for business purposes.

Other links might change the policy pursued by the tributary state; for example, a Chinese princess was often given in marriage to a vassal king. We have seen this diplomatic ploy in action with the Wusun; it was also used on the Xiongnu. Thus, in 33 B.C. Wang Zhaojun, one of the imperial concubines, was given in marriage to the *Shanyu* Huhanxie.

The principal advantages of the tribute system to the vassal states were economic. Indeed, the annual tribute sent by the states was repaid in imperial gifts of far greater value than the tribute. In 51 B.C., when he visited Chang'an, Huhanxie received weapons, a chariot, 15 horses, 20 *jin* of pure gold, 77 outer garments, 8,000 rolls of silk, 6,000 *jin* of floss-silk and 34,000 *hu* of grain. In 33 B.C., when he returned in person, the gifts were doubled. Gifts, especially silk, reached their maximum in 1 B.C., with 370 garments, 30,000 rolls of silk and 30,000 *jin* of floss-silk. Besides gifts, another substantial benefit was the economic aid that China gave its tributaries. Finally, permission to trade directly with the Chinese was no mean attraction; however, contraband trade profited from the system to at least the same extent as legal commerce.

On the Chinese side the ultimate aim of the system was to bring the Xiongnu—and other 'barbarians'—to total submission. The idea was to paralyse them by offering them, in the form of these barbed gifts, a superior material culture and the luxury of Han life. But China paid extremely dearly for this policy, for the cost of the system was enormous, including as it did expenses incurred in transportation and lodging for foreign princes and the price of gifts charged to the public purse. Yü Ying-shih[1] has calculated that the system absorbed 7 per cent of the total revenue of the empire, not counting the military and administrative expenses that resulted.

For all its advantages to China—in the submission of the barbarians and the guarantee of peace—the tribute system, symbolized by the presence of hostages at court, was by its very nature unstable. To make it work it required a kind of political, military and economic balance between the two parties, and that balance was precarious since it was threatened by any change in the circumstances of either partner. Nor did they deal as equals. China always considered herself superior to her neighbours and regarded the cultural superiority that she claimed as moral superiority. In this sense, the submission of the barbarians and the tribute system accorded perfectly with the political ideal and order of the Confucians as advocated by the scholars of the *Yantielun*. In terms of this philosophy, the number of vassal states paying homage was a sign of imperial virtue and of China's civilizing mission. The system, consequently, became even more fragile, for it could only function for as long as China was powerful enough to impose herself and the system. We shall see that even within the Han period itself this was not always the case.

For the time being, in the mid first century B.C. and after a long break of eighty years, the Xiongnu were once more overwhelmed with gifts from the Han, including gold, cash, clothing, silk and rice. The Noïn-Ula tombs, thought to date from about the beginning of the Christian era, give some idea of the new wealth that the Xiongnu were deriving from the tribute system.

Noïn-Ula, one of the Xiongnu centres, lies in the heart of the modern People's Republic of Mongolia, some 100 kilometres north of Ulan Bator. The remains discovered by Kozlov in 1924–5 were those of *kurgan*, important tombs of the Xiongnu

maps, pp. 221, 223

73
Belt-hook: a barbarian is attacked by a tiger.
Bronze, inlaid with turquoises, L. 12.4 cm, first century B.C.
Kunstindustrimuseet, Copenhagen.

74
Detail of a felt rug.
Appliqué motif of a griffin attacking an elk. The rug was on the floor of the antechamber of the sixth *kurgan* at Noïn-Ula, People's Republic of Mongolia: Xiongnu art, end of the first century B.C. or beginning of the first century A.D.
Hermitage Museum, Leningrad.

lated to the famous gold belt buckle found in tomb No. 9 at Sogam-ni in the former commandery of Lelang and to a very similar buckle excavated from tomb No. 7 at Shizhaishan in the kingdom of Dian in Yunnan province.[2]

The Xiongnu were not satisfied simply to import goods; Chinese craftsmen worked among them, creating chariots, coffins, parasols, etc., the remains of which have been found in the Noïn-Ula burials. At the same time, woollen cloth with embroidered ornament borrowed directly from the Hellenistic repertoire was imported from Central Asia or made at Noïn-Ula by deported craftsmen.

The first impression, therefore, is of the cosmopolitan appearance of the Noïn-Ula burial goods. The felt hangings are the one truly native contribution—they seem to have been in use for some time before they were buried—their ornamentation, although adapted, closely following the animal style of the steppes. As a whole, however, the abundance of imported goods and the employment of craftsmen from China und Central Asia suggest that Xiongnu art, as exemplified at Noïn-Ula, was not a major art.

The North-Western Garrisons

We have to imagine the north-western frontier as a vast region embracing several lines of defence with fortresses and garrisons. The outer edge of this frontier zone was again protected, at least in theory, by subject 'barbarians' organized into dependent states (*shuguo*).

Thus today the Gansu corridor is still strewn with the remains of Han fortifications made of unfired bricks alternating with fascines, rammed earth and sometimes stone blocks; they comprise parts of the Great Wall, fortresses, watch-towers

aristocracy, covered by rather low tumuli. Below each tumulus, at the bottom of a pit, was the burial chamber. The chamber was wood-framed, constructed very much on the Chinese model and that of the burials of Lelang commandery in Korea—which were probably contemporary—and was often hung with felt cloth. It contained a lacquered and painted wooden coffin, which would appear to have been made by Chinese craftsmen, and burial goods in which the traditions of the steppes are mingled with Chinese imports and influences, as well as some from Hellenized Bactria.

The silks, lacquers and jades found in the Noïn-Ula *kurgan* probably came from the Chinese court. Similarly, a number of the bronze, gold and silver ornaments, many of which were inlaid with turquoise, seem to have been made in China in the 'barbarian' style for the vassal princes. Some are re-

75
Belt-buckle.
Gold set with turquoises, L. 9.5 cm, W. 6.5 cm, dragon motifs in relief, from tomb No. 9 at Sogam-ni, former Lelang commandery, Korea, first century B.C. or first half of the first century A.D.
National Museum of Korea, Seoul.

122

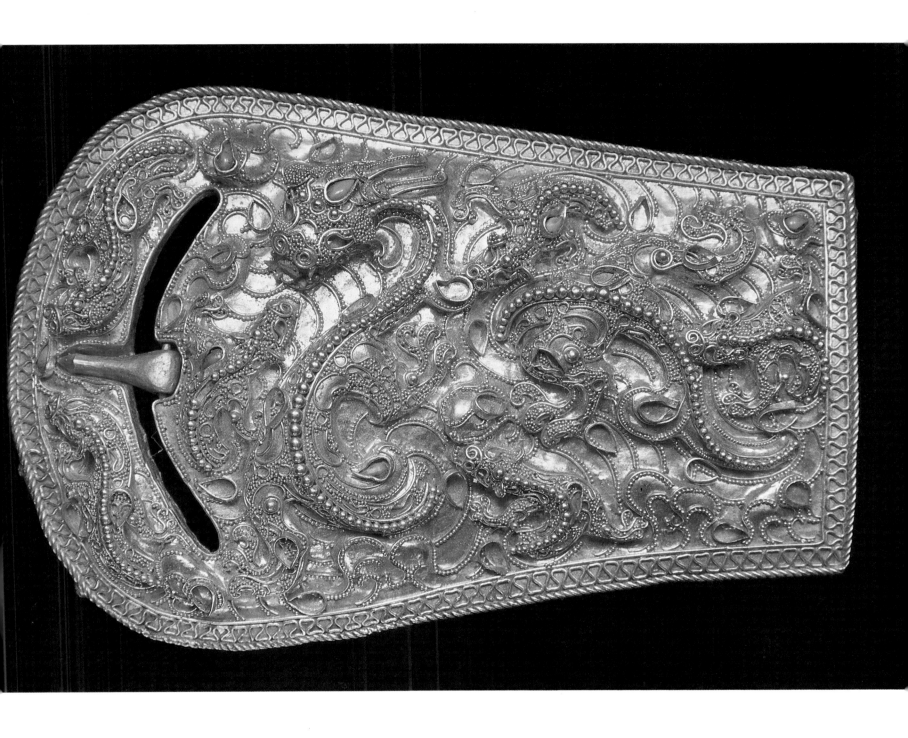

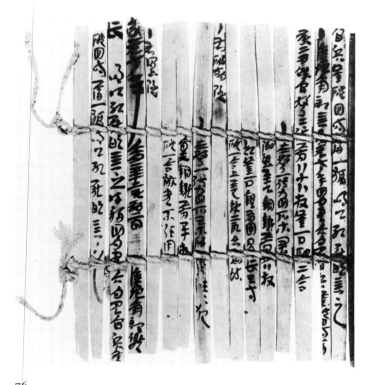

these regions since the beginning of the century. Most of these documents come from the regions of Dunhuang (in particular some thousand collected by Sir Aurel Stein between 1900 and 1915), from Juyan (Etsin-gol)—some 10,000 slips found by the Sino-Swedish expedition of 1927–34, and nearly

76
Wooden slips joined by hempen cords.
L. (slips) *c.* 23 cm, writing in a simplified form of *lishu:* an inventory of the equipment of two infantry sections for the second quarter of A.D. 95, provenance: Juyan, Gansu. (See Lao Kan, *Juyan Han,* vol. I, p. 574; vol. II, p. 191).

77
Two fragments of a letter of recommendation, on silk. L. (larger fragment) 12 cm, W. 6 cm. An officer named Zheng stationed on the northern frontier recommends one of his colleagues to an officer of his acquaintance garrisoned at Dunhuang. Provenance: Dunhuang, Gansu, (See Chavannes, *Les documents chinois,* no. 398), first century A.D. British Library, London.

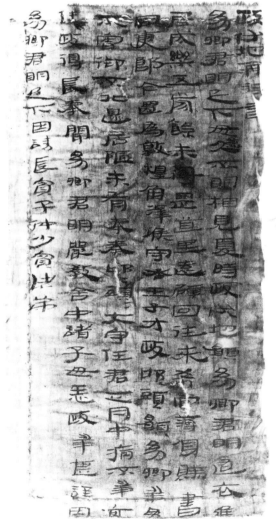

and city walls. The main lines of defence extended east and west, but an important line followed the course of the Etsin-gol for 250 kilometres from south to north and consisted of 10 fortresses, 156 watch-towers, not counting palisaded enclosures and fortified villages.

The garrisons' duty in this vast region was to defend not only the actual frontier, but also the agricultural settlements *(tuntian)* and the stud farms that had been established there; they also defended and controlled the new diplomatic and commercial route that linked Chang'an to the oases of Central Asia.

The military organization of the frontier zones, the conditions in which the garrisons lived and the way in which despatches and official documents were carried are known from numerous wooden and bamboo slips that have been discovered in

124

20,000 discovered since 1972[3]—and from Wuwei (dig of 1959) in Gansu province.

The slips from the Dunhuang and Juyan regions are remains of the archives of the garrison posts and extend in date, according to the sites, from 102 B.C. to A.D. 137. They include reports, inventories regulations, instructions and soldiers' letters and demonstrate the discipline and conscientiousness in the performance of everyday tasks and in the care of weapons and equipment that the hierarchy endeavoured to maintain and on which the military defence of the Han rested in great part. It seems very likely that the *Pax Sinica* of the first century B.C. favoured the meticulous keeping of registers in the regional posts, the compiling of detailed reports and the creation of vast archives—all features that have characterized Chinese bureaucracy down the centuries.

Military authority inside each commandery was held by one, or later by several, constables general *(duwei)*, who, like the governor *(taishou)*, were appointed by the central government. The *duwei* were responsible for organizing defences and garrisons, also for the agricultural work that was part of the duty of the military colonists.

Most of the troops drafted to defend the frontiers were conscripts *(zu)*. There were also volunteers and convicts whose punishment had been commuted to military service. Tours of duty might be of considerable duration, as suggested by many of the slips and the letter from one Zheng, who complains that he has been stagnating for over five years at Chengle, near modern Helingeer in Inner Mongolia. Officers and men were often joined by their families.

The troops were divided into sections *(sui)*, platoons *(hou)* and companies *(houguan)*. Each section (between 2 and 10 men) was responsible for a watch-tower or a small fortress. As the Dunhuang slip illustrated here indicates, the first duty of the soldiers of the section was to keep guard and when there was an alert to give the alarm by lighting a pile of faggots; the signal was received at the neighbouring post and passed on. As in the Roman empire, there was a distinction between day-time faggots *(feng)*, designed to produce a great deal of smoke, and night-time faggots *(sui)*, which burned with a bright flame to penetrate the darkness. There were other signals based on a compli-

78
Wooden slip.
L. 23.1 cm, W. 1.2 cm. One of a group of several slips giving instructions for signalling beween posts: '. . . the order will be put up where it can be seen by the soldiers of the section [*sui*] of each post [*ting*] so that all may know it by heart and understand it; a close watch is to be kept and as soon as there is a fire signal [*feng*] the section of the post shall light one in turn . . . .'
Provenance: Dunhuang, Gansu, (See Chavannes, *Les documents chinois,* no. 432), first century B.C. or first century A.D. British Library, London.

cated code by which news was passed from one post to another.

The troops had also to provide the postal service, to manufacture unfired bricks and to construct and maintain the defensive works. Those who were not employed on defence had to till the soil.

As most of the troops were illiterate, intellectual life can hardly have flourished in these little military colonies of the north-west. The fragments of books found among the official documents are treatises on divination, collections of medical recipes and vocabularies for those learning to read and write.

43 An inhospitable terrain of sand and gravel, a trying climate, hard living conditions, pay that was often meagre and was supplemented by trade in the local markets on the part of both officers and men—such was the lot of the soldiers at the northern and western frontiers; it was a monotonous life in peacetime and became hazardous when the raids 77 resumed. As Officer Zheng wrote, '. . . the distance is long; contacts are rare; my rank is low and my person is humble; exchanges of letters are difficult. I apologize; I apologize. . . .' And, further on, after recommending to his correspondent a colleague who had been sent to Dunhuang, he adds, 'on the northern frontier, I am living in a wretched country and I have nothing to tell you. I apologize, I apologize. . . .'[4]

map, p. 223 ## The Silk Road in the First Century B.C.

The entry of the southern Xiongnu into the tribute system in 53 B.C. considerably enhanced Han prestige in the western regions. Since the year 60 the Chinese controlled both the southern and the northern routes of the Silk Road. From then onwards Han initiative was concentrated on expanding their diplomatic and commercial activities in Central Asia.

The Silk Road started at Chang'an and led across 43 the Gansu corridor by way of Wuwei, Zhangye, Jiuquan and Dunhuang. After Dunhuang it divided. One route crossed the Yangguan Pass to the south-west and led westwards, skirting the southern edge of the Tarim Basin. Among other king-doms, it passed through Shanshan (the former state of Loulan, south of the Lobnor, the name of which the Han had changed in 77 B.C.), Jumo, Khotan (Yutian), and Yarkand (Suoju). From Yarkand the caravans crossed the Pamir Mountains to reach Bactria, whence they travelled either to India or—by way of Bactres (Balkh), Merv, Ecbatana, Ctesiphon and Palmyra—to the Mediterranean world. The other route, leaving the Yumen Pass (Yumenguan) behind it to the north-west, led westwards, skirting the northern edge of the Tarim Basin. The road proceeded via Turfan (former kingdom of Jushi), Karashahr (Yanqi), Wulei, Kuchâ (Jiuci), Gumo (Aksu) and Kashgar (Sule). From Kashgar it made the difficult crossing of the Pamir Mountains to reach Ferghana. It rejoined the road to Antioch and the Mediterranean at Merv.

The inclusion of the city-states of Central Asia in the tribute system, the creation in 60 B.C. of a Protectorate General of the Western Regions (Xiyu duhu) with its headquarters at Turfan, the fostering of the agricultural colonies (tuntian) run by the military, and especially the establishment of a vast international trade, brought prosperity to the oasis towns. Throughout the Han period Central Asia remained the pivotal point of trade to India—whence goods were consigned on to the west by the sea route—as well as to the Parthian empire and from there to the Mediterranean.

The Chinese commodity for which there was most demand was, of course, silk. In the early days of Chinese conquest in Central Asia silk seems to have been exported in the main by government agents. The Han court used silk for the gifts exchanged for tribute from the allied princes; it was also used to pay troops' wages, for services, and ambassadorial presents, and it seems probable that all or some of these gifts of silk were resold by the recipients. But fairly early, as soon as the demand from the Roman empire began to assume sizeable proportions, a genuine trade developed. It was never direct, but, during the first century B.C., was carried on mainly by the merchants of the caravans and of Central Asia, then, further along the Silk Road, by Sogdian, Parthian and Indian middlemen and finally by Palmyran, Nabataean and Syrian merchants.

Although silk was already popular in Rome by

79
Reconstruction of a wooden tomb model of a junk.
H. 20.6 cm, L. 80.6 cm, found in a tomb of the end of the
Former Han in Canton. (See Zhongguo kexueyuan ..., *Xin
Zhongguo,* p. 79, no. 2).

the death of Julius Caesar in 44 B.C., it was not imported in large quantities until the reign of Augustus (27 B.C.–A.D. 14). At that period it reached Rome both as woven silk from China itself or from Syrian workshops, and as skeins of silk thread. The precious threads were mixed with other fibres to obtain a mixed weave; woollen and cotton garments were decorated with pieces of silk.

Also by the Silk Road the Chinese imported horses, furs, woollen cloth and jade (nephrite) from the region of Khotan, and perhaps glass beads made in Syria or Alexandria. But the volume of these imports was small compared with the demand for Han silk. This was mainly paid for in gold, so

that China and, to a lesser degree, her agents in Central Asia, together with India, absorbed a large part of the gold reserves of the Hellenistic, and later the Roman, world.

Although the Silk Road was by far the most important trade route between China and the west in the first century B.C., the sea route was not entirely unknown to the Han. Chang'an received commodities (pearls, rhinoceros horns, tortoise-shell and spices) from the Indian Ocean, India and South-East Asia. These were transported in 'barbarian' vessels and arrived after many trans-shipments on the coast of Vietnam or in Canton. Thence they were carried northwards by river and overland. Chinese silk was exported to India by the same sea route. But it was not until the first or second century A.D. that a flourishing international maritime trade grew up and that this artery, extending from the Mediterranean to the China Sea, linked the great empires of the period.

79

Chapter III

From Learning to the Governing of Men

The Study of the Classics and Intellectual Trends in the First Century B.C.

The reign of Xuandi (73–49 B.C.) was a golden age in the study of the Classics. Twelve scholars representing twelve different schools of interpretation taught the Five Classics (the *Yijing, Shijing, Shujing, Chunqiu* and *Liji*) at the Grand School. These masters taught the version known as the 'modern text' *(jinwen)* of the Classics, that is to say, they used texts that had been recopied by Han scholars in modern characters. Versions written in old characters had just been discovered, but these so-called 'old texts' *(guwen)* were not recognized officially until a little later, although many scholars of the first century knew and had studied them. Thus, while teaching the *Shujing* from the modern-character text, Kong Anguo was simultaneously engaged in editing the old-character text of the same work, which had been found when the wall of Confucius's house was demolished.

During the reign of Xuandi, the divergences between the different schools of the modern texts seem to have depended on whether the masters came from Lu or Qi. Although during the fourth and third centuries philosophy flourished in Qi to a remarkable extent, Lu, where Confucius was born, lovingly preserved the memory of his teaching and the performance of the rites. It would also appear that the best tradition of interpretation of the *Shijing* had been kept alive in Lu. In fact the differences between the Qi and Lu schools were not

great. Lu stressed the rites and etiquette, Qi miraculous phenomena and marvels.

These differences between the commentaries on the Classics, especially on the *Chunqiu ('Spring and Autumn Annals')* resulted in a debate set up in the capital by Xuandi, who summoned the best scholars to attend. The discussions lasted for two years, from 53 to 51 B.C., and took place in Shiqu Pavilion, inside Weiyang Palace. The results of the council were published; out of them came the official interpretation of the Confucian Classics; this was the only version taught at the Grand School and was compulsory study for all candidates for government appointments. Nevertheless the other interpretations were not proscribed.

While the known texts were being edited and interpreted, a great effort was being made to collect and classify lost books and early copies of the Classics. This culminated in the reign of Chengdi (32–7 B.C.) in the compilation of the catalogue of the imperial library. The work was entrusted to a group of scholars under the direction of Liu Xiang (79–8 B.C.), who was made responsible for the sections of canonical books and books of philosophy and poetry and for co-ordinating the whole undertaking. At his death he was succeeded by his son, Liu Xin (*c.* 32 B.C.–A.D. 23). The catalogue was incorporated in the form of a bibliographical treatise *(yiwenzhi)* in Ban Gu's *Hanshu ('History of the Former Han')*.

The Classics were not regarded as mere historical documents, nor were they studied with the aim of acquiring objective historical knowledge. They were holy writ, containing messages and instructions from a golden age, and must therefore be preserved and transmitted with respect and studied with piety; they contained rules of wisdom that must guide everyone in the conduct of their lives and the sovereign in conducting the life of his people. The purpose of exegesis and interpretation—metaphysical, ethical and political, but never philological—was to render the philosophical content of these texts intelligible to the generation of the day. From this point of view 'oral instruction was as necessary as the written Book; it was complementary to it and was the orthodox explanation without which the disciples would have gone astray'.[1]

Until the end of the first century B.C. the dominant ideology remained that of the school of Modern Texts founded by Dong Zhongshu. Parallel with the exegesis of the Classics, in a spirit on the whole fairly close to this ideology with its basis of mysticism and cosmology, a literature of so-called apocryphal writings *(Chanwei)* developed. The term covers two originally distinct groups of texts: oracle books *(chan)* and esoteric 'readings' of the Classics *(wei)*. The *weishu* claimed to complement the *Yijing ('Book of Changes')* and the other Classics, to approach the truth and explain the world from a different angle. Speculations on the theory of *Yin-Yang* and the Five Phases formed the basis of these writings in which history, myth and speculation on numbers and presages were quite happily mingled.

By the use of systems of classification, symbolism and correspondences, the apocryphal literature satisfied that need for an explanation of the universe as a whole which characterized the period. It was widely read in the first century B.C., but because, from the fifth century A.D. onwards it was repeatedly proscribed, it has, unfortunately, survived only in fragments.

In the vast intellectual melting-pot of the end of the Former Han dynasty, the apocryphal writings absorbed many old non-Confucian beliefs, as well as a number of precise observations, which went to enrich the exposition of the Classics. Moreover, the *weishu* in themselves provided such answers to contemporary questions as were often more effective and better suited to the spirit of the age than were the Classics.

Han Interest in Omens and the Habit of Consulting Them

Contemporary thought was permeated with occult speculation and magical practices, all aimed at interpreting signs, foreseeing and predicting the future.

These practices were not confined to the *fangshi* (diviners, magicians) but extended to their detractors and rivals, the Confucians *(ru)* who, for their

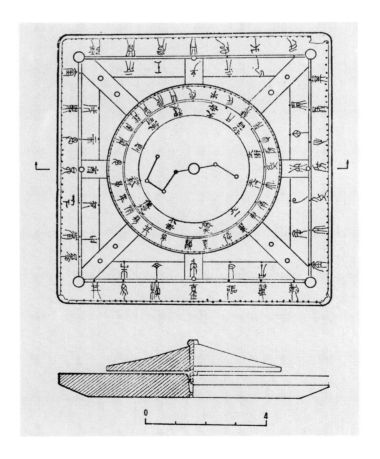

80
Drawing of an astrological instrument *(shipan)*.
Lacquered wood, D. 9 cm, from tomb No. 62 at Mojuzi, district of Wuwei, Gansu. The tomb dates from the period of Wang Mang; the *shipan* may be dated to the early years of the Christian era. (See *Wenwu,* no. 12 [1972]: 14–15).

part, predicted on the basis of the Classics. Dong Zhongshu and, following him, Sui Hong had consulted the *Chunqiu;* others, like Jing Fang (77–37 B.C.), predicted and interpreted marvels from their reading of the *Book of Changes.*

In fact all the schools vied with another, and all the arts of number—astrology, the calendar, the Five Phases, the yarrow and the tortoise, the interpretation of dreams—were put to the service of divination and prognostication. Thus the diviners had perfected a device *(shipan)* that seems to have been very fashionable at the end of the Former Han and several examples of which have been found recently in tombs. It consists of a square terrestrial board *(dipan)*, on which a celestial board *(tianpan)* in the form of a movable disc pivots round a bamboo axis. The *tianpan* consists of three concentric zones: in the centre is a diagram of the Great Bear constellation with one of its stars on the axis of the device; the second zone bears the names of the 12 lunar months, and the outer zone those of the 28 constellations or positions of the moon *(xiu)*. The signs of the denary and duodenary series are marked on the terrestrial board, with the 28 *xiu* repeated on the outer rim. On the perimeter of the square are 182 engraved dots, perhaps related to the 365¼ days of the year. The instrument symbolized the cosmos—heaven, earth and the four seasons. The diviner set the bearings of the terrestrial board on the four directions and pivoted the celestial board to correspond with the position of the sun. The Great Bear constellation gave the answer to the question by pointing to one of the lunar months.

These devices and many other methods of interpretation were based on the ancient Chinese concept of the indissoluble unity of man and the universe. 'Everything moves and changes on three parallel levels and in close correlation: Heaven, Earth and man. The stars move on the celestial vault; this movement is the *Dao* ['way'] of Heaven; the *Dao* of the Earth and the *Dao* of man are linked to it. A disturbance of one of them has repercussions on the other two. This repercussive force is a kind of vital magical potential'.[2] Observation of the heavens—of the stars, the movements of the five planets, their positions relative to the twenty-eight constellations, coronas round the sun and the moon, eclipses, comets, meteorites and emana-

tions—gave rise to prognostications about life on earth and the affairs of the State.

At the same time, the appointed place of the sovereign in the cosmos, his responsible position in the good order of the universe, played into the hands of astronomer-astrologers and scholars of every complexion. Since the sovereign was the Son of Heaven, it was natural to believe that Heaven employed unusual phenomena to warn its son of coming danger, to hold him responsible or even to punish him—through his subjects—for his own or his ministers' misconduct.

Thus the science of calamities and marvels *(zaiyi)* developed. They comprised both celestial (eclipses, falling stars, etc.) and terrestrial phenomena (droughts, floods, locusts). Different methods were used by the different schools to interpret such phenomena, often with contradictory results. But the explanation was never neutral or unmotivated; marvels and ill omens were used mainly as political weapons by one faction against another, more generally by scholars in criticizing the sovereign and, at the end of the first century B.C., by those engaged in predicting and calculating the end of the dynasty.

An example of the right to criticize the sovereign on account of calamities and marvels, manifestations of his wrongdoings, occurs in the biography of Jing Fang (77–37 B.C.). Jing Fang spoke thus to Yuandi in 43 B.C., 'Since the accession of Your Majesty, the sun and the moon have lost their brightness; the stars no longer follow their normal courses; mountains collapse; springs overflow; the earth trembles; rocks crumble. It freezes in summer, and thunder rumbles in winter; in spring everything withers, and in autumn everything is ablaze.... Does Your Majesty think that there is peace or trouble in the Empire?' At the emperor's embarrassed reply Jing Fang suggested that those responsible were to be found among the emperor's ministers. Those who felt that they were being criticized then tried to oust Jing Fang. But still invoking marvels, Jing Fang persisted in his criticisms. In the end he was beheaded.[3]

Such disguised curbs on despotism and censure of the government sometimes had more positive results than had that of the unfortunate Jing Fang. When all is said and done, predictions were used mainly by factions in their struggles for power.

A Desire to Clean Up
Religious and Court Life

Xuandi's patronage of classical studies and of the establishment of orthodox teaching, through which State officials were trained, laid the foundations for the triumph of Confucian ideology and for the growing influence of the Confucians at the heart of the government during the second half of the century.

The *Yantielun ('Debates on Salt and Iron')* of 81 B.C. had already shown that the scholars represented a force to be reckoned with. The council of Shiqu Pavilion (53–51 B.C.) confirmed them in their rôle as guides. As the masters of knowledge and teachers of the future administrators of the nation, it was only logical that they should become the emperor's counsellors. The first step was taken by Yuandi (48–33 B.C.), who adhered wholeheartedly to the ideology of the scholars. This allowed his Confucian counsellors to recommend and implement a series of reforms and economic measures aimed at a return to the simplicity of early times. Work in certain imperial factories that supplied the court, in particular the silk factories in Shandong province, was suspended or cut. Similarly, the emperor reduced the number of court ladies and musicians; several of the palaces in Shanglin Park were closed down and some of the park land returned to the people. The emperor also reduced his expenditure on food and on his stables. To complete these economies nearly 200 ancestral temples were closed.

The ancestral temples of the dynasty in the capital, in the commanderies and in the kingdoms did indeed represent a very heavy charge on the government. Each temple, dedicated to the soul of an emperor, an empress or even a dead prince of the imperial line, was the site of a cult in which food offerings were made daily and sacrifices on appointed dates some thirty times a year. These cults involved enormous expenditure on food (the *Hanshu* speaks of over 24,000 dishes of food offered annually), and the costs of upkeep and staff (over 60,000 guards, intercessors, sacrificers and musicians) were extremely high. Besides suppressing the temples, the reform produced a new set of regulations that restricted the right to a separate cult to

the five generations of ancestors preceding the reigning emperor, although three emperors—the Founder (Gaozu), Wendi and Wudi—retained their cults.

Another series of measures relating to the imperial cults was set in train at the beginning of the next reign. In 32 B.C. sacrifices to the Supreme Unity, the Five Emperors and the Earth, which had taken place outside Chang'an—at Ganquan Palace and at Fenyin and Yong—were brought back to the capital, where sites in the north and south of the city were established for them. A simpler ritual was introduced at the new sites. At the same time many provincial cult sites were closed.

The scholars sought by these means to reform religious practices, which they condemned for

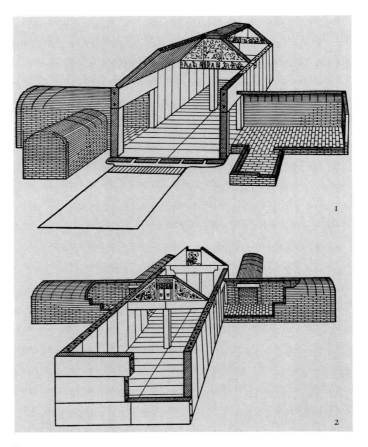

81
Drawings of cutaway views of tomb No. 61 at Luoyang. (1) east-west view looking towards the back of the burial chamber, (2) west-east view looking towards the entrance door of the chamber, second half of the first century B.C. (See *Kaogu xuebao*, no. 2 [1964]: 110).

82
Large hollow brick from a tomb.
Grey earthenware, H. 35 cm, L. 1.28 m, impressed decoration in low relief composed of symbolic motifs and images intended to ward off evil spirits, probably from the region of Zhengzhou, Henan, *c.* 50 B.C.–A.D. 50.
Musée Turpin de Crissé, Angers.

their pomp and luxury. They presented the measures as a return to sound observance and to the purity of antiquity, and recentred the cult round Heaven and the Earth.

The steps taken by the Confucian 'reaction' in regard to economy and morality in religious and secular life affected another institution that had been patronized by Wudi: the Bureau of Music. Having suffered when the pomp of the imperial banquets was reduced in 70 B.C. and again in 48 B.C., the Bureau was finally abolished in 7 B.C. The reason given by its critics was that it encouraged and practised a corrupt form of music, whereas morally uplifting music should be revived. Of the 829 musicians—singers, instrumentalists, craftsmen and musicologists—who made up the Bureau at the time of its abolition, only those who played the 'old music', those who played at certain official ceremonies and audiences, and specialist instrumentalists were retained and allocated to other government departments.

The Common Outlook
as Seen in Burial Decoration

Moving down from the various circles of scholars, *fangshi* and reformists, right-thinking or the re-

verse, to the world of the petty official or the small landowner, the picture changes slightly. One of the sources of information for the period in question—and a source that has remained relatively untouched by the later manipulations of scholars—is tomb decoration and burial goods. A burial programme is a fair indicator of the beliefs, fears and some of the concerns of the living.

Middle-class tombs in the region of Guanzhong and of Guangdong province at the end of the

83
Tomb No. 61 at Luoyang.
Detail of the painting on the back wall (left half) of the main chamber, depicting an exorcist (right, part only) with bear's head, and assistants, second half of the first century B.C.

84   ▷
Figure of a woman.
Grey earthenware, H. 35.5 cm, max. W. 15.3 cm, second century B.C.
Royal Ontario Museum, Toronto.

132

Former Han were conceived as dwelling-places in the next world and were often designed to take both coffins of a married couple; they were built of large hollow bricks, sometimes, when the tomb had additional chambers, combined with small solid bricks. In such cases the burial chamber housing the coffin or coffins was faced with large hollow bricks and had a flat or pitched roof, while the adjoining chamber or chambers were constructed of small solid bricks and had tunnel-vaults. The burial goods naturally varied according to the wealth of the deceased. They consisted largely of everyday articles, such as vessels made of ordinary grey fired clay, sometimes decorated with painted motifs or with a green lead glaze produced by copper oxide. This ware, which was used only for burials, was designed, with its dark green glaze, to imitate bronzes, for which it was a cheap substitute. These tombs also contained a growing number of earthenware models *(mingqi)* of everything that the deceased might need to continue in the next world a life that differed little from his life on earth; they included storehouses, stoves and wells, also statuettes of servants. Bronze articles included a few pieces of personal adornment (belt-hooks), a few weapons, ornaments for vehicles, cash (often in quite large quantities), one or two mirrors, and sometimes a censer.

    The really luxurious feature of these burials was the wall decoration. Only the burial chamber was decorated; motifs were either impressed★ or painted★★ on hollow bricks. More modest tombs were decorated with simple impressed geometric orna-

81

86

84

82, 85★

83, 87–9★★

85
Burial pillar.
Grey earthenware, H. 1.28 m, (sides) 24.2 cm, decorated on three sides with impressed geometric motifs and dragons, sculpted top representing a crouching guardian spirit, its body, legs and arms appearing in relief on the sides of the pillar, first century A.D.
Metropolitan Museum of Art: Gift of Abby Aldrich Rockefeller, 1942, New York.

86   ▷
Wine jar in the shape of an owl.
Earthenware, painted, D. (at base) 14 cm, H. 35 cm, first century B.C. or beginning of the first century A.D.
Musée Cernuschi, Paris.

87
Tomb No. 61 at Luoyang: west side of the lintel and partition pediment of the main chamber. Paintings on hollow bricks: on either side of a half-open door two Immortals ride on the backs of dragons, second half of the first century B.C.

88
Partition lintel and partition pediment of the main chamber of a Luoyang tomb.
Paint and ink on hollow bricks, H. 73.8 cm, W. 240.7 cm, *c.* 50 B.C.–A.D. 50.
Museum of Fine Arts: Denman Waldo Ross Collection, Boston.

ment repeated along the length of the walls and ceiling. In the most luxurious tombs geometric motifs were combined with figural scenes, impressed and framed. Impressed geometric motifs might sometimes be combined with painted decoration. 82, 85

83, 87

The major themes of the figural decorations, both painted and impressed, centre round the ascent of the deceased to the world of the Immortals, representations of Heaven (sun, moon and constellations) and, especially, the protection of the deceased, his tomb and his ascent.

In its main concepts, therefore, the burial programme was similar to that which governed the decoration of the Dai family tombs a little over a century earlier. Yet ideas had evolved. There seems to be less emphasis on the ascent and more on the concern for protection, which appears throughout, together with representations of material goods and pleasures that it was hoped would be enjoyed in the next world, and, in some tombs, depictions of the Confucian virtues.

The images of protection of the tomb are often concentrated on the doorway, the separating pediment and the end wall of the burial chamber. They depict exorcists (*fangxiangshi*) with the heads and skins of bears or pigs—presumably a reminiscence of the exorcists who wore masks and animal skins in the rites for warding off demons—guardian spirits, *tingzhang* (post-masters) or guards armed with shields, who, serving as defenders against robbers and as guardians of the roads in this world, are expected to act similarly against the demons and robbers who threaten the deceased. Further protection is afforded by animals (rams, tigers) and 83

85

82

objects *(bi rings)* with apotropaic powers: the four
beasts of good augury *(siling)*, dragon, tiger,
phoenix and stag, who are guides, protectors and
intercessors, are always present, as is the theme of
the dragon ridden by the Immortals who receive
the soul of the deceased on its journey to paradise.

A deity whose popularity was to become more
general during the period of the Latter Han begins
to appear in the tombs of the first century B.C.
among this crowd of exorcists, protectors and
guides. She was Xiwangmu, the Queen Mother of
the West, who was believed to bring immortality
and to rule the cosmos; she is already depicted in
these tombs, accompanied by her acolytes (the
three-footed bird, the fox with nine tails and the
hare pounding the herb of immortality). Her appearance in the burials of Luoyang and Zhengzhou[4] may not be unconnected with the messianic
movement of the year 3 B.C., to which we shall return.

References to the pleasures of life—harnessed
chariots, cash, images of the estate (the door, the
que towers flanking it and the masks adorning it)
and hunting scenes—are conceived both as stating a
social position and expressing desires that complement the burial goods in the tomb; the trend
towards this type of representation became more
marked during the first and second centuries A.D.

Another innovation dating from the end of the
Former Han and certainly related to the spread of
the Confucian ideology was the painting of historical scenes and portraits of heroes, sages and
meritorious officials on the lintels of the partitions
between the two parts of the burial chamber. Such
lintels occur in two tombs at Luoyang. Their
themes are related to paintings of Confucian inspiration in the palaces and were designed to extol
good government and ethical values. These two
lintels sound what is perhaps the only frankly Confucian note among the motifs of hundreds of
tombs of medium importance from the end of the
Former Han excavated in the regions of Luoyang
and Zhengzhou. As regards the official ideology of

the *Yinyang wuxing shuo* formulated in the second
and first centuries, only the old cosmological basis
that inspired it would appear to occur here. The
four beasts of good augury *(siling)* remain in
favour, as in the tomb of the Marchioness of Dai,
and have not yet entirely given place to the symbolic beasts of the four directions,[5] which were to
be depicted so regularly and always in the same
positions in later tombs.

The mental images reflected in the iconography
of these tombs thus seem fairly remote from the
view of the world that the scholars were trying to
establish. The new themes that appeared, like the
moralizing ones borrowed from the past, became
grafted on to a stock of religious beliefs and superstitions, some of which triumphant Confucianism
rethought, while channelling and systematizing
those it could not dislodge.

89
Detail of the partition lintel in Pl. 88 from the main chamber
of a Luoyang tomb.
Paint on hollow brick, H. 19.5 cm, overall W. 240.7 cm, *c.* 50
B.C.–A.D. 50.
Museum of Fine Art: Denman Waldo Ross Collection,
Boston.

Chapter IV

Tensions of a Society in Crisis

New Forces in Control

The triumph of the Confucian scholars was anything but absolute at the heart of government. They had to reckon with the 'inner court', that parallel government established by Wudi inside the palace to secure direct control of affairs for himself. As it happened, in the reign of Yuandi (48–33 B.C.) this system, for which the eunuchs had been made responsible, gained an autonomy that in its turn endangered the emperor's prerogatives. A sick man who devoted all his time to music, Yuandi unloaded the affairs of State on to a eunuch, Shi Xian. Shi Xian governed the 'inner court' and manipulated the emperor. The high civilian posts were left to the Confucian scholars, while Yuandi's maternal relatives controlled the army.

In subsequent reigns, the empresses' families seized the key posts in the government. The top position was now that of *Dasima* (Commander-in-chief), a kind of regent with unlimited political and military powers. In this redistribution of rôles, the Grand Counsellor *(Chengxiang)* and the Grand Officer of Censorship *(Yushidafu)* were relegated to administrative posts carrying no decision-making powers. They were chosen from among elderly Confucians and lent the government an air of virtue.

This system lasted until the dynasty was overturned by Wang Mang, a member of one of the maternal clans. The Wang clan, to which Chengdi's (32–7 B.C.) mother belonged, controlled both outer and inner courts—the eunuchs having been

removed from the latter—almost without interruption. Aidi (6–1 B.C.) and Pingdi (A.D. 1–5), both colourless figures, died without heirs. Wang Mang, a nephew of Dowager Empress Wang, was regent, as a prelude to usurping power. The career of Empress Wang is the extreme example—from the point of view of length—of the ascendancy assumed at court by the maternal relatives in the face of weakened central power. Empress Wang entered the court in 54 B.C., became Yuandi's empress and mother of Chengdi; she died in A.D. 13 at the age of eighty-four, having maintained her position for over sixty years through all the court intrigues and bloody rivalries in which the period abounded.

Poverty of the Peasants Contrasted with the Luxury of the Rich

The most marked social division throughout the Han period was that between the landowners (officials and nobility) and the poor peasants (smallholders, tenant farmers, agricultural workers). All the social conflicts of the period originated in the economic domination of the ruling class over the down-trodden peasantry.

The seizure of land by rich families, which had begun by the beginning of the dynasty, gathered momentum during the first century B.C. Landed property was considered the safest investment, and all officials bought estates. Thus by the end of the Former Han most of the well-irrigated ground belonged to the great landowners. Trade in this land was free and it was therefore an easy matter to take advantage of the poverty of lean years to buy cheaply from the penniless peasants. The ground was cultivated by salaried workers, especially when the owner was a retired official living on his estate and directing the work; when the official was still employed and therefore absent, the estate was let to tenant farmers, who shared the profits of the produce on a fifty-fifty basis with the owner.

The Han government was unable to check the growth of large estates. An edict of 7 B.C. was drafted to limit the size of landed estates to 3,000 *mu* and to restrict numbers of slaves (a maximum of 200 slaves for the owners of royal fiefs, marquisates and princes, 100 for metropolitan dignitaries, and 30 for officials and private individuals). The edict was opposed by the great influential landowners and was never promulgated, let alone applied. The officials had no intention of damaging their own position in the public interest. This is how the enduring ambiguity of the Chinese governing class came about: the bureaucracy belonged at once to the machinery of the State and to a body of landowners whose immediate private interests conflicted with those of the central government, of which it formed part and in which it coveted appointments in order to draw the maximum profit from the government.

As the officials seized more land, which they tried to expunge from the tax registers, taxes became more difficult to collect. As a result of the reduction in revenue from the land tax, great public works (such as irrigation) financed by the State became fewer and productivity declined. For the smallholder this deterioration coincided with an increased demand from the (Confucian!) officials, who tried to make him pay what they ought to have paid themselves. The natural result was that the vulnerable peasants required credit, which the backer (usually a large landowner) was only too pleased to advance, since his usurious rates of interest prepared the way for expropriation.

The concentration of land and the accumulation of enormous fortunes were a danger to the State, and a danger that it was powerless to check since the State bureaucracy was composed of the very families that should have been most strictly controlled.

After the abundant harvests of the years 86–48 B.C., natural catastrophes multiplied, bringing famine and exposing the peasants to the greed of the landowners. Some have thought that the large estates were developed by slaves. In point of fact, even when slavery was at its height in the first century B.C., slaves in China were preponderantly domestic. And as we have seen, agricultural development was entrusted to labourers or tenant farmers. In a country in which the population was increasing rapidly, in which there were more hands than cultivable soil available and few prospects for the rural proletariat outside agriculture, there was no point in employing slaves.

During the second half of the first century B.C. there were several hundreds of thousands, perhaps a million, private and state-owned slaves in China, i.e. about 1 per cent of the total population. Free men were reduced to slavery for having committed crimes, or were sold at times of economic distress, or were enslaved illegally, or imported from abroad to be sold. Those enslaved for crimes always became state-owned slaves, while economic distress (women and children were sold in times of famine) and kidnapping provided private slaves —at least at the first sale. Both government and private individuals acquired foreign slaves—from Central Asia, as well as from the barbarian countries of the south (Bo, Yue, Dian). Slaves formed a very mobile class and could move from the government to private families and vice versa, be bought, given or requisitioned.

Private slaves formed the domestic staff of a household; they were servants and, in great families, guards, armed militia, mounted escorts, musicians, acrobats, dancers and singers. Young slave girls trained for variety spectacles were undoubtedly chosen for their beauty, and references to sexual relations between slaves and masters abound, many slaves becoming legal or *de facto* concubines in their master's house. Domestic slaves seem, on the whole, to have been well treated.

State-owned slaves were employed on public works, forests, stud farms, State arsenals and especially in the imperial workshops, forming an enormous body of officials of over 130,000 individuals by the end of the century. They were also used in the departments (as scribes, accountants, messengers and porters) and for service in the palace.

Thus the system as a whole retained a patriarchal character. The growing number of slaves owned by private individuals was a sign of the times: the poor were too poor and the rich too rich. The upper classes made a display of their luxury and slaves were an integral part of their life-style. To enable them to live in grand style, landowners did not hesitate to pressurize their tenant farmers, to persuade the government to grant them ever more substantial subsidies, to take bribes and to go into business. Those less ambitious and more honest were content to ensure that the land they had developed was productive and to indulge in the most highly prized of pleasures—good food, wine, the company of women, music and dance—against a rural background. Yang Yun, grandson of Sima Qian through his mother, was one such. An honest official, disgraced in the year 56 B.C., he retired to his country estate: 'As a relaxation from my labours as a landowner,' he wrote to a friend, 'on the *Fu* [sixth month] and *La* [twelfth month] feast-days, I have a sheep simmered, a lamb roasted and I draw a *dou* of wine. I come from Qin [Shaanxi] and so I can play the music of Qin; my wife comes from Zhao [Shanxi] and plays the *se* zither very skilfully; many of my slaves sing. When the wine has warmed my ears, I turn my head skywards and beat time on the clay drum as I cry *wu wu!* ... On these occasions I am extremely happy; I shake my garments, flick up my cuffs as I bend and stand up again; I beat time with my foot and begin to dance. Certainly it is licentious and unseemly, but I do not want to be told so. Luckily I still have money....'[1]

The writer of this letter with its bucolic ring appears not to regret his disgrace nor to trouble himself about Confucian morality. Certainly his revels and misdemeanours seem extremely modest compared with the life of pleasure, libertinage and debauchery that reigned in certain royal palaces and even in the imperial palace. Certain economic measures recommended by the reformists during the 40s were more than necessary, but the fact remains that the Confucians would have to work hard to restore a semblance of moral order to a world dominated by extravagance, wastefulness, ostentation and extreme over-refinement. The great entertained themselves in a thousand different ways. Hunting remained highly fashionable, as is testified by the rhyme-prose *(fu)* of Yang Xiong (53 B.C.–A.D. 18), the great poet of the end of the century, and by much figural decoration on bronze vessels, especially the wine jars used by the nobility. The *Yantielun* had already censured the fondness of the rich for the gardens which they had laid out for them on their estates, with ponds and artificial lakes. They strolled, held horse races and archery contests, played ball games and picnicked in their gardens. But the banquets accompanied by concerts, dancing and variety spectacles *(zaji)* were perhaps the quintessence of pleasure. Musicians, singers and dancers, both men and women, were joined by strolling players from Central Asia and their imitators. Like the dancing, the exotic performances of the wrestlers, acrobats and illusionists were accompanied by music.

The earthenware group found to the north of Yinan in 1969 represents one of the variety spectacles that so greatly delighted Han society. The tableau comprises 21 figures: 7 spectators stand on either side; in the centre are 4 acrobats and a standing man, whose rôle is not clear (he may be the leader of the orchestra and the protagonists); behind him are 2 female dancers shaking the long narrow cuffs of their richly decorated dresses. At the back, its rhythms synchronizing the movements of dancers and acrobats, is the orchestra, consisting of, from left to right, 2 female players of mouth-organs *(sheng)*, a zither player *(se)*, a small drum, 2 bells hanging on a stand, and a large drum with 2 men beating it.

In this context—declining conditions of life for the peasants, insolence of the rich, intrigue and debauchery at court—it is not surprising that at the end of the first century B.C. evil omens, peasant revolts and messianic movements proliferated.

From the time of the reign of Chengdi (32–7 B.C.), a succession of reports of catastrophes and prodigies of evil augury reached the court. These reports were critical of the government and also constituted a barometer of popular discontent and anxiety. In a memorandum to the throne in the reign of Aidi (6–1 B.C.), Bao Xuan expresses the situation well: '... the people are scattering and perishing, abandoning the cities; robbers and brigands appear from nowhere; officials become oppressors and scoundrels; from year to year the situation worsens'.[3]

In the year 3 B.C., following a serious drought, there was a mystical uprising of the people of Shandong province. They marched in their thousands, holding a piece of straw or hemp, which they called 'the slip of the imperial order' and passed from one to another. On reaching the capital they 'gathered in the quarters and the alleys, offering sacrifices and setting up boards [for divination] and worshiped Xiwangmu with songs and dances'.[4] A document was passed round in which the goddess assured her faithful that they would not starve and would attain immortality.

This movement, which may be considered the first messianic and millenarian movement in the history of China, coincided with a spate of prophecies sustained by the theory of the Five Phases, which foretold the end of the dynasty.

A strong man arose to take advantage of the social crisis and the eclipse of imperial power. This was Wang Mang, nephew of Dowager Empress Wang; at the death of Aidi his aunt appointed him Commander-in-chief, and he governed the country in the name of the new emperor, Pingdi, who was nine years old. At Pingdi's death in A.D. 5 Wang Mang became the official regent for the crown prince, who was still an infant, and finally himself ascended the throne in A.D. 9.

For eight years Wang Mang manipulated public opinion—beginning with the world of scholarship—with great skill, preparing it for a seizure of power that he presented as a renaissance. He began by eliminating potential rivals, the clans of all the imperial relatives, except his own. At the same time he gained the aura of a 'sage' by refusing—in the best Confucian tradition—titles and honours proposed by those nearest him at his own suggestion. He acted the part (perhaps deceiving himself as well) of the Duke of Zhou, the illustrious ruler whom Confucius adopted as his ideal. In the same spirit he revived so-called Zhou institutions; for his dignitaries he borrowed from the Classics titles imbued with literary and magical connotations.

In the year 4, thinking to return to the sacred government of antiquity, Wang Mang had a *mingtang* (sacred hall), a *biyong* (palace of the encircling moat) and a *lingtai* (transcendent terrace) built in the southern suburb of Chang'an. The remains discovered in 1956–7 (see p. 142) were probably map, p. 224 those of his *biyong*, the site where the royal virtue was believed to manifest itself. A hypothetical reconstruction shows a three-storeyed central palace raised on a rectangular earthen platform measuring 42 metres square, itself situated in the centre of a circular base of rammed earth measuring 62 metres in diameter. The central structure was surrounded 91 by an outer wall measuring 235 metres square,

90
Acrobats, dancers and musicians perform before seven standing spectators.
Painted earthenware, H. 22 cm, L. 67.5 cm, W. 47.5 cm, provenance: Yinan, Shandong, period of the Former Han.

with four gateways and additional buildings at the four corners. A moat full of water surrounded the whole complex and was connected with a canal to the north.

Wang Mang was an ardent Confucian and acted on his principles; in contrast to the great ones of the court, and especially the members of his own clan, he led a frugal life, from which all extravagance was excluded. Following as it did the reign of Aidi, an incompetent and corrupt 'playboy' totally manipulated by his favourite catamite, Wang Mang's attitude could not fail to win over the Confucian ministers and many scholars seeking to oppose superstition and establish a stricter morality. Wang Mang completed this movement by gaining the loyalty of the great scholar Liu Xin (*c.* 32 B.C.–A.D. 23), who had succeeded his father, Liu Xiang, in the work of cataloguing the imperial library. Liu Xin admired everything that had descended from the Zhou and this included the old-character texts *(guwen)* that were said to have been rediscovered. Similarly, he examined certain previously neglected commentaries including the *Zuozhuan* (commentary on the *Chunqiu*), which were superior to the commentaries that had been taught until then by the so-called modern-text schools *(jinwen)*. He succeeded in getting the *Zuozhuan*, the *Mao* version of the *Shijing*, the *Zhouli (Ritual of the Zhou)* and the text of the *Shujing* in old characters taught at the Grand School and incorporated into the programme for the examinations by which officials were recruited. Like the other scholars who defended the 'old text' *(guwen)*, Liu Xin censured the modern-text schools for their mystical theories, their use of the *weishu*, and their manipulation of the Classics for purposes of prophecy and divination.

The 'old-text' school inspired a renewal of classical studies, which had become bogged down in sterile theorizing. At the same time and more immediately, it provided those given to forecasting the future, of whom Wang Mang was one, with elements to feed their speculations and hopes. Liu Xiang and Liu Xin believed that the Han dynasty reigned by the virtue of Fire. Now Wang Mang claimed descent from no lesser monarch than Huangdi, the Yellow Emperor, whose virtue was Earth; Earth is born of Fire. When Pingdi died in A.D. 5 it was genuinely believed that the virtue of

Fire had been extinguished. Had not an astrologer of the first century B.C. calculated that the Han dynasty would end after a period of thrice 70 years, i.e. in A.D. 4? From this it was deduced that the Earth Phase would follow, according to the natural cycle. Since Wang Mang possessed the virtue Earth it was logical that he should inaugurate a new dynasty. Most of the Confucians approved; moreover, the way for his decision had been prepared by hundreds of prodigies and auguries of good fortune, including appearances of phoenixes and dragons and discoveries of objects bearing inscriptions revealing what was described as the will of Heaven. Assisted by a number of adventurers turned forgers for the occasion, Wang Mang had become the elected of Heaven. He ascended the throne on the 10 January in the year A.D. 9, founded the Xin dynasty and changed the calendar.

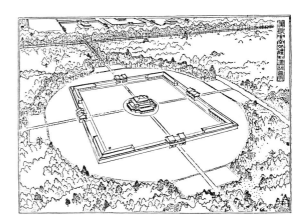

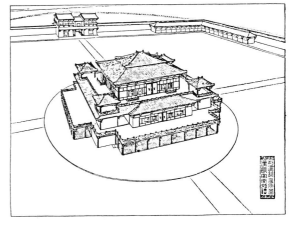

91
Tentative reconstruction of the *biyong* ('palace of the encircling moat') built by Wang Mang in A.D. 4. (See Liu Dunzhen et al., *Zhongguo*, p. 47).

Chapter V

The Interregnum of Wang Mang (A.D. 9–23)

Radical but Ineffective Reforms

Monetary Reforms

Before he came to the throne Wang Mang had issued new, lighter cash, and this devaluation had resulted in more counterfeiting. He also nationalized gold. Only vassal kings were allowed to possess gold; the other noblemen and ordinary citizens were compelled to lodge their gold in the Imperial Treasury, which gave them bronze currency-knives in exchange.

I (no. 5)

Once in power, Wang Mang changed the whole coinage on several occasions (A.D. 9, 10, 14). These reforms did not consist simply of introducing new coins. Their main result was a depreciation of the currency; the weight of metal in a coin did not correspond to its value: thus a cash contained 1 *shu* of bronze while a currency-spade worth 1,000 cash contained only 24 *shu* of bronze.

I (no. 7)

I (no. 6)

Punishment for counterfeiting was severe. Those who held on to the old cash were also punished, by death or exile. At each new reform certain coins were dropped altogether; others were exchanged for new ones at a clearly disadvantageous rate. Given that the coins were melted down, this situation encouraged people to forge coins rather than lose over the exchange.

When gold was nationalized, the aristocracy had been compelled to exchange their gold for currency-knives made of gilt bronze. In A.D. 9, when gold was restored to circulation and the currency-knife dropped, the same noblemen were obliged to exchange their knives, which were now worth only their weight in bronze. Thus Mang stripped the Han nobility of a large part of its wealth and accumulated an enormous reserve of precious metal in the coffers of the Imperial Treasury. Part of the gold reserve came from Siberia, but much of it had entered China as payment for Chinese silk exports. Since the Chinese were used to having gold in square ingots they were obliged to melt down the western coins which they received.

The classes worst affected by Wang Mang's monetary reforms were the rich, especially the aristocracy and the merchants; in the latter group the small tradesmen and pedlars who did not possess the machinery of counterfeiting and whose stall or shop was easy to keep under surveillance suffered most severely. The peasants were quite unaffected; they stored their grain, selling small quantities in order to buy goods in the market and so using little currency, except when they had accumulated a small surplus of wealth.

Agrarian Reform

At once, in A.D. 9, Wang Mang addressed himself to the major economic problem: so many peasants working on estates did not pay tax that there were too few taxable agricultural labourers to feed the state coffers. So the new emperor suppressed the large estates and nationalized the land. Trade in land was forbidden; the area allocated to each family was fixed, and the surplus distributed among neighbours, relatives and the peasants with the smallest plots.

At the same time an effort was made to introduce the system of the old 'agrarian draughtboard' *(jingtian),* in which an area of 1 *li* was divided into nine equal squares of 100 *mu.* Eight families each cultivated one square for its own use; in addition, each cultivated one-eighth of the central square, the produce from which was paid in kind as tax to the government. By this system, therefore, the peasant paid one-tenth of his harvest to the government, which represented an increase compared with the period of the Former Han. The ideal of the 'agrarian draughtboard' may have been tried out in antiquity over a small area and within a simple social structure, but it was impossible to apply on a large scale, since the ground could not be divided into equal squares and was not uniform in quality. Nor was the system viable in as complex a society as that of the Han.

In the same series of measures private slaves were freed and slavery was prohibited.

In fact agrarian reform had to be abandoned after three years. Private individuals found ways of buying and selling land again and of owning slaves. As regards the latter, in a new effort to exact revenue, Wang Mang simply imposed in A.D. 17 a tax of 3,600 cash on each slave owned. The measure mainly affected aristocratic houses that kept large staffs of domestic slaves.

Monopolies

The third part of the economic measures of A.D. 9 concerned monopolies; since, as we have seen from the *Yantielun,* the Confucians were opposed to monopolies, Wang Mang used the word 'controls' *(guan).* Thus he re-established six controls, five of which concerned salt, iron, fermented beverages, the striking of coinage and produce of the mountains and marshes. This fifth control did not deprive the poor of the countryside, who pursued secondary occupations—such as fishing, hunting, fruit-picking, silkworm culture, etc.—of their livelihood, but it required them to pay for permission to pursue it; therefore, it represented an additional tax on the poor.

The aim of the sixth control was to avoid fluctuations in prices. As early as 54 B.C., under Xuandi, 'storehouses of constant prices' *(changpingcang)* had

been built in the frontier commanderies. These storehouses bought grain when it was cheap and sold it at prices favourable to the peasants when the rate had risen. The measure appears to have been unsuccessful, and the storehouses were abolished in 44 B.C.

Wang Mang revived the idea and used it to control prices in the markets of the six largest cities of the empire: Chang'an, Luoyang, Handan (in Hebei), Linzi (in Shandong), Wan (modern Nanyang in Henan) and Chengdu (in Sichuan). Warehouses were to buy goods (especially grain and textiles) when prices were low and to sell when prices had risen. The system could also lend to persons in need at rates below those offered by usurers. In fact the measure known as the 'five equalizations' *(wujun)* failed because those responsible, fearing to lose money, bought only at rock-bottom prices, below the normal rate; so the peasants sold to them only when they were destitute and the equalizing warehouses remained empty.

Revolutionary, Enlightened Innovator or Opportunist? Wang Mang's Motivations and the Causes of his Downfall

As H. Bielenstein[1] has shown, Wang Mang's reforms have been the subject of endless discussion. The true intentions of the usurper and the causes of his downfall are still disputed. Was he a revolutionary, a socialist before the term existed, an idealist or a skilful intriguer? It is apparently impossible to decide. His reign was short and punctuated by catastrophes that rendered his—dangerously radical—activity totally ineffective.

Wang Mang's usurpation is easily explained by the conditions that prevailed at the end of the Former Han; the court was corrupt; the clans and cliques were in contention; imperial prestige was becoming increasingly weakened; large fortunes were being amassed; the life-style of the aristocracy was one of extravagant luxury. But such conditions could favour equally a man of ambition thirsting for power and an enlightened individual confident of his mission as a saviour. Wang Mang was probably both at the same time, just as he was at once a sincere Confucian and a votary of diviners, sorcerers and those who promised immortality, their accomplice as well as their plaything.

Nor can there be any doubt that the reformist policy commended by the Confucians in the first century B.C. gave Wang Mang the ideological authority on which he relied. His reforms were aimed essentially at the great landowners who lived in the capital on the income from their lands and at the rich merchants, but his uncoordinated fiscal and monetary measures also suggest that he tried to exploit all possible sources of revenue without worrying overmuch about the effects. He earned the hatred of the nobility and, more generally, of the moneyed classes; the new taxes were unpopular, as were certain administrative measures. But it seems to have been a series of natural disasters, bringing famine, crime, rebellion and finally civil war in their wake, which dealt the death-blow to his régime.

According to the earliest surviving census, dating from A.D. 2, the population of the empire was of the order of fifty-eight million. It was distributed unequally, being concentrated in the Wei valley in Shaanxi province (in the region of the capital), in the Great Plain, especially south of the Yellow River, and in the region of Chengdu in Sichuan province. The whole of China south of the Yangzi was regarded as colonial land; it was sparsely populated and remained so until the great north-south migration that marked the period of the Latter Han.

Guanzhong (central Shaanxi) round Chang'an had been the key economic zone during most of the Former Han; but the irrigation system, having been rather poorly maintained, gradually ceased to work after the reign of Wudi. The metropolitan zone did not escape the serious droughts and consequent famines that affected various regions of northern China from A.D. 11 onwards. However, the major disaster of this period was the breaching of the dikes of the Yellow River in A.D. 11. In even more dramatic form the breach was a repetition of that of 132 B.C. in the same region. Between A.D. 2 and 6 the river broke out of its silted-up bed and flooded much of the plain, sending an arm into the Huai River; new breaches in the year 11 flooded the eastern zones. Instead of flowing, as before, into

the sea near the city of Tianjin, the river now formed two arms, one of which flowed into the sea immediately north and the other just to the south of the Shandong peninsula. Five provinces were affected by this series of disasters, especially Shandong. The breaches were not sealed until A.D. 70. Famine and a vast migration of people fleeing from the disaster zones followed the floods.

The refugees organized themselves into bands, pillaging and disrupting the regions through which they passed, causing famine as they went. In c. A.D. 20 several bands had been formed in the commanderies of Jiangxia and Nan, to the south-east and south of modern Nanyang. Other bands had formed in Shandong, the heart of the disaster area. These different bands of starving peasants rebelled and, from A.D. 18 onwards, the troubles they caused were sufficiently serious to attract the attention of the court. Known as Red Eyebrows, from their red-dyed eyebrows, they successfully opposed the government troops sent to quell them. Following their victory in A.D. 22 the Red Eyebrows left Shandong in separate groups and headed west.

Other rebellions, directed unambiguously against Wang Mang, had broken out before his accession to the throne, in the years 6 and 7, and again in 9. But all these uprisings, in which members of the Liu clan (the Han imperial family) were implicated, had been put down. They had been organized and implemented by the aristocracy and lacked popular support. A new revolt of aristocrats began in 22 in Nanyang commandery; this one allied itself to the peasant bands that had been driven out by famine and proved decisive.

Nanyang commandery (modern southern Henan and northern Hubei provinces), with its capital Wan, had a population of nearly two million in A.D. 2. The fertility of the soil, the many dams that had been built on the rivers in the south of Henan on the initiative of local officials, had helped to make this commandery a prosperous economic zone at the end of the Former Han, supplanting Guanzhong in importance. It is not surprising that the region contained many rich clans connected by intermarriage. The landowners could count on a vast clientele of 'guests' (ke), who were also partisans. One of these clans, the Liu, were descended from Jingdi. The rebels, aided by armed bands from the south (Jiangxia and Nan), appointed an emperor (known by his reign-title as Gengshi), took Wan, then attacked Luoyang and Chang'an. Short of troops, surrounded in his bastion of Guanzhong and cut off from the populous regions of the Great Plain, Wang Mang tried to defend the capital. But on 4 October the rebels entered the city; on 6 October Wang Mang was killed, together with his co-defenders.

The true cause of the fall of Wang Mang would thus appear to have been the alteration in the course of the Yellow River, with the consequent famine and disorder.[2] The peasant revolts which then flared up from Shandong to Hubei formed the determining factor on which the aristocratic rebellion of Nanyang was originally based. Given these conditions of famine, crime and confusion, it is difficult to see how the economic reforms launched by Wang Mang could have become established. With the death of the 'usurper', his dynasty collapsed, and the Liu clan could proclaim the return of legitimacy. Nevertheless, China had to endure thirteen years of civil war before the whole empire was united by Guangwudi of the Latter Han.

Part IV

The Latter Han (A.D. 25–220)

Chapter I

The Empire in the Hands of the Great Families

Restoration of the Han

In A.D. 25 the Red Eyebrows too provided themselves with an emperor—another member of the Liu clan—entered Chang'an, murdered Gengshi, who had been chosen by the Nanyang clan, and installed their own man. But since the year 24 Liu Xiu, the future Guangwudi, who with his elder brother had instigated the Nanyang rebellion, had controlled most of the fertile plain north of the Yellow River. In 25 his relatives proclaimed him emperor, and on 27 November he entered Luoyang, which he made his capital. It was from Luoyang, former capital of the Eastern Zhou, that this dynasty acquired the name of Eastern or Latter Han as distinct from the Former or Western Han, whose capital had been at Chang'an.

Civil war dragged on for eleven years, until the end of A.D. 36. Having conquered the Great Plain and Shandong province, Guangwudi turned to attack his rivals in the west and the Red Eyebrows. In 26 the latter, having exhausted supplies in Chang'an, pillaged and set fire to part of the city, robbed the imperial tombs and made off southwards, returning to Chang'an at the end of the same year. In 29 Guangwudi gained control of all the southern regions, except for Sichuan, which was not reconquered until 36.

One of the features of the civil war was its strictly regional character. This first break-up of the empire foreshadows the final collapse, which was to bring about the downfall of the Han

dynasty less than two centuries later. The efforts of the first emperors of the Latter Han—Guangwudi, Mingdi and Zhangdi—failed to arrest the process. The worm was in the bud, and it would have taken a radical change in the socio-economic structure to destroy it; like Wang Mang before them, the new masters of China were unable to effect such a change.

Guangwudi, a man of intelligence, though of no great breadth of vision, and an accomplished strategist and tactician, devoted the rest of his reign (25–57) to consolidating his administration and reconstituting a powerful central government on the model of that of Wudi of the Former Han. But he also revived the old and dangerous tradition of enfeoffing members of the imperial clan. It was not long before these kingdoms, concentrated in the southern part of the Great Plain and in the Shandong peninsula, began to present problems. Similarly, the policy of increasing the number of marquisates was economically highly injurious to the government because the marquises took as revenue part of the taxes that the families of their fiefs paid to the State.

More generally and more seriously, under the first emperors of the Latter Han, those trends which were in due course to bring radical changes to Chinese society either began or gathered momentum: the exodus to the south, the concentration of private estates, the government's economic laissez-faire, and the formation of a new ruling class more firmly entrenched in its rights and more powerful than the upper classes had been under the Former Han.

Shifts of Population

From the beginning of the first century A.D. migration southwards swelled to a great torrent. Having begun in the north-east after the Yellow River altered course (A.D. 2–11), the movement continued in the north-west under pressure from the Xiongnu in Shanxi and the Qiang in Gansu. The migrations followed the main north-south routes, especially the great river-valleys, depopulating northern China in favour of the central and southern regions. The consequent reversal of equilibrium between the north and south of the empire showed up clearly in the census of A.D. 140: northern China had sustained heavy losses in both density and number, with a particularly dramatic drop in the north-north-west, which the colonists had abandoned as the shepherds settled inside the frontier line and frequently rose in rebellion; in the north-east (modern Hebei) the population thinned out in the area affected by the alteration in the course of the Yellow River; the fall in the Wei valley seems to have been due as much to the economic decline of the region as to the transfer of the capital to Luoyang. By contrast, the population of the southern provinces showed a considerable increase; numbers on the register increased by 66 per cent in Sichuan and Yunnan, quadrupled in Jiangxi and Hunan and trebled in Guangdong.

This shows that the shift of the demographic and economic centre of gravity from the north to central and southern China, which was to culminate a millennium later, had already begun in the Han period. In the short term the void left in the northern marches of the empire had serious consequences, inasmuch as it left the political and economic centres of Chinese civilization unprotected.[1]

The government, both central and provincial, failed to appreciate the scale of the phenomenon. It knew that the peasants were abandoning their land, and this caused concern since it meant that the new 'vagabonds' were evading taxation, but it was unaware of the exodus that was taking place. Some of the economic migrants in search of land developed the southern regions where colonization had been recent; others went to increase the manpower of the great estates.

92
Model of a three-storeyed watch-tower.
Earthenware with pale-green iridescent lead glaze, D. 43.4 cm, H. 94 cm, crossbowmen on guard on the parapet of the second-floor balcony, second century A.D.
Fogg Art Museum (Gift of Mr and Mrs Earl Morse), Harvard University, Cambridge, MA.

Concentration of Privately Owned Land and Government Non-Interference

The Latter Han looked for support to the great land-owning families of the central plain, for the emperor belonged and owed his success to this class. The vast estate of the Fan (Guangwudi's maternal grandfather's family) near Nanyang extended over 300 *qing* (some 1,370 ha) and was self-supporting in all the necessities of daily life. In addition to agriculture, the owners engaged in stock-raising, fish-farming and commerce. Estates of this sort were often protected by walls and watch-towers, defended by an armed militia and possessed their own market. The landowner employed a large labour force consisting of farmers, agricultural labourers, guards and domestics, both free men and slaves.

During the first and second centuries the struggle of the independent peasants against competition from these vast enterprises became increasingly hard. Living from day to day on his patch of land, powerless to build up reserves, continually at the mercy of rising prices or bad years, perennially in debt, the small farmer was an easy prey to the great landowner, who would expropriate him or employ him as a tenant farmer at a rent that might be as much as two-thirds of the harvest.

Production on large estates was more easily organized. Crops could be chosen and diversified according to the quality of the soil, and methods of production (including irrigation, manuring, rotation of crops, greater use of draught animals) could be improved. With the financial means at the disposal of the great landowners the inventions developed under the Former Han were used more widely and were improved (tools became more solid, larger and better designed). The first reference to rice-growers in northern China pricking out their plants occurs in the *Simin yueling ('Monthly Instructions for the Four Social Classes')* by Cui Shi (*c.* 110–70), although it may have been practised in the Yangzi valley earlier. Shi recommends planting the rice during the rains in the third month, followed by dividing and pricking out the plants in the fifth month. New crops (sesame, lucerne) were planted more generally. In the same region north of the Huai River, which remained the centre of agricultural production, the landowners took advantage of the rapidly growing—largely urban—fashion for foods based on wheat-flour (noodles, filled bread), put more land down to wheat and invested in water-mills and grinding equipment.

Self-sufficient in times of unrest, the economy of the great estates was frankly commercial in aim in peace-time. As Cui Shi recommends, the landowners speculated in grain on a seasonal basis and sold some of their agricultural produce, as well as the craft-work and industrial products of the estate.

The government's laissez-faire economic policy greatly favoured the large landowners and rich merchants, the two groups becoming ever more closely linked, despite the fact that the merchant class was still regarded as socially inferior—at least officially. The salt and iron monopolies were not reintroduced; instead, the local administration in the areas of production was made responsible for the salt tax and for iron-smelting—but only for fairly short periods. More often, rich landowners and merchants returned to running the salt works privately and supported the smelting works to their own advantage.

The policy of economic laissez-faire favoured the growth of the provincial centres of craft-work, particularly in central and southern China. It also favoured trade, which was served by an excellent road network augmented by the network of rivers and canals. Nearly all rivers of any size were arteries of trade and most of the prosperous towns—Luoyang, Linzi, Handan and Shouchun in Anhui, the junction for communications to the south, Jiangling in Hubei, Chengdu, Changsha and, of course, Canton—were situated on or near these waterways. Privately owned inns sprang up along these routes, increasingly replacing the state-owned establishments.

Thus the dealings of the great estates where agriculture and industry were combined extended far beyond their immediate neighbourhood. In contrast to the small independent concerns, the great estates as organized at the end of the Han remained the model for agriculture and the basis of the economy in northern China for centuries.

92

The Power of the Great Families

At all events the first emperors of the Latter Han supported the political power of the great families. This new and dominant class was made up of different groups. Some owed their influence to their connections with the central power; these were the members of the imperial clan and of the families of the empresses and eunuchs. Others—high officials, magnates and local notables—had made their fortunes through their own efforts. But hard and fast distinctions are usually misleading, and nine out of ten empresses of the Latter Han period were themselves members of great families (the Ma, Dou, Deng and Liang). The status of the eunuchs, who from the beginning of the first century onwards occupied all the positions inside the palace, improved, and their influence increased from the end of the century, when some were ennobled. From that time on they were permitted to adopt sons who would inherit their rank; they placed their relatives in key administrative posts, entered commerce and grew rich and gathered dependants round them, thus forming further powerful families.

Local magnates *(haoqiang)* placed their sons in local government, and it was from among these middle-ranking officials from rich families that most of the 'Filial and Honest' *(xiaolian),* whom the local high officials recommended annually and sent to the capital, were chosen. Recommendation, which had been occasional under the Former Han, became a regular practice and the preserve of the local élite, leaving candidates from modest families little chance of being chosen. This closed circle generated a whole web of ties of recognition, tacit promises of loyalty between inferiors and their superiors, and a sense of allegiance, which fed the system of patronage of the period.

Complicity therefore existed between the officials of the highest echelons of the hierarchy and the rich local families of which most were members. At the same time these families sought to extend their family relationship to the palace nobility.

The prosperity of all these influential groups was based on their possession of large estates, and their political power on their control of local government, on their near monopoly of promotion in public office, and on an increasing number of partisans or 'guests' *(ke)* who paid for the protection they enjoyed under the aegis of the clan by services ranging from regular guard duties to conducting vendettas. By the end of the second century these 'guests' constituted veritable private armies *(buqu)* in the pay of the great families.

Rival Factions

From the reign of Hedi (89–105) the delicate balance that had been preserved in the palace between the eunuchs and the 'outside relatives' *(waiqi)* was upset. For a century successors to the throne were child-emperors and totally incompetent, prey to the efforts of the eunuchs and families of the empresses to control and manipulate them. Several families dominated the government in succession; they were the Dou under Hedi, the Deng and the Yan under Andi (107–25), and the Liang under Shundi (126–44). But at the same time, thanks to their intimacy with the emperor and dowager empress, the eunuchs exerted a continuing influence. The high officials, including members of the 'outside relatives', who saw the emperor far less often, could not compete with those State servants of plebeian origin who, at least to begin with, had no ties with any clan outside the palace and in whom the young emperor therefore believed he could place his trust. Thus it was the eunuchs who in 159 assisted Huandi to liquidate the Liang clan, whose influence had prevailed since 125. Liang Ji, general-in-chief and regent, who had been in power since 141, was arrested and forced to commit suicide; all his relatives and some of his dependants were exterminated; his possessions were confiscated and resold for 300 million cash.

However, the high officials belonging to the great landed families and the less rich intelligentsia were extremely unhappy to see themselves losing real power decade after decade, the State in the hands of parvenus, and the situation worsening in the empire. Moved both by class feeling and by a degree of concern for public order, sensible of the corruption that was sapping the strength of the government, the scholars—those, that is, who had not elected to escape from public life and retire to the country—reacted and formed a league. They kept up incessant criticism of the vices of the régime: favouritism, misappropriation of public funds, injustice, oppression and chaos. In 166 their leaders were arrested and the movement dissolved. In 168 a second attempt to eliminate the eunuchs, in which the scholars and students of the Grand School allied themselves with the family of the dowager empress, also failed. Some hundred officials were executed and another six or seven hundred dismissed for life.

Messianic Uprisings at the End of the Han Dynasty

While the courtiers were tearing one another to pieces, the landed aristocracy was prospering and local government stepping up its demands. In the countryside poverty was appalling; crime was on the increase and migrations were renewed, especially at times of drought or flood, both of which caused famine. During the years 140 to 160 several politico-religious peasant revolts flared up, and messianic and millenarian movements nurtured on Taoism spread through the countryside, in both the east (on the borders of Henan and Shandong provinces) and west of China. The revolt came at a moment when predictions of the end of the world and the coming of a new era were becoming more frequent throughout the country.

The movement of the Yellow Turbans (Huang-jin), the most important in eastern China, was led by Zhang Jiao and his two brothers. They were quacks and propagandists and went about proclaiming the renewal of the world, the inauguration of the Great Peace (taiping), a return to the golden age and universal equality. They instituted communities with collective ceremonies, public confession of misdeeds, magico-religious curative practices and distributed healing amulets and medical charms. In a few years it had become a genuine mass movement. Zealots rallied in hundreds of thousands and Zhang Jiao set up a military organization. In A.D. 184, a jiazi year, that is, the be-

ginning of a new cycle of sixty years, the insurrection was launched and set the whole of the Great Plain ablaze; wearing yellow turbans as their rallying sign—yellow being the symbolic colour of Earth, the phase which would follow the Fire of the Han—the rebels attacked and seized the sub-prefectures, killed or drove out the officials and appointed new ones in an attempt to institute a theocracy—some structures of which were modelled on those of the Han, whom they hoped to dethrone. Repression was swift and violent. In the single year of the rebellion it left half a million dead.

The movement of the Celestial Masters or the Five Bushels of Rice (Wudoumi dao), also inspired by Huanglao Taoism, was confined to Sichuan province and the high valley of the Han River, but lasted longer. The sect was organized as a popular church under the direction of Zhang Daoling, succeeded by Zhang Lu. As with the Yellow Turbans, the ideology was a communal one, and they dreamed of the Great Peace, the Great Equity, of the restoration of primordial purity, with which

93
Model of a fortified dwelling place.
Earthenware, H. 29.6 cm, W. 41.2 cm, found in a tomb in Canton dated A.D. 76. (See Zhongguo kexueyuan ..., Xin Zhongguo, p. 89).

they associated the search for longevity—all ideas that expressed the popular consciousness of the age. The Church created what amounted to a small independent state, which survived for some thirty years until it was quelled by Cao Cao in 215. There were many natives among its adepts, and it had instituted a communal life with a morality based on spontaneity, sharing and free circulation of property. Equity hostels, modelled on the official relays, offered rice and meat to travellers; disease was regarded as the natural punishment for errors and excesses, and the sick person must therefore seek his cure through public confession and atone by repairing roads and bridges. For all the spontaneity there was a genuine administrative system, a hierarchic and authoritarian organization of the community, often modelled on the official bureaucracy. Nor was the Church of the Celestial Masters extinguished when it was suppressed in 215; on the contrary, it developed considerably during the third and fourth centuries.

The Collapse of the Dynasty:
The Reign of the Military Leaders

Although the rebellion of the Yellow Turbans was soon crushed, it left the country disrupted from end to end and the dynasty finally weakened. The opposing factions continued to struggle at court, and in 189 Yuan Shao, the leading spirit of the party opposed to the eunuchs, urged He Jin, the empress's half-brother, to suppress them. This time the conspiracy succeeded, and two thousand eunuchs were exterminated. But the triumph of the scholars and nobles came too late; Dong Zhuo, a soldier and one of the vanquishers of the Yellow

Turbans, took over the puppet emperor. After 190, the existence of the Han as a dynasty was merely nominal, and the control of the country was in the hands of local leaders who belonged to rich land-owning families such as Yuan Shao, Yuan Shu, Cao Cao (155–220), Liu Bei (161–223) and Sun Quan (185–252).

The struggle for power between these *condottieri* lasted some thirty years. During the civil war, the urban centres of the northern plain were destroyed, beginning with Luoyang, which was sacked by Dong Zhuo in 190; the city—palace, temples, ministries, private residences—was pillaged and set on fire; the imperial tombs were desecrated. The Han libraries and archives disappeared in the blaze, representing a perhaps more irreparable loss than the Burning of Books ordered by Qin Shi Huangdi.

In the general anarchy the empire broke up; owners of estates lived as self-sufficient units, fortified their manors and recruited troops to defend 93 them. Generals seized whole regions: Sun Quan the lower basin of the Yangzi and the provinces south of the river, Liu Bei—a descendant of the imperial Han clan—Sichuan. But it was the formidable figure of Cao Cao, who was gradually making himself master of northern China, which dominated the first quarter of the third century. At once a remarkable strategist, a poet and a statesman, he remains the embodiment of a new type of great captain and adventurer.

In A.D. 220 his son Cao Pi deposed Xiandi, ascended the throne at Luoyang and founded the Wei dynasty (220–65). His rivals in turn assumed the title of emperor, one instituting the Han dynasty of Shu (221–63) at Chengdu, the other the Han dynasty of Wu (222–80) at Nanking. With these 'three kingdoms' *(sanguo)* a new era opened; it has often been called the Chinese Middle Ages.

Chapter II

China and the Outside World during the First Centuries A.D.

Difficulties in Controlling and Integrating Non-Chinese Peoples

The major concern of the Latter Han was no longer expansion, but how to integrate and Sinicize the subjugated populations, how to control them and coexist with them. From now on increasing numbers of non-Chinese ethnic groups lived within the empire. In the third century A.D. in provinces like that of modern Shaanxi nearly 50 per cent of the population were barbarians. Thus these groups, with whom the Chinese were living side by side in many regions, both north and south, needed to be integrated without upsetting the internal order. Conquered barbarians entering the provincial systems came under the direct control of an imperial official; this meant that their chief was stripped of all power. The barbarians became taxable like every Chinese; above all, they became mercilessly liable to the corvée. Many were enslaved; others were conscripted to the frontiers to fight invaders or quell rebellions by other barbarians. There can be no doubt that exploitation, exaction and oppression, of which these peoples were usually victims at the hands of local government, considerably delayed the process of Sinicization and accounted for the large number of barbarian revolts during the period of the Latter Han.

As for the steppe lands, these no longer constituted a unified and powerful empire as they had done in the second century B.C. From now on they embraced various barbarian groups, who, although divided, were in a continual state of turbulence both inside and outside the Chinese frontiers. In their effort to control these groups the Han government played off barbarians against barbarians, provoking and feeding armed conflict and encouraging reciprocal attacks. These tactics were designed to prevent the re-formation of a union of non-Chinese ethnic groups; this proved, however, to be a two-edged weapon, for at the end of the Han the Chinese frontier system was shattered by continual warfare between these foreign populations. Furthermore, because from the first century onwards the northern barbarians had been allowed to settle inside the frontier line, the Chinese population moved away, and the population of the vast northern frontier zone became almost wholly barbarian. Add to this the increasing volume of recruitment of non-Han personnel to the garrisons and the treatment meted out to the conquered ethnic groups and it becomes obvious that all the conditions required for the outbreak of the barbarian revolts of the fourth century were to hand.

Although Chinese weaponry had not changed 56, 94–95 fundamentally, it did improve during the period of the Latter Han: crossbows became more powerful; armour was better designed, etc. Under the Former Han armour made of plaques (shaped like scales) had been used with, or instead of, plate armour. The trend accelerated during the first centuries A.D. From then onwards armour consisted of a kind of cuirass with attached sleeves (liangdang- 95 kai), and plaques and plates were now made of steel. Horses too began to be armoured.

But the edge was taken off these advances by the fact that the Chinese no longer enjoyed exclusive use of their weaponry. The watch kept on the frontiers was now less vigilant, and smuggling became so active that large quantities of Chinese weapons passed into the hands of the barbarians. At the same time Chinese casting techniques were introduced into many of the surrounding states.

The Situation in Northern China

The Xiongnu took advantage of the disorder and civil war that followed the fall of Wang Mang to resume their raids. In A.D. 39 over 60,000 people had to be evacuated from the north of Shanxi province, and the Xiongnu occupied the territory they had abandoned, inside the Chinese frontier. In 44 another area, north of the loop of the Yellow River, was abandoned, and the population surged back to the south of Shanxi province. But internal dissension among the Xiongnu reversed the balance of power in favour of the Han. And in 48 the Xiongnu again split into two branches, a northern and a southern. The southern Xiongnu then re-entered the tribute system. Living along the frontiers and in the north-west of the empire, growing rapidly in numbers, the southern Xiongnu became increasingly dependent on the Chinese, not only for luxury goods, but also for the most basic commodities, including the livestock that was considered to be their special economic resource. The northern Xiongnu began by stepping up their raids on the south but were soon compelled to migrate westwards under the threefold pressure of the Xianbei to the east, the southern Xiongnu to the south-east and the Han, who, under Mingdi, abandoned Guangwudi's wait-and-see policy and turned to the attack.

During the first century B.C. in the north-west, the Qiang had migrated to Gansu province, inside the Chinese frontier; during the years of disorder (A.D. 23–36) their numbers steadily increased and with them friction between the Chinese and the Qiang. Indeed coexistence between the two ethnic groups had been difficult from the start. The Qiang were semi-nomadic and lived mainly from stock-raising (cattle, horses and sheep) and secondarily from agriculture. From the moment of settling in Gansu the Qiang had suffered serious economic exploitation at the hands of the Chinese

94
A cavalryman holding a halberd *(ji)*.
Bronze, H. 53 cm, from a tomb at Leitai, district of Wuwei, Gansu, end of the second or beginning of the third century A.D.

95
Incised stone slab from Sunjiacun, Tengxian, Shandong.
H. 58 cm, W. 62.5 cm, (upper register) battle scene, (middle register) prisoners of war are presented, (lower register) hunting scene, Latter Han. (See *Corpus des pierres sculptées Han,* vol. II, p. 89, Pl. LIX).

96
Rubbing of the lintel on the façade of a tomb at Yinan, Shandong.
Incised stone depicting a battle against the 'barbarians', L. 2.86 m, end of the Latter Han. (See Ceng Zhaoyu et al., *Yinan gu,* Pl. 24).

(who stole their cattle, their women and children, etc.). This worsened under the Latter Han. As early as A.D. 33 the historian Ban Biao (3–54) gave a lucid description of the situation: 'At the present time conquered Qiang live in Liangzhou [Gansu], retaining their barbarian manner of life; nevertheless, they co-habit with the Chinese. Since the two peoples have different customs and do not speak the same language, Chinese petty officials and crafty persons take advantage of this to rob the Qiang of their possessions. There is nothing the Qiang can do; they are exasperated and they revolt. One could almost say that this is the cause of all the barbarian rebellions'.[1] Ban Biao's was a true assessment of the situation, and Qiang revolts became more frequent during the second century. Their raids were usually directed towards the Wei valley, but on two occasions (in 108 and 111) they penetrated as far as the Great Plain. The fighting devastated the north-west of the empire, accelerated the flight of the Chinese colonists and disorganized the economic life and military control of the region.

In the north-east of the empire two branches of the Donghu, the Wuhuan and the Xianbei, who were probably proto-Mongols from western Manchuria, shook off the Xiongnu yoke in A.D. 49. A large group of the Wuhuan now went to pay homage to the Han court, taking as tribute slaves, cattle, bows and skins. They settled along the frontier lines, and the post of Colonel Protector of the Wuhuan *(Hu Wuhuan xiaowei)* was restored at Ningcheng (Shanggu commandery, in north-western Hebei province, near Inner Mongolia) to take charge of the affairs of the Wuhuan and the Xianbei, including organizing trade, presenting gifts and taking hostages. While relations with the

97
Cavalry battle: detail of the lower part of the east wall of the chamber for offerings at Xiaotangshan.
(Above) battle between barbarians and Han warriors, (below) hunting scene, Xiaotangshan, Shandong, *c.* A.D. 100. (See Chavannes, *Mission archéologique,* vol. I, Pl. XXVIII, no. 50).

Wuhuan remained fairly good until about the 150s, contacts with the Xianbei proved more difficult. They too had formed a confederation, and their traditions were very similar to those of the Wuhuan, but they appear to have been much stronger militarily and were therefore more dangerous. Very soon they settled the territory abandoned by the northern Xiongnu when they migrated westwards. They occupied almost the whole of the present-day People's Republic of Mongolia, and being unable to support themselves economically, they took to trade and plundering. During submissive periods they sold horses to China in exchange for food supplies, mirrors, ceramics, lacquers and silk. But as the empire weakened they stepped up their raids. Thus the northern and north-eastern provinces were subject to incursions at intervals throughout the period from 87 to 186.

95–7 The barbarians of the north and north-west were depicted on the walls of tombs and votive chambers belonging to certain rich families in northern China, for example at Yinan, at Xiaotangshan, and at Sunjiacun in Shandong province. In what appears to be a very conventional way all these scenes glorify the activities of the deceased in his appointed official post. The Chinese can be recognized on these engraved stones by their head-dresses and cuirasses. The barbarians always wear a pointed cap, like a kind of Phrygian cap. At Xiaotangshan a man sits with his elbow on an arm-rest in front of an encampment of tents, from which archers emerge (at the right). The engraved inscription behind him identifies him as the 'King of the Hu' *(Hu wang);* but this remains somewhat vague as the term *Hu* was used at the time to designate all the non-Chinese populations from Liaodong to Xinjiang.

Southern China

From the beginning of the first century B.C. the colonization of the south-west in Yizhou commandery, the former kingdom of Dian, began to call for reconsideration. Revolt succeeded revolt (86 B.C., 83 B.C., A.D. 14, 42–5), and all were severely repressed. Following these uprisings the ancient kingdom disappeared altogether, and its ter-

98
Soldiers and peasants of the military colonies *(tuntian).* Painting on bricks, H. 66 cm, W. 1.01 m, from tomb No. 3 at Jiayuguan, Gansu, A.D. 220–316 (See *Han Tang bihua,* p. 52).

ritory became an ordinary administrative district of China. Revolts started again in the second century, often prompted, as in the north-west, by the exactions of the Han officials.

By contrast, due to considerable flexibility on the part of the governors, the south-east at first accepted co-existence with the Chinese colonists more readily. The situation deteriorated with the wave of migration in the first century A.D. On arriving in the south, the new Chinese colonists occupied the fertile land of the great river valleys, forcing the indigenous populations to abandon ground that they considered to be theirs. At the same time the Han officials interfered increasingly in local affairs and sought to impose 'civilization' Chinese-style. Besides repressing revolts, Sinicizing the natives was the prime task of officials posted to the south. The natives were expected to adopt the Chinese language, customs (especially marriage and burial rites), beliefs and methods of production; schools claiming to be centres of Confucianism and Chinese culture and designed to civilize the barbarians were established. In fact, colonization remained fragile, as the incessant rebellions prove, and in-depth Sinicization occurred extremely slowy, by a process that is still continuing in certain areas.

In the year A.D. 40 a serious revolt broke out in Vietnam, led by the Trung sisters, daughters of a local chief from the delta of the Red River. Ma Yuan (14 B.C.–A.D. 49), known as 'general tamer of the waves', was despatched to the area and crushed the rebellion in 43. The Han seizure of Vietnam was reinforced, but the Trung sisters have continued to be venerated as symbols of national independence until modern times.

In this climate of difficult settlement, some local chiefs of the south-west—Ailao of the Upper Mekong and Shan of Upper Burma—did surrender, presumably because they were attracted by the luxury articles that arrived by the Burma road.

International Trade and Cultural Exchanges

Reconquest of Western Regions

During Wang Mang's interregnum part at least of Central Asia had again come under Xiongnu domination. In A.D. 46, threatened by the hegemony of Yarkand, certain states requested the empire to accept their surrender and asked for a Protector General to be appointed. Not much caring to become involved in new wars, this time to reassert control of Xinjiang province, Guangwudi declined. Faced with this blunt refusal, the king of Shanshan (formerly Loulan) surrendered to the Xiongnu, as did Turfan. In the years that followed, the Xiongnu took possession of the whole of the eastern half of the Tarim Basin, including Kuchâ. Here, as on the northern frontier, Guangwudi would appear to have lacked vision and perspicacity, sacrificing long-term imperatives to immediate advantages. This policy of non-intervention came to an end in 74, after the Xiongnu attack in Gansu province. Mingdi then launched an offensive against the northern Xiongnu that was intended to free the states of Central Asia from their tutelage and to re-establish security and trade in the

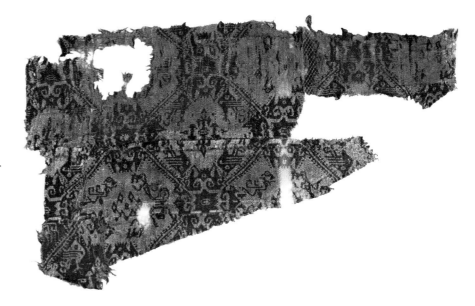

99
Strip of polychrome silk.
H. 17.5 cm, W. 23 cm, decorated with stylized birds in lozenges, provenance: Dunhuang, Gansu, c. first century A.D.
British Museum: Stein Collection, London.

region—all to China's advantage. He established a military commandery under a Protector General at Yiwu (modern Hami). At the same time Ban Chao (32–102), brother of the historian Ban Gu, was sent on a mission to Shanshan, then to Khotan and Kashgar. In a few years he won back for China the submission of all these states and control of the southern route of the Silk Road. But in this region, where every battle won has to be won all over again, the situation tottered once more in 77 in the face of a joint attack by Turfan and the Xiongnu. Ban Chao struggled for thirty years (73–102) to re-establish Chinese supremacy over the western kingdoms. Indefatigable, omnipresent and nearly always victorious, he fought his way from one oasis to the next. He had to face not only the local potentates but also, in A.D. 90, the Kushans, whose dynasty had just carved out a great empire extending from the north-west of India to Sogdiana.

Following his victory over the Kushans, Ban Chao was appointed Protector General and established the seat of the protectorate at Kuchâ. In 102, now old and sick, he was finally permitted to re-

map, p. 223

turn to his own country where, on reaching Luoyang, he died.

After 107 revolts broke out again in Central Asia and the northern Xiongnu again seized the advantage. The situation was restored, this time by Ban Yong, a son of Ban Chao, between 123 and 127. The last attack by the Xiongnu was in 150, and relations between the Han court and the western marches were severed.

Throughout the period of Ban Chao's administration and until c. 150, trade flourished on the routes of the Silk Road. The domination of the region by the two empires of the Han and the Kushan undoubtedly guaranteed the caravans of the time the peace and security they required for their dealings.

The empire of Kushan, its dynasty descended from the Yuezhi who had conquered Bactria in the second century B.C., lay at the meeting point of three great trading routes: the road to India and on to the Mediterranean by sea, the Silk Road linking China with Parthian Iran and Roman Syria, and the road to the Black Sea by the north of the Caspian Sea or by the Caucasus. This position, the mosaic of races that made up the empire, the steppe origins of much of the population, the former

presence of Greece on its soil and, finally, commercial facilities, all favoured the development of a cosmopolitan culture sustained by foreign imports. At Begram in Afghanistan on the site of a former residence of the kings of Kushan, Greco-Roman bronzes, Alexandrian glass, Indian ivories and Chinese lacquer have all been found.[2] A little further north, at a site that is now in the Soviet Union, jewellery and gold ornaments from India and Central Asia have been discovered side by side with Chinese silks and mirrors.

Continuing west from the Kushan empire by the land route, the traveller, as in the Former Han period, was bound to traverse the Parthian empire, which derived much of its revenue from controlling and exploiting commodities that passed in transit through its territory.

Chinese silk was still the principal commodity in this trade, and specimens dating from this period have been found in the Crimea and in Syria (Palmyra) as well as in Central Asia. Another commodity seems also to have reached the Roman empire at this period. Speaking of the different qualities of iron, Pliny the Elder says that the best is that made by the 'Seres' (the Chinese). Iron-smelting works have been discovered at the oasis of Niya, east of Khotan, in Xinjiang province; it is therefore perfectly possible that at the period of the Latter Han articles made of Chinese iron were exported, together with certain techniques, and reached the Roman empire by way of Central Asia.

99

100
Tomb model of a boat.
Earthenware, L. 55 cm, from a tomb at Shahequ in Canton, period of the Latter Han.

China kept the secret of silk, the middlemen (Kushans, Parthians, Syrians and Greeks) that of the trade routes. Everyone benefited, except for the Roman empire, which eventually paid enormous sums in gold, silver and copper coins for this luxury. Writing in the mid first century, Pliny states that the annual cost of Roman imports from the east (mainly silk and spices) amounted to 100 million sesterces (22,000 Roman gold pounds).

The Sea Route (map, p. 223)

In Pliny's day the overland route was not the only one by which silk was imported. It could be bought in Palmyra or Petra, having been shipped from distant Indian ports. In the reign of Claudius (41–54), a Greek pilot from Egypt hit on the idea of using the regular monsoon winds—familiar to Indian and Arab sailors but unknown in the west at the time—to sail directly from the Red Sea ports to India.

Navigation was still difficult: sailors followed the coast-line by day and took their bearings from the stars by night. But, just as Indian ships sailed to Vietnam and Canton, so it became possible for the Romans to transport men and merchandise from the Mediterranean to China, thus short-circuiting the obstacle that was Parthia.

In A.D. 120 minstrels and acrobats from Da Qin (Roman Syria) disembarked in Burma, whence they were taken to the emperor of China, by way of Yunnan. In 166 a so-called Roman embassy from Marcus Aurelius arrived at the Han court. Its members were presumably merchants who had disembarked in Vietnam and passed themselves off as emissaries from the Roman emperor. The presents they brought and which they had probably purchased at one of their ports of call—elephant tusks, rhinoceros horns and tortoise-shell—aroused little admiration at court, since the Chinese imported these commodities regularly from Vietnam and southern Asia.

Few Roman merchants can have travelled as far as China. Similarly, proof that Chinese ships reached Indian trading posts at this period is still outstanding. It is very likely that sailors and merchants specialized in a single sector of the network along this sea route. The actual commodities travelled long distances. In the entrepôts of southern India, Roman goods were transshipped and despatched with local goods to South-East Asia. Thus at Oc-eo, a port much used at the time in the Cambodian kingdom of Funan in southern Vietnam, Roman medals of the second century A.D. have been found together with Indian jewellery, intaglios and a fragment of a Chinese mirror; again, a Roman bronze lamp has been discovered at P'ong-tük, near Kanchanaburi in Thailand, and ceramics from Arezzo have been unearthed at Virapatnam near Pondichery on the east coast of India.

It seems probable that from the end of the first century A.D. most of the silk imported by the Roman world went by the sea route and not overland across Parthian Iran.

At the other end of the chain, the Vietnamese ports of call and trading posts in this international commerce certainly enjoyed considerable prosperity; the country produced and exported pearls, ivory, tortoise-shell and incense.

Panyu (Canton) was the most important port—being both a sea and a river port—on the south coast of China. Silks, ceramics and cinnamon were shipped for export, while cargoes from overseas were unloaded and redespatched northwards to the capital by river, together with tropical fruits. Canton also possessed shipyards. One of these, dating from the Qin or the beginning of the Han period, was discovered in 1975.[3] The pearl fisheries of Hepu, the second port, rivalled those of Jiaozhi in northern Vietnam.

Exclusively Chinese maritime traffic seems to have been concentrated in Chinese waters, mostly in the East China Sea; it was largely coastal, but there was also trade with Korea and the islands of Japan. Envoys from the minor kings of the north of the island of Kyushu, the *Woren* of the Chinese texts, brought pearls in tribute and received silk, gold, bronze mirrors, articles made of iron and cash in exchange.

It seems, however, that the high seas did not represent an irresistible attraction during the Han period. Official China remained a nation of landsmen, of continentals. They peopled islands in mid-ocean with Immortals, imagining them as highly desirable but inaccessible paradises, and this is the only context in which the sea appears in Han

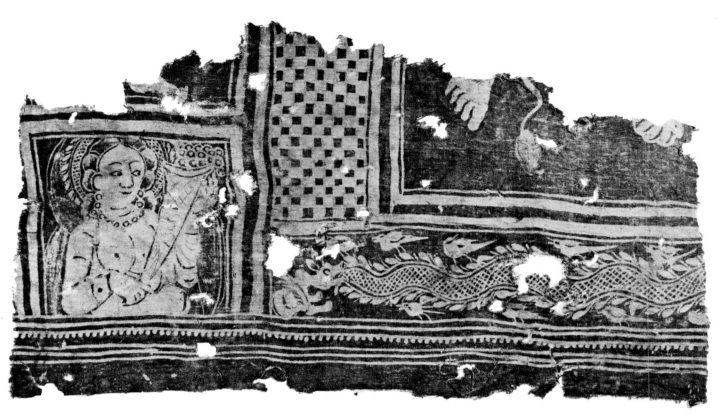

101

Printed cotton (batik): female deity holding a cornucopia.
L. 86 cm, W. 45 cm, provenance: Niya, Xinjiang, second or
third century A.D. (See *Xinjiang chutu wenwu,* p. 35).

literature. This does not mean that a certain
amount of maritime trade had not developed, but
it remained marginal and was usually carried on by
non-Chinese peoples—the Yue, for example—
who, in taking to the sea, were merely following
an ancient tradition. The higher realms of Han
government did not figure in these movements,
and the remark of the scholars of the *Yantielun:*
'Must we abandon the earth, from which we live,
to sail upon the Ocean river?'[4]—fairly sums up the
Han lack of enthusiasm for maritime adventure.

Contacts and Cultural Imports

Their very lukewarm feeling for the sea, and for
distant exploration in general, did not prevent the
Chinese of the Latter Han from coveting barbarian
commodities and customs even more avidly than
their ancestors of the second and first centuries B.C.
From the west they obtained glass jewellery and
other articles, woollen cloth, coral and pearls from
the Red Sea, amber from the Baltic and *styrax of-
ficinalis* ('Storax') resin. From Central Asia and
Parthian Iran came grape wine, furs, carpets and
woollen coverings, jade, printed cottons and new 101–2
plants, such as sesame. By sea from the countries of
the south came pearls, tortoise-shell, incense,
spices (ginger, cloves and nutmeg) and slaves.

Their taste for the exotic also led them to adopt
certain techniques that were new to them, such as
granulation in goldsmiths' work. But such bor- 103
rowings do not seem to have been very numerous.
In the second century A.D. four empires reigned
supreme: the Roman, the Han, the Parthian and
the Kushan; the first two—which were the richest
civilizations of the period—tried, but failed, to

102   ▷
Fragment of woollen cloth.
24 × 12 cm, provenance: Niya, Xinjiang, period of the Latter
Han. (See *Sichou zhi lu,* p. 15).

162

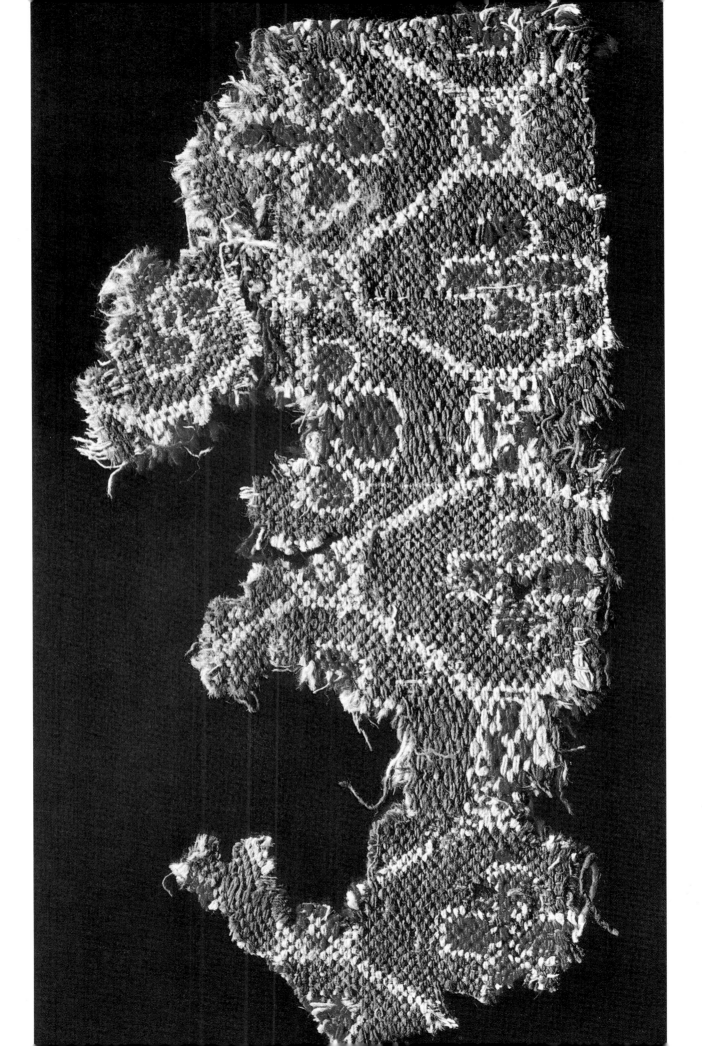

forge direct links. In *c.* 100 Maès Titianos, a Macedonian merchant, financed caravans to explore the roads of Central Asia; in 197 Ban Chao sent one of his lieutenants, Gan Ying, out to reconnoitre. Gan Ying halted at the edge of the Persian Gulf, but returned with a little information about the kingdom of Da Qin (the Roman empire, in fact, Roman Syria), which traded with the Parthians and India. Gan Ying said that the king of Da Qin wished to establish relations with the Han government but was prevented by the Parthians, who intended to retain the monopoly of Chinese silk. His and other accounts lent support to the utopian vision, widely held in China at the end of the Han dynasty, of Da Qin as a wonderful country and the model of a well-governed state.

In reality, nothing in the way of thought and life-style passed between the Roman west and China: contacts were too difficult, changes of language too numerous, intellectual worlds too far apart. At this period the Chinese encounter with other cultures took place in Central Asia, where the oases of the Silk Road were the favoured meeting-places of the Greek, Iranian, Indian and Chinese civilizations.

Western influences are apparent in the wall paintings at Miran discovered by Sir Aurel Stein at the beginning of the present century, also on textiles that are closely related in style, like the fragment of batik found at Niya. The treatment and attributes of the female divinity, who may represent Demeter or the Greek Tyche personifying good fortune, remain within the Hellenistic tradition. Through this young woman with nude breasts, large eyes and a slightly aquiline nose, a scrap of Greek civilization has filtered through Kushan to reach the frontiers of China.

From the Kushan countries too, and spreading through Central Asia, came the great stream of Mahayana Buddhism. Merchants and missionaries travelled in convoy carrying the scriptures and luxury articles and the images of Indo-Greek inspiration that were in vogue at the Kushan court.

The first mention of Buddhism in the Han empire dates from the year A.D. 65 and concerns a Buddhist community established at the court of Prince Ying of Chu, at Pengcheng, in the north of Jiangsu province. The earliest Buddhist sculptures known in China were also found in this region.[5]

They are images dating from the end of the Latter Han or the period of the Three Kingdoms, carved and engraved in the rocky cliffside of the Kongwangshan, at Lianyungang, in the extreme northeast of the province.

Before penetrating into Jiangsu province, Buddhism became established in the great trading centres of northern China, where there were many foreigners. It first found a response and patronage in aristocratic circles, the only ones able to afford the luxury goods that were brought by the merchants from Central Asia and, by the same token, the only ones exposed to foreign influences.

The Buddhist community of Luoyang had already become important by the mid second century A.D. and was presumably fairly well established at the court, for in 166 Huandi made offerings to Laozi and the Buddha in the palace. The combination is indicative of the confusion that attended the dissemination of Buddhism in China in its early days: the new doctrine of salvation was regarded as a barbarian variant of Taoism, and its devotees were recruited from among the Taoists. Thus Prince Ying of Chu, patron of the Pengcheng community in Jiangsu, was a Taoist.

In 148, also at Luoyang, An Shigao, a monk of Parthian origin, founded a school and began to translate the sacred Buddhist books.

The penetration of Buddhism by sea would seem to date from the end of the Han dynasty, and again foreign traders were the intermediaries. Communities became established at that time in the commercial centres of northern Vietnam and at Canton.

103 ▷

Box and cover.

Gold, D. 8.1 cm. Decoration consists of areas of granulated surface delimited by soldered gold wire; some other areas are empty and may originally have contained semi-precious stones, end of the Latter Han.

William Rockhill Nelson Gallery of Art—Atkins Museum of Fine Arts, Kansas City.

Chapter III

A Distinctive Art of Living

The extravagant burials of their contemporaries were condemned by moralists throughout the last two centuries of the Han dynasty. Their words went unheeded, and everyone of any substance continued to build expensive underground dwelling places and to decorate and furnish them, sometimes at great cost, to the immense advantage, not only of tomb-robbers, but also of the historians of posterity. Indeed, what would we know of material life at the period of the Latter Han without the copious evidence provided by its funerary art? We should have to rely on contemporary writing, which is usually deceptive in this sphere, being imprecise and somewhat conventional. The tombs take over from the texts, for the rich Chinese of the first centuries A.D. has left an endlessly lively and varied picture of his way of life and his activities. The frantic desire to outlive the body's death, to flaunt one's life-style and social rank, to surround oneself in the grave with familiar or precious objects, and to make sure of one's material comfort in the next world is part of an extremely ancient tradition in China, but round about the beginning of the Christian era the phenomenon became more general and began to affect the middle classes.

Tombs

The commonest form of burial at the time consisted of a hypogeum built of small solid bricks. These were easier to handle and facilitated more flexible and complex solutions than the large hollow bricks of the Former Han. This underground architecture often consisted of a whole complex of subsidiary chambers placed at different angles round a principal chamber, itself sometimes divided into a vestibule, a central and a rear chamber.[1] It had a barrel vault that might be stilted to varying degrees, a rib vault or a dome. The dividing brick walls might be decorated with impressed geometric motifs, with cash or with phrases of good augury; they might also carry paintings of everyday scenes, fabulous beasts or mythological themes.

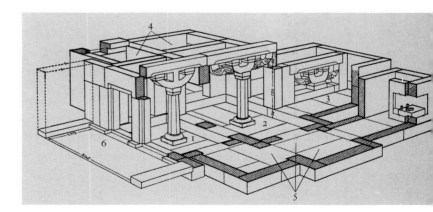

104
Reconstruction of a cutaway view of a tomb at Yinan, Shandong.
Central axis: (1) antechamber, (2) central chamber, (3) rear chamber, (4) chambers on the left lateral axis, (5) chambers on the right lateral axis, (6) entrance; end of the Latter Han. (See Ceng Zhaoyu et al., *Yinan gu,* p. 4).

105
Two-leafed door of a rock tomb to the south of Chengdu, Sichuan.
Sandstone, H. 1.295 m, decorated in flat low relief with masks, the tiger of the West (left-hand leaf), the dragon of the East (right-hand leaf), wading birds and pheasants, second century A.D.
Museum Rietberg: Collection Eduard von der Heydt, Zurich.

were decorated with engraved motifs, sometimes heightened with pigment.

Tombs made entirely of stone slabs with engraved decoration were common in the provinces north of the Yangzi and more frequent in Henan, Shangdong, Jiangsu and Sichuan provinces. Most were hypogea of some considerable size, the most perfect example being the tomb at Yinan in Shangdong province. Conceived as a complete underground residence (8.70 m in length N-S, by 7.55 m in width E-W), it was divided into eight compartments, comprising three chambers (vestibule, central and rear chambers) on the central axis, surrounded by three lateral chambers to the right and two to the left. The beams were supported by thick columns surmounted by capitals in imitation of timber-framed buildings. Various techniques—incising, engraving in low relief, sculpture in the round—were used for the decoration, the repertoire being borrowed from real life or an imaginary world. 96, 114

104

A third type of tomb, which was very popular in Sichuan province in the valley of the Min River,

Very large tombs—that at Leitai measures 19.2 metres in length by 10.3 metres maximum width and 4.5 metres in height, that at Helingeer 19.85 metres in length by 3.6 metres to 4 metres in height—seem sometimes to have been conceived as true family vaults, the chambers being constructed at different times.

A second type of tomb, found mainly in northern China was made of brick and stone slabs combined, or of stone only. Broadly speaking, the chambers were arranged on the same principle as the brick tombs. Decoration was impressed on the bricks and engraved on the stones, or it might also be painted. Thus in the north of Shaanxi, doors, lintels and columns were made of stone, while brick was used for walls and ceilings. Stone slabs

106
Brick with impressed motif showing *que* ('towers') flanking a gateway.
Earthenware, 46 × 41 cm, provenance: Chengdu, Sichuan, second century A.D. (See Rudolph and Wen You, *Han Tomb Art,* p. 86).

107
Pillar known as the pillar of Gao Yi: front of left-hand pillar and buttress at the entrance to the burial precinct of the tomb of Gao Yi, governor of Yizhou commandery (d. A.D. 209). Sandstone, H. 5.75 m, Ya'an *xian,* Sichuan.

108
Lion from the avenue of a tomb.
Grey limestone, H. 1.45 m, L. 1.50 m, second century A.D.
Musée Guimet, Paris.

109
Red bird, the emblem of the South.
Low relief on the front of the right-hand pillar at the entrance to the burial precinct of the tomb of Master Shen, sandstone, second century A.D., Quxian, Sichuan.

110   ▷
Model of a house.
Painted earthenware, H. 1.29 m, second century A.D.
William Rockhill Nelson Gallery of Art–Atkins Museum of Fine Arts, Kansas City.

169

was the rock tomb. For the largest tombs the rock might be hollowed out to a depth of between 30 and 40 metres. As in the brick tombs, the whole complex comprised a vestibule, several main chambers and annexes, and passage-ways. Here again several coffins (made of stone or earthenware) were often placed in the same tomb, which thus served as a family cemetery, the various chambers being excavated as required.

Except in the case of the rock tombs, the grave was surmounted by a tumulus. It was surrounded by a sacred precinct forming the burial area, the size of which depended on the rank and means of the deceased. On the central axis of rich tombs one, two or four paths led to the tumulus. At the entrance to the burial area this 'spirit path' (shendao) was marked by a pair of columns (que), recalling the towers that flanked gateways of cities, palaces and estates, or the gates in the encircling walls of the imperial tombs. These columns with their abutments marked the limits of the precinct, and inscriptions gave the name and titles of the de-

ceased. They were decorated with different scenes and images of the Beasts of the Four Directions, whose presence—they are also found on tomb doorways—situated the burial in space and related the deceased to the universe through the whole network of correspondences of the *Yinyang wuxing shuo* (see p. 99). Stone lions were sometimes placed in front of the columns. Inside the burial area the 'spirit path' was bordered by statues, stelae and columns. A sacrificial chamber, usually open-fronted and consecrated to the cult of the deceased, was situated in front of the tumulus. A stela carrying the genealogy and a eulogy of the deceased stood in front of the sacrificial chamber.

111
Residential complex consisting of courtyards, reception hall, storeyed pavilion, galleries and well.
Impressed brick, 45 × 40 cm, second century A.D. (See Liu Zhiyuan, *Sichuan Han,* p. 64).
Sichuan Provincial Museum.

112
Pigsty and lavatories.
Tomb model, grey earthenware, H. 25 cm, first or second century A.D.
Tenri Museum (Tenri sankōkan), Tenri, Japan.

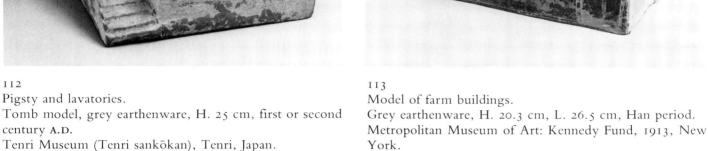

113
Model of farm buildings.
Grey earthenware, H. 20.3 cm, L. 26.5 cm, Han period.
Metropolitan Museum of Art: Kennedy Fund, 1913, New York.

114
Reconstrucion of a view of a house and courtyards.
Based on an incised stone slab from a tomb at Yinan, Shandong, end of the Latter Han. (See Ceng Zhaoyu et al., *Yinan gu*, p. 103, no. 1).

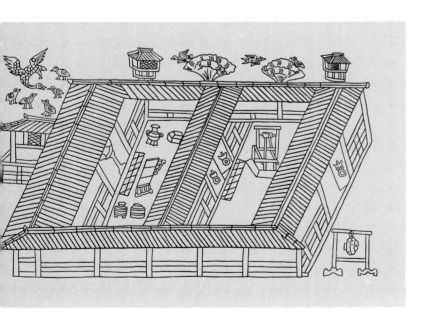

Dwellings

The tombs themselves, their decoration, the 104 funerary models they contained, constitute our best source of information about Han dwellings and their architecture, from modest farm buildings 112, 113 to the storeyed and galleried pavilions of high society.

Medium-sized residences were usually built round one or more courtyards. Two examples seem particularly significant: one is a reconstruction of the house of a landowner of average means 114 in Shandong province; the other belonged to a land-owning official or a merchant in Sichuan 111 province. The former house is all on one level. A 114 half-open door gives on to a courtyard containing the well. At the top of a few steps another door—its leaves decorated with masks like those of the first—leads through the first wing of the building to a second courtyard. A low table, a box and various ordinary receptacles stand in this courtyard. Like the first, the second wing is raised on a terrace and undoubtedly houses the private apartments,

115

Model of a two-storeyed pavilion.
Red earthenware with green glaze, H. 1 m, W. 0.46 m, end of the Latter Han.
Museum of Fine Arts: Charles B. Hoyt Collection, Boston.

116

Wall painting: 'the officer in charge of the kitchens and the table' *(gongguan yuanshi)*, preparing a banquet to be given by the Colonel Protector of the Wuhuan, west wall of passageway connecting the antechamber and the north lateral chamber.
1.20 × 1.02 m, from a tomb at Helingeer, Inner Mongolia, *c.* A.D. 150–66 (See *Han Tang bihua*, p. 27).

with a wing or pavilion behind it at right-angles. The upper storeys of two watch-towers or pavilions rise above the roof of the right-hand lateral wall. The Sichuan house is surrounded by a wall enclosing four courtyards separated by covered galleries. The main wing of the house stands on a terrace at the end of the second courtyard on the left. The hall opens on to the courtyard and is a three-bayed chamber with a pitched roof supported by columns and beams. Two men sit conversing in the hall while two cranes—birds of manifold symbolism—dance before them in the courtyard. The right-hand side of the complex is also divided into two courtyards: the front one contains a kitchen, a well and a wooden frame for drying washing; in the second courtyard, where a servant sweeps, stands a tall pavilion on a square ground-plan and with a hipped roof, which probably

172

118
Incised stone slab: fishing scene and pavilion above a pond. 87.5 × 82.5 cm, from Liangchengshan, south-east of Jining, Shandong, period of the Latter Han. (See *Corpus des pierres sculptées Han,* vol. I, p. 34, Pl. XXXI).

119
Stone slab from a tomb.
Sandstone, H. 88 cm, W. 1.19 m, chamber for offerings belonging to the Dai family at Qingbing *xian,* Shandong, dated A.D. 114.
Museum Rietberg: Collection Eduard von der Heydt, Zurich.

117
Incised stone slab: the sun bird carries the sun on its back (above), the moon with its inmate the toad (below); constellations surround the moon.
From a tomb in the region of Nanyang, Henan, first or second century A.D. (See *Wenwu,* no. 6 [1973]: 25).

120
Rubbing: detail from an incised stone slab from one of the chambers for offerings of the Wu family *(Wuliang ci)*.
(Detail) 61.5 × 50.5 cm, (upper register) Jing Ke tries to assassinate the king of Qin (the future Qin Shi Huangdi), who escapes and is seen to the right of a column into which a dagger has been thrust; (lower register) Fuxi (right) holds a set square; Nügua (left) holds a compass; Immortals in the centre, district of Jiaxiang, Shandong, *c.* A.D. 150 (See Speiser, Goepper and Fribourg, *Chinese Art*, vol. 3, no. 116, p. 249).

121
Rubbing: woman seated at a loom (scene depicting Zeng Shen, a paragon of filial piety, and her mother).
Detail of an incised stone slab from one of the chambers for offerings belonging to the Wu family *(Wuliang ci),* district of Jiaxiang, Shandong, *c.* A.D. 150. (See Nagahiro et al., *Kandai gazō,* p. 74).

housed residential quarters and a watch-tower. These tall towers with timber-framing and brick

115 walls were very much the fashion in the Han period; they rose to several storeys surrounded by

115–16, 118 balustrades and constituted the private part of the dwelling. Some pavilions of this type were large and were interconnected by storeyed galleries and covered ways. The top storey served as a watch-tower and fort, when there was no free-standing

92 building for the purpose.

110 Some of the houses belonging to members of high society were decorated with paintings on doors, walls, beams and external capitals.

The houses of the rich, especially country-houses, were surrounded by gardens or pleasure

118 parks, with kiosks overlooking ponds whence the inmates watched the fishing and gathered to make music or admire the landscape.

The interiors of these houses were painted in bright colours, their themes deriving from the same source as the painted, impressed and engraved decoration of the tombs and sacrificial chambers, i.e. mythological and cosmological fig- 117, 119–20 ures, legendary and historical scenes, moralizing portraits, and everyday scenes. 120–1

Furniture remained unchanged from the time of the Former Han; now, however, instead of a mat, the seat of honour was often a low dais accommodating one person, sometimes with a canopy 122, 124 above it. The use of folding screens of several leaves surrounding such daises seems also to have become more common and would become more frequent still after the Han period. 123, 140

The Seasonal Round

The tombs inform us not only about Han dwelling places, but also about the layout of markets and of- 126 ficial buildings in some towns. However, com- 125

174

pared with rural and estate life, urban activities are
33–4, 36, not often depicted. All the agricultural processes
3, 127, 129 are represented, including tilling the soil, harvest-
ing, hulling and winnowing and garnering, and
some industrial activities. Models of wells,
7 granaries, pigsties, mills—all quintessential symbols of Han activity—occur again and again in the
tombs of land-owning officials. The wheelbarrow
might also have figured, for it had been invented,
possibly by the end of the Former Han, and was

122

Secretary-annalist *(zhujishi)*.
Painting, H. 91 cm, W. 65 cm, from the entrance chamber of
tomb No. 1 at Wangdu, Hebei: (left) inkstone in front of the
dais; the ink, in the form of a pellet, was crushed on the inkstone with a small pounder (this one is conical and is painted
black) and moistened with water; (right) cylindrical water
pot, second half of the second century A.D. (See *Han Tang
bihua*, p. 8).

123

Fragment of a painted screen: figures of emperors, famous
generals, virtuous women, pious sons and high dignitaries.
Red lacquer ground, (bottom register) imaginary portrait of
Chengdi (32–7 B.C.) riding in a palanquin, H. *c.* 80 cm, W. 40
cm, from the tomb of Sima Jinlong (d. A.D. 484), Datong,
Shanxi. (See Zhongguo kexueyuan ..., *Xin Zhongguo*, p.
135).

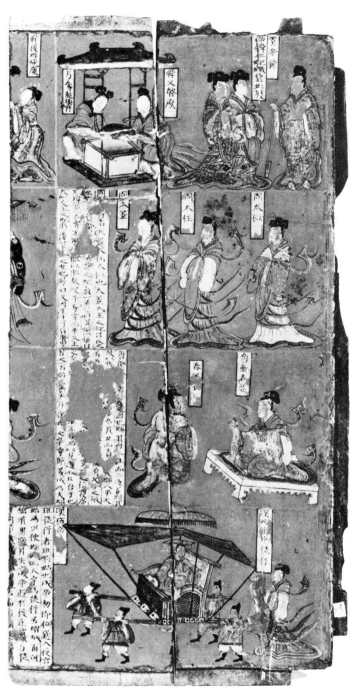

175

124
Master and disciples.
Impressed brick, 41 × 39.5 cm. The master (left) is seated on a dais; his pupils are seated on mats and hold slips. Provenance: Chengdu, second century A.D. (See Liu Zhiyuan et al., *Sichuan Han*, p. 33).
Sichuan Provincial Museum.

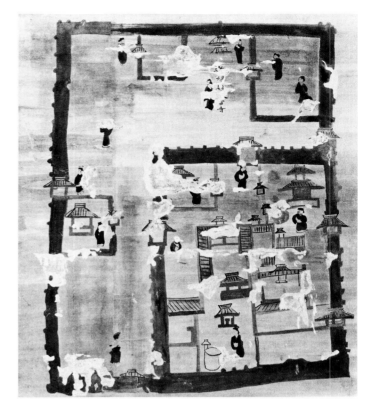

125
Administrative buildings of the sub-prefecture of Fanyang, Hebei, where the occupant of the tomb had been sub-prefect. Wall painting from the central chamber of a tomb at Helingeer, Inner Mongolia, A.D. 150–66 (See *Han Tang bihua*, p. 22).

widely used in agricultural work during the early centuries of the Christian era.

128 130–1, 133 The tombs contained a similar number of objects reflecting the home and women's chores, including lamps, stoves, wine jars, large glazed jars, cooking vessels and, in general, anything connected in any way with the sacrosanct preparation 116, 132 of food.

134–5 No less lively a picture of domestic economy has survived in the *Simin yueling* of Cui Shi (*c.* 110–70). Cui Shi came of an old family of officials and land-owners in Hebei province. His father, a writer and a renowned calligrapher, had been a friend of Zhang Heng (78–139), Ma Rong (79–166) and Wang Fu (*c.* 90–165). Himself well versed in the Classics and a good calligrapher, he was recom-

mended to the capital, where he served for some years before being appointed to a post in Wuyuan commandery, north of the loop of the Yellow River. But such were the tensions at court and so corrupt the government that in 161 he decided to retire. His surviving works are a treatise *On Government (Zhenglun)*, in which he recommends realist and legalist solutions to the problems of his time, and the *Simin yueling ('Monthly Instructions for the Four Social Classes')*, a kind of family almanac in which he gives precise month-by-month instructions for agricultural work, silk production, the preparation of medicines, preservation of food-stuffs, social activities and the rites. The writer shows himself to have been an enthusiast for family economy and methods of production. He may

176

be said to have transferred to the private estate his ambition as a local administrator concerned for the economic well-being and the security of his district.

The landowner to whom the *Simin yueling* is addressed is no official residing in the capital or in a distant city, but the master who cultivates his own land, where the men and women of the family work alongside peasants and servants, the men helping in the fields and the women in the running of the house. For the landowner of average means, living on his estate, surrounded by men of his clan, close to the tombs of his ancestors, the *Simin yueling* represented a kind of breviary. It helped him to plan the work, to organize military training for his

126
Market scene.
Impressed brick, 47 × 27 cm, (left) east gate of the market; near the gate a restaurant-keeper stands behind his oven; (centre) sellers and their customers, (right) market tower, with a drum hanging on the upper storey and two men conversing on the ground floor, provenance: Guanghan *xian,* Sichuan, second century A.D. (See Rudolph and Wen You, *Han Tomb Art,* p. 93).
Sichuan Provincial Museum.

127
Impressed brick from a tomb.
46 × 42 cm, (upper register) hunting wild geese as they fly over a pond, (lower register) reaping, (left) a figure brings a meal for the reapers, second century A.D., Chengdu, Sichuan. (See Rudolph and Wen You, *Han Tomb Art,* p. 76).

128
Bird lamp.
Earthenware with green glaze, H. 50.7 cm, period of the Latter Han.
Tenri Museum (Tenri sankōkan), Tenri, Japan.

130
Model of an oven.
Earthenware with dark green glaze, H. 9 cm, L. 31.8 cm, W. 26.8 cm; (on oven top) many cooking utensils modelled in relief, including an *an* tray, with *bei* bowls and food, first or second century A.D.
Royal Ontario Museum, Toronto.

129
Inscription on barn wall: 'barn belonging to the Colonel Protector of the Wuhuan'.
Wall painting, 1.30 × 0.65 m, west wall of the entrance chamber of a tomb at Helingeer, Inner Mongolia, A.D. 150–66. (See *Chūka Jimmin Kyōwakoku Kan Tō*, p. 29).

131
Vessel *(guan)*.
Earthenware with impressed decoration, D. 16 cm, H. 12.9 cm, from a Han tomb in Vietnam, period of the Latter Han.
Musées Royaux d'Art et d'Histoire, Brussels.

132
Cook or fishmonger.
Red earthenware with an iridescent green glaze, H. 20.3 cm, end of the Latter Han.
Yale University Art Gallery (Gift of Wilson P. Foss, Jr.), New Haven, CT.

133
Tripod vessel *(ding)*.
Earthenware, D. 19 cm, H. 15.5 cm, from a Han tomb in Vietnam, period of the Latter Han.
Musées Royaux d'Art et d'Histoire, Brussels.

peasants to prepare them to fight off robber-bands, to make ready the seasonal festivities and sacrifices and to care for the comfort of the very poor.

The year was punctuated by religious feast-days and sacrifices to the ancestors, the most important festivities being those of the New Year, which took place roughly between 16 January and 20 February. This long period began with the ceremony to expel pestilences *(Nuo)*, conducted on the eve of 136 the *La* feast by the exorcist *(fangxiangshi)*. The exorcism was intended to purge everything old and bad so that the family might enter the New Year in a state of purity. At burials the exorcist also expel-

led evil spirits from the tomb. At the celebrations for the New Year, sacrifices were offered to the an- 137 cestors and to the five tutelary spirits of the house (the porch, inner door, well, stove and impluvium). At this season of transition and renewal, wishes for the long life of the head of the family were expressed and congratulatory visits paid to superiors, elders and friends—it was in short a period of rejoicing. Other important festivities were held at the equinoxes and solstices, with, again, sacrifices to the ancestors, preceded by purification rites and followed by family banquets and friendly gatherings.

134
Kitchen scene.
Painting on brick, 36×17 cm, from tomb No. 5 at Jiayu-
guan, Gansu, A.D. 220–316. (See *Chūka Jimmin Kyōwakoku
Kan Tō*, p. 72).

135
Water carriers.
Painting on brick, 36×17 cm, from tomb No. I at Jiayu-
guan, Gansu, A.D. 220–316. (See *Chūka Jimmin Kyōwakoku
Kan Tō*, p. 38).

136
Exorcist *(fangxiangshi)* as a tomb guardian.
Grey earthenware with traces of white slip and pigment,
H. 39.4 cm, third century A.D.
Asian Art Museum: Avery Brundage Collection, San Fran-
cisco.

137   ▷
Tray.
Earthenware, D. 38.2 cm, H. 1.6 cm, painted decoration depicting four figures bearing offerings and four animals (ram,
cock, pig and duck) in red and black on white slip. In the central roundel are a water bird and a fish. First or second century A.D.
William Rockhill Nelson Gallery of Art—Atkins Museum of
Fine Arts, Kansas City.

138
Basket from a tomb known as the tomb of the Painted Basket.
Bamboo, painted and lacquered, H. 21.5 cm, L. 39 cm, (main motif) pious sons and heroes of antiquity, first century B.C. or first century A.D., former Lelang commandery, northern Korea.
Pyongyang Museum, Korea.

Moral Education

The *Simin yueling* lays great stress on the education of the young. Obedience, deference and politeness towards one's elders was inculcated from infancy. At ten years of age a boy began lessons with a master. He studied first *The Classic of Filial Piety (Xiao jing)*, the *Analects (Lunyu)* of Confucius and arithmetic, before starting, between fifteen and twenty years of age, to read the Classics, though without the commentaries. At this point the young man was often sent to complete his education in the capital, where he acquired a certain refinement of manner.

Separated from her brothers at the age of seven, a girl stayed at home and learned to prepare hemp and silk, to cook and to sanction payment for and prepare sacrifices. Humility, gentleness and self-control were the major virtues that were impressed upon her. As Ban Zhao wrote (*c.* 48–117), 'A man (who is *yang*) is honoured for his strength; the beauty of a woman (who is *yin*) depends upon her gentleness'.[2] Women were considered inferior to men and were expected to obey their fathers when they were children, their husbands when they married, and their sons when they were widowed. Girls married at fourteen or fifteen, thus uniting two families, but the main purpose of marriage was to maintain service in the ancestral temple and the continuity of the family line. Despite the narrow scope for initiative left to women in the Confucian society of the Latter Han, there can be no doubt that their individual destinies varied according to the hazards of birth even more than those of men. While female infanticide was practised widely among the poor, the status of girls was comparatively liberal in the ruling class, especially in educated circles. Thus the advanced education received by Ban Zhao, daughter of the historian Ban Biao and sister of Ban Gu (32–92) and Ban

139
Mirror back.
Gilt bronze, D. 21.4 cm, decorated with TLV motifs, animals of the four directions, the twelve characters of the duodenary cycle *(dizhi)* and an inscription of good wishes, *c.* A.D. 100.
Tenri Museum (Tenri sankōkan), Tenri, Japan.

140

Mirror back.

Bronze, D. 17.5 cm, decorated in high relief with the Animals of the Four Directions, Immortals and scenes from the legend of King Wen of Zhou, father of the founder of the Zhou dynasty; inscription of good wishes on one of the outer concentric bands: 'Tian made this mirror; the barbarians of the four regions surrender. Great are the benefits of the dynasty and the people know peace. The foreign barbarians have been destroyed and the empire restored. May wind and rain come without excess at the proper season and the five cereals mature. May you long keep your father and mother, thanks to the heavenly power. May this pass to future generations with endless joy', end of the Latter Han.

Freer Gallery of Art, Washington, D.C.

Chao (32–102), enabled her to continue the historical work begun by her father and brother and to become governess of Hedi's young empress and her ladies-in-waiting. She was a historiographer and counsellor at the palace, and a woman of letters, writing the *Lessons for Women (Nüjie)* for her own daughters of marriageable age. While this little treatise on feminine morality echoes the well-mannered Confucian ideas of her own family background, Ban Zhao recommends that all girls should receive the education that she had enjoyed, i.e. between eight and fifteen years of age the same

for girls and boys, and access for women to education based on Confucian principles, an advantage then reserved for men. Unfortunately her advice went unheeded.

Confucian morality, praised by the Ban family among others, preached courtesy, modesty, self-control, submission and subordination to superiors in the hierarchy and to one's elders, sincerity between equals, and justice and benevolence towards inferiors. Each member of this society had his allotted place that he must recognize and to which he must keep, ideal relations being based on respect for the rites and proprieties, on the cult of the family and the ancestors. Together with exaltation of filial piety, the paragons of which are depicted endlessly in art and literature, great importance was attached to charitable duties towards the underprivileged in one's circle, though close and distant relatives were clearly differentiated. 121, 138

Another aspect of respect for the rites was the art of harmonizing conduct with the universal order, of preserving equilibrium between *Ying* and *Yang* and the Five Phases, the ideal being for man to maintain in perpetuity his correct position within the cosmos, related to and in harmony with it. Many mirrors from the tombs of the period are explicit in this regard. They are often decorated with motifs (T L V) that are related to those of the astrological devices *(shipan)* and those of the games of *liubo,* or with the Animals of the Four Directions *(sishen),* the characters of the duodenary cycle and a votive inscription: 'the *shangfang* workshop has made this mirror to keep all misfortunes away; skilled craftsmen have engraved the decoration and inscription; the dragon on the left and the tiger on the right keep harmful influences away; the red bird and the "black warrior" [*xuanwu* = tortoise and snake] accord with *Yin* and *Yang*. May you have children and grandchildren in great number and may you reside in the centre. May you long keep your two parents and know joy, wealth and prosperity; may your life be longer than that of metal and stone, as is fitting for a marquis or king'. 139, 80, 139

The passage contains all the leitmotifs of the morality and cosmological beliefs of the period. The illustrations of *Yin* and *Yang* and the Five Phases in the form of animals correctly positioned on the mirror have, of course, a prophylactic power; they ward off demons and are sources of happi-

141
Variety spectacle.
Wall painting, colours: red, black, brown and white, (top left) seated spectators, (right) musicians, (centre) two men beating a drum. Round the drum are dancers, acrobats, minstrels and jugglers. From a tomb at Helingeer, Inner Mongolia, A.D. 150–66 (See Nei Menggu, *Helingeer Han,* pp. 140–1).

ness, prosperity and longevity. They represent a perfect and thus beneficent world, enlivened by a harmonious play of correspondences, a kind of properly adjusted 'magic square', within which man, living or dead, enjoys the most luxurious conditions. This perfect rightness leads naturally to the dual comfort of accomplished filial piety and an assured posterity.

Other mirrors from the end of the dynasty, characterized by their edifying historical or legendary references executed in high relief, also show the Animals of the Four Directions, together with Immortals—intermediaries between men and 140 the celestial world—and a votive inscription.

From Official Life to the Scholar's Pleasures

As we have seen, wall decorations in tombs constituted a kind of picture book with accompanying inscriptions. These texts (giving the name of the place and person, name of office and identification of the subject illustrated) were added to avoid confusion and to identify an image that was often fairly conventional; through the magic of the written symbol they often also intensified the reality of the representation. The deceased, who was usually an official of some importance, was thus evoked by the names of the posts he had filled and was accompanied by his subordinates. In his tomb or 122 sacrificial chamber were illustrations of the towns 125, 129 he had governed, his estates and storehouses, the 56, 95–6 battles he had fought and his travels. All this was depicted without much concern for individualization, but rather in order to assert his rank, worldly means and the respect and consideration that were due to him.

But besides his official life, which was often full of traps for the unwary, pleasanter memories were called up; these might include hunting, banquets, variety entertainments, evenings of music and 95, 97, 116 dance with wine-drinking as the central attraction, 127, 141–4 recitations by story-tellers and games of chess *(liubo)*.

There are references, too, to calligraphy, a rarer pleasure. Although not masters like Zhang Zhi or Cai Yong (133–92)—scholar, calligrapher, painter and musician—many scholars of the first and second centuries A.D. practised the art of calligraphy—as inkstones found in tombs testify. Some are sumptuous, others modest but of symbolic 146 significance; all take the form of a shallowly con- 147 cave receptacle standing on feet and with a lid, in which the ink stick—made of soot, usually from pine—was crushed. From the time of the Former Han at latest a calligrapher used an extremely sensitive brush—its rigidity or flexibility depending on 122

142   ▷
Two *liubo* (chess) players.
Earthenware with green glaze, H. 24.2 cm, W. 19.2 cm, from tomb No. 3 at Lingbao, Henan, second century A.D.

143

Impressed brick from a tomb: a scene of music-making and dancing.

46 × 42 cm, (left) a man plays a *qin* zither, surrounded by spectators, (centre) between a dancer with long sleeves and a drummer (?) stand vessels for warming and pouring wine, provenance: Chengdu, Sichuan, second century A.D. (See Rudolph and Wen You, *Han Tomb Art*, p. 77).

144

A pair of dancers.

Grey earthenware, H. 11.5 cm; 11.1 cm, period of the Latter Han.

Minneapolis Institute of Arts: Bequest of Alfred F. Pillsbury.

145

Tomb figure: a story-teller.

Earthenware, H. 56 cm, from rock tomb No. 3 at Tianhuishan, Chengdu, Sichuan, period of the Latter Han. (See Zhongguo kexueyuan ..., *Xin Zhongguo,* p. 86).

146 ▷

Inkstone with cover in the shape of a fabulous beast.

Gilt bronze inlaid with turquoises and coral, L. *c.* 23 cm, provenance: Xuzhou, Jiangsu, end of the first or first half of the second century A.D.

147
Inkstone with cover in the shape of a tortoise.
Grey earthenware, H. 10.2 cm, L. 25.4 cm. Incised on the tortoise's shell, which forms the cover, are the Eight Trigrams of the *Yijing*. First or second century A.D.
Minneapolis Institute of Arts: William Hood Dunwoody Fund.

what hair was used—with which he could produce downstrokes and upstrokes in all their variety. Though difficult to use, the favourite surface was silk; the calligrapher wrote on long horizontal bands of silk, which were rolled on to a wooden stick for storage. Paper, also on rolls, came to be used more widely by the end of the dynasty. But it

had been invented earlier, as is shown by the discovery in 1957 of fragments of coarse proto-paper made from hemp fibre in a tomb dating from the reign of Wudi; further fragments have been unearthed more recently in tombs of the end of the Former Han and the beginning of the Latter Han. Improvements and widespread use of the new material came slowly, and for a long time it remained unsuitable as a surface for ink. The tradition that attributes the invention of paper to the eunuch Cai Lun shows that there was a watershed at the beginning of the second century. In fact, the method of paper-making presented to the emperor in A.D. 105 was presumably simply a synthesis of and improvement on earlier experiments. From

148 a/b
Vessel *(gui)* with cover.
Porcellanous stoneware with olive-green glaze, incised trellis pattern under the glaze, (on the cover) three rams couchant, modelled in high relief, and an appliqué central ring, south-eastern China, first century B.C. or first century A.D.
Yale University Art Gallery: Gift of Mrs William H. Moore, New Haven, CT.

149
Unicorn charging.
Painted wood, H. 38.5 cm, L. 59 cm, from tomb No. 22 at Mozuicun, district of Wuwei, Gansu, first or second century A.D.

150
Belt-hook.
Bronze, inlaid with gold and silver, L. 16 cm, decoration: a monster holding a fish in its paws, facing a dragon whose head forms the hook; inscription on the reverse, end of the Latter Han.
Musée Guimet, Paris.

then on different types of paper were perfected, some made of vegetable fibre mixed with rag, some of bark and hemp. Since these papers were far less expensive than silk, the demand for them continued to grow, and by the end of the century, they had become extremely popular.

151
Dog.
Red earthenware with amber-brown glaze, H. 37.5 cm, L. 34.2 cm, probably from Hunan, period of the Latter Han. Asian Art Museum: Avery Brundage Collection, San Francisco.

152
Ring *(bi)*.
Green jade, H. 25.5 cm, disc surmounted by openwork decoration of *chi* dragons, discovered in 1959 at Beizhuang, Dingxian, Hebei, in the tomb of Liu Yan (d. A.D. 90), fifth son of Guangwudi and king of Zhongshan.

◁
153
Mirror back.
Bronze, D. 23 cm, decoration: Taoist motifs, second or third century A.D.
Museum für Kunst und Gewerbe, Hamburg.

154   ▷
Galloping horse, its right hind foot resting on a flying swallow.
Bronze, H. 34.5 cm, L. 45 cm, from a tomb at Leitai, district of Wuwei, Gansu, end of the second or beginning of the third century A.D.

The Growth of Craftsmanship, Diversity and Regionalism

The glorification of the family and of filial piety was presumably not unconnected with the spread of a very elaborate form of burial formerly reserved for those close to the court—tombs became larger, more richly decorated, and burial goods more abundant and more varied. It is also certain that this extension to the levels of officialdom, land-owners and merchants was a great stimulus to local craftsmanship. Stone-cutters, sculptors and engravers on stone, makers of bricks and stamps, 149 painters, potters who made vessels and tomb 103, 146, 150 models in earthenware, wood-carvers, carpenters, lacquerers of coffins, bronze-workers and goldsmiths, jade-workers, workers in glass, lacquerers, weavers, iron founders—all these craftsmen worked for a wider market than they had done under the Former Han. The market was wider but also more widely dispersed. Indeed, although the centres of political, economic and cultural life remained in the zone to the south of the middle reaches of the Yellow River, in the region of the former capital and in Sichuan and modern Jiangsu provinces—as is confirmed by the map of the richest known burials of the period—the establishment of many families in the south contributed to the growth of regional craftsmanship, for, like those in the north-west, officials posted to the southern commanderies became clients and sometimes promoters of the local workshops.

In a way, the requirements of burial art furthered the decentralization of craftsmanship. While the rôle of the official manufactures was becoming less clearly defined, local centres were being created or developed; these specialized in stone-engraving in 56, 95–7, 105, Shandong, Henan and Sichuan provinces, pottery 107, 109, 117– in Zhejiang, Jiangsu, Hunan and Guangdong prov-118, 120, 148, inces, mirror-making in the Shaoxing region of 153 Zhejiang and model-making, carving and designing impressed bricks in Sichuan province. These 127, 145 centres perfected their own techniques, styles and repertoires, developing a synthesis of the ancient traditions of the locality with the conventions of the time. Similarly, the need to adapt to local materials, to economic conditions and methods of manufacture, modified many of the creations of the first two centuries A.D. For example, there can be no doubt that the flowering at this period of the art of the stone-cutters and engravers of Shandong and Henan provinces, an area rich in good sandstone, was closely connected with the development of the region; advances in the technique of extracting the stone, due to improved iron tools, meant that it could be used on a vast scale for hydraulic works, such as dikes, etc. Once quarries were open and workmen trained, the use of the same material for building tombs followed fairly naturally.

The art of the Latter Han can thus be approached equally well from the point of view of its unity of inspiration, programme and artistic intention as from that of the diversity of its manners, styles of expression and regional variations—though these last do not imply any compartmentalization, since objects, styles and techniques circulated continuously between one centre and another.

The comparative popularization of burial art also accounts to a great extent for three characteristics of the products of the period. The first is the primacy of the arts of firing, on which the architecture of the tombs and their furniture mainly depended. While earthenware with green or brownish-red lead glazes continued to be made in northern China and was sometimes imitated in 142, 151 central China, glazed porcellaneous stoneware was 148 produced in south-eastern China. The most important kilns, and those with the longest tradition, were situated in the north of Zhejiang province (Shaoxing region) and in Jiangsu. The kilns in the region of Changsha (Hunan) and in Guangdong developed in imitation of these. At the time when these two types of ware were being made—both conceived originally as imitations of bronzes—pottery vessels for everyday use were continually improving in quality, and bricks, tiles and figurines, often heightened with pigment, were being made virtually everywhere.

The second characteristic feature was the search for cheap substitutes for rare or expensive items, which meant that ceramics were made to imitate bronze and glass to imitate jade. Side by side with imported pearls, the Han used beads and objects moulded in opaque glass—such as ritual objects (*bi* rings, etc.), sets of jewellery—that are overt imitations of the same forms in jade. Chinese glass, the lead and barium content of which differs from that of western glass, was also used for inlays in bronzes, especially belt-hooks.

Like the second feature, the third has to do with the character and worth of the article. Indeed, one often feels that in order to meet the constantly growing demand, quality has been sacrificed to quantity. For example, gemstones engraved in series based on a stereotyped repertoire, wall paintings rapidly and carelessly executed without any real artistic effort and batches of burial models sometimes eclipse totally successful pieces of outstanding quality.

56, 97
116, 129

113, 136
96, 109–10
139–40, 145–6,
149, 154

Chapter IV

Luoyang and Intellectual Life

The Capital of the Latter Han
(map, p. 225)

Luoyang was the capital from A.D. 25 until 190. With an *intra-muros* area of 10.10 square kilometres, it was, after Chang'an (33.48 km²) and Rome (13.80 km²), the largest city of the ancient world. H. Bielenstein[1] estimates its population (within and without the walls) at 500,000, which would make it the most densely populated city of its time.

The city inside the walls was rectangular, lay on a north-south axis and was surrounded by a wall of rammed earth with twelve gateways, as at Chang'an, though here they were painted in colours that accorded with the cosmology of the *Yin Yang wuxing shuo*. The city was encircled by the Gu River; wooden bridges crossed the river in front of the gates, except that the bridge outside the upper eastern gate *(Shandong men)* was made of stone. Apart from some religious buildings, the city outside the walls consisted largely of working-class quarters and markets.

Luoyang inside the Walls

The city possessed two palace complexes—a northern and a southern—each occupying an area of some 50 hectares and surrounded by its own walls. The two complexes were linked by a raised, roofed avenue of three lanes, of which the central one was reserved for the emperor. The north-south avenue cut the city in two, an eastern and a western half, which communicated by roadways that passed under the raised avenue.

The southern palace contained audience halls, offices, the imperial apartments, pavilions and the *Hongdumen xue* ('school by the gate of the vast capital'), a kind of academy founded in 178, which trained young men in the art of calligraphy, in drafting official documents and composing rhyme-prose *(fu)*. The Dongguan, the most famous of the imperial libraries of Luoyang, was also housed in the southern palace; it was not only a library but also a literary centre, where historians and scholars continued to work for nearly two centuries.

In addition to official and private buildings, the northern palace contained gardens and ponds, which made it the more attractive of the two palaces. The court resided in the southern palace from A.D. 25 to 65, in the northern one from 65 to 125 and from 147 to 189, and alternately in one or the other between 125 and 146.

Outside the two palace complexes, the city inside the walls was divided into quarters where the aristocracy and high officials lived. Besides, it contained thirty-two official inns *(ting),* which were also posts for the police whose duty was to maintain order, a number of ministerial offices, prisons, places of worship—the dynastic ancestral Temple *(Zongmiao)* and the Altar of the gods of the soil and of grain *(Sheji)*—and the arsenal and Great Granary, near the upper eastern gate and the mouth of the Yang canal.

One of the *Nineteen Old Songs* describes the city and its bustle:

In the city of Luo, great is the bustle,
Officers chasing one another, vying for speed.
Crisscross of avenues, branching of lanes,
Of princes, marquises, many are the mansions.

From afar the two palaces gaze at one another,
The two entrance towers exceed a hundred feet.
By exhausting all pleasures the soul is distracted...
But what can be this disquiet that haunts one?[2]

The Suburbs

Two of Luoyang's principal markets were situated outside the city gates. Further out in the southern suburb lay several important groups of buildings erected under Guangwudi: the *lingtai, mingtang, biyong* and the Grand School *(taixue)*. The *lingtai* ('transcendent terrace') was the main imperial observatory. Scientific and cosmological observations were conducted there; there too the emperor came to examine the cosmic breaths (the *yin* and *yang* cycle) by vibrating the resonant tubes of the twelve months. In the *mingtang* ('sacred hall') the emperors sacrificed to the Five Emperors. The archery ceremony that preceded a banquet was conducted in the *biyong* ('palace of the encircling moat'). A little further east the Grand School formed a vast university campus, housing lecture rooms, a library and lodgings for masters and students. After the repairs and additions of A.D. 131 there were 240 buildings and 1,850 rooms. During the second half of the century up to 30,000 students attended its courses.

The Altar of Heaven *(Nanjiao)* lay to the south of the city beyond the Luo River; Heaven was worshipped there, as well as a multitude of divinities; these included the five Planets, the five sacred Peaks, the twenty-eight Stations of the moon, the Duke of Thunder and the first Labourer. The Altar of the Earth *(Beijiao)* appears to have stood to the north of the city. The seasons were ushered in at five other altars, the *Wujiao* ('five altars of the suburbs'), which surrounded the capital to the east (spring), south (summer), west (autumn) and north (winter); the fifth altar, symbolizing the centre, was situated to the south-west of the city.

The overcrowded city of Luoyang under the Latter Han was no match for the splendours of Wudi's Chang'an. The city was smaller and more austere, though still impressive. During the renaissance of the reigns of Guangwudi and Mingdi (25–75) the new capital seems to have been the symbol of moderation, quiet elegance and refined frugality—at least in the eyes of Ban Gu (32–92) and Zhang Heng (78–139), who celebrated it in their rhyme-prose, contrasting it with the megalomania, unwholesome luxury and parvenu magnificence of Chang'an under the Former Han. In the minds of these right-thinking Confucians, who despised excess, vulgarity and the display of wealth, Luoyang was to mirror the ideally organized society of antiquity, which they dreamed of bringing to life again.

From Criticism of Orthodoxy to Criticism of Society

Guangwudi's restoration was cultural as well as political. He abolished the chairs of the 'old texts' *(guwen)* of the Classics, for they were a reminder of Wang Mang, the usurper, and re-established the schools of 'modern texts' *(jinwen)*, with the privileges they had previously enjoyed. Orthodoxy became more rigid than ever in official ritual, in everyday morality and also in literature. At the same time the apocryphal writings *(weishu)* continued to be used to interpret the Classics and as the source of oracles, to be consulted before all important decisions. The emperor himself remained a fervent believer in presages and prognostications.

Official science was becoming submerged in totally sterile verbiage. A reaction came from the rationalist school of the 'old texts', which had already won fame in the person of Yang Xiong (53 B.C.–A.D. 18) at the end of the Former Han. Huan Tan (*c.* 43 B.C.–A.D. 28), and especially Wang Chong (27–*c.* 100), were two of the most illustrious representatives of this line of sceptical philosophers of the first century A.D. In his *Xinlun* ('New Treatise') Huan Tan was the first to criticize the cabbalistic interpretation of the Classics by the supporters of the 'modern texts' and their idealization of antiquity. Wang Chong developed this criticism in his *Lunheng ('Critical Essays')*, jettisoning many superstitions, legends, beliefs and theories to which his contemporaries were giving credence. Wang Chong's refutations, which were usually based on accurate observation of natural phenomena, were part of his desire to break down errors, re-establish truth and encourage his contemporaries to return to a purer morality. 'I have written these essays on death and on the errors concerning death to show that the deceased has lost his consciousness and cannot be transformed into a ghost. Thus I hope that when my readers have understood this they will hold less extravagant funeral ceremonies and will conduct themselves more economically in this regard'.[3] Wang Chong argues against the concept of immortality and belief in the prolongation of life; he differs on this point from the Taoists, from whom elsewhere—as Yang Xiong and Huan Tan had done before him—he borrows certain ideas, in particular the notion of spontaneity as a law of nature. Yet this eclectic materialist, with his interest in the sciences, still remained a captive of the ideas of his time, including the *yin-yang* theory and the theory of the Five Phases, belief in signs—which, however, he thought appeared spontaneously and were not sent by Heaven—and many superstitions.

Nor were the 'old-text' philosophers slow to criticize the quibbles and empty verbiage of the scholars' studies, their excessive use of the *weishu*, blind veneration of the past and refusal to adapt to the changes in society. Their criticisms culminated in the debate of the Pavilion of the White Tiger (*Baihu guan*), which took place in A.D. 79 under the patronage of Zhangdi, a passionate enthusiast for classical studies and champion of the more objective and rational school of the 'old texts'. But the debate failed to solve any problems; the supporters of the 'modern texts' came out of it comforted, and the *Baihu tongyi,* a summary report of the discussions edited by Ban Gu (32–92), reads like a kind of catechism of the Confucian orthodoxy of the period.

Disquiet merely increased with the political and moral decay of the second century, while many honest scholars stood by powerless. These men, many of whom abandoned public office to live in retirement, rediscovered answers to contemporary problems in the philosophical thinking of the third century B.C. Some turned to Legalism, others to Taoism.

Of the thinkers who returned to the school of the Laws, Wang Fu (*c.* 90–165) in his *Qianfulun ('Criticisms of a Hermit')* set himself up as a severe judge of his time. The work of Cui Shi (*c.* 110–70) in the next generation was even more insistent in its desire for a realistic policy suited to contemporary circumstances and in its appeal to the severity of the law. In his *Sincere Remarks (Changyan)* of the beginning of the third century, Zhongchang Tong (180–219), counsellor to Cao Cao, called for an authoritarian government. All these men rejected traditional values and government by virtue, declaring that the only possible way out of the crisis was the application of absolute and egalitarian laws.

At the end of the Han, in opposition to the revival of Legalism that inspired Cao Cao's policy, came the first stirrings of a renaissance of the metaphysical Taoism of the *Laozi (Daodejing)* and the *Zhuangzi,* which was to blossom a few years later.

The Path of Individual Salvation

The quest for immortality and the cult of the Immortals was very much alive at the time of the Latter Han; it was reflected in the wishes inscribed on talismans and mirrors, in figural representations and in biographies of Immortals such as the *Liexian zhuan.* Art and literature are thronged with Immortals *(xianren, yuren).* With hairy, downy or feathered bodies, wings for arms and streaming hair, they fly among the clouds and journey to the land of the gods.

Taoism had spread to all classes of society and offered its devotees a religion of salvation based on moral values, spiritual asceticism, as well as on forms of hygiene, medicine and alchemy. The immortality offered by the Taoism of the time was a bodily immortality attainable through countless medicinal, gymnastic and dietetic formulae designed to prolong the life of the body. Aspirants must abstain from wine, meat and cereals, practise embryonic respiration and controlled breathing—comprising exercises for circulating the breath that would gradually replace the gross elements of the body with light, pure breathing—and

120, 139–153

155
Detail from one of the stelae on which the authorized text of the Confucian Classics was incised in three different styles of writing: *guwen, zhuanshu* and *lishu*.
Engraved under the Wei dynasty from 240–8.
Fujii Saiseikai Yūrinkan, Kyoto.

body. That body would live in the world of the Immortals, where it would be ranked according to its progress on the path of holiness.

The conquest of immortality was long, costly and difficult; it was not accessible to all and certainly not to those who had to work to survive from day to day. Just as Buddhism was moving into China, some Taoist centres had the idea of instituting, for the salvation of the faithful (both rich and poor), collective religious festivities, in which groups of zealots could redeem their sins and create for themselves in advance and here below, a living substance that would await them in the other world. They needed only to perform good actions, follow religious exercises and repent of their errors. A popular church that became well established among retired scholars *(yimin)*, lower officials, village notables and, through them, the peasants, gradually formed round this religious life, which called for voluntary poverty and venerated Huanglao (a synthesis of Huangdi and Laozi) as the supreme deity. This church inspired the movements of the Yellow Turbans and the Celestial Masters. In the confusion of the second century it reached even the court, when, in 166, Huandi worshipped both Laozi and the Buddha.

In contrast to Confucianism, which was concerned only with man in society, Taoism offered morality and a way of individual salvation that was accessible to all. This accounts for its popularity and impact, even among those scholars who were uninterested in alchemy and continued to subscribe to Confucian doctrines.[4]

take cinnamon and drugs; and the end-result of these techniques would be purification and mutation, which would lighten the body and make it immortal. This régime was accompanied by meditation. The adept concentrated his mind on the gods within the body, which was a kind of microcosm; in this way he retained the gods, whose departure would mean death. While practising hygienic techniques and interior vision, the adept was to live a pure life and to do good works, which were essential to the attainment of immortality.

An adept who had achieved immortality was able to fly. He only appeared to die; the body that was buried according to the rites was not the real

Philological and Historical Writings

During the end of the first century and throughout the whole of the second, the official learning, that of the 'modern texts' taught at the Grand School, remained in force and—except for the work of He Xiu (129–82)—became submerged in empty scholasticism, quibbles over interpretation and contradictions. By contrast, the learning of the school of the 'old texts', though not recognized officially, developed brilliantly round the remarkable philologists Jia Kui (30–101), Ma Rong

(79–166) and Zheng Xuan (127–200). At the same time the deciphering of the texts in *guwen* and the interest shown in the old forms of writing must have been the inspiration behind Xu Shen (30–124), compiler of the first Chinese dictionary, the *Shuowen jiezi (c.* 100). The work contains 9,353 characters under 540 radicals, and Xu Shen analyses the old characters from the etymological and semantic standpoint. He also draws attention to the discrepancies that existed among the ancient texts. Basing their studies on texts written in old characters in an attempt to understand them, Ma Rong and Zheng Xuan sought to eliminate the contradictions and to establish a consistent interpretation of all the canonical books; theirs was the earliest piece of critical philology. Their commentaries and teaching—each inspired a school in his native region—were immensely successful and famous; so much so that, at the fall of the Han, there was no resisting their teaching, and its victory spelled the rapid and total disappearance of the school of the 'modern texts'.

There was a parallel desire in official circles to start afresh from a better established text, as a result of which some of the Classics were revised from a philological standpoint and the corrected texts engraved on stone. The enterprise was directed by Cai Yong (133–92) and involved the *Shujing, Yijing, Shijing, Liji,* the *Chunqiu* with commentary by Gongyang, and the *Lunyu.* The texts, written by Cai Yong, were engraved between 175 and 183 on the backs and fronts of stone slabs. The stelae were set up to the east of the lecture room of the Grand School and immediately attracted many scholars, as well as the merely curious, who came to admire and copy them. The triumph of the 'old-text' school led the Wei dynasty to order the engraving (240–8) of a new series of stelae, on
155 which the texts now appeared in three scripts.

The enormous labour of engraving the Classics on stone continued until the eighth century and helped to preserve and disseminate the works of ancient literature; it made a fixed and standard text available to all, and its spread was further facilitated by the invention of block-printing some time between the second century and the beginning of the fifth—the date is still a matter of controversy.

Historical studies were made famous at the time of the Latter Han by the appearance of the *Hanshu*

156
Rubbing: detail from the stela known as *Kongmiao liqi bei,* with *lishu* script ('the scribal hand').
Dated A.D. 156, Qufu, Shandong (See Speiser, Goepper and Fribourg, *Chinese Art,* vol. 3, p. 201).

('History of the Former Han Dynasty') by the Ban family. Authorship of this monumental work, the first of the Chinese dynastic histories, is usually attributed to Ban Gu (32–92), the principal author; however, it was begun by his father, Ban Biao, and finished by his sister, Ban Zhao (c. 48–117), assisted by Ma Xu, brother of Ma Rong.

The work is in 100 chapters, opening with the birth of Gaozu, founder of the Han, and closing with the death of Wang Mang. The plan follows that of the *Shiji* by Sima Qian and consists of four sections:

- twelve annals *(ji)*, which recount the principal events of the dynasty, reign by reign in chronological order;
- eight synoptic tables *(biao)* giving a chronological survey of nobles, high dignitaries and eminent personalities;
- ten treatises *(zhi)*, corresponding to the *shu* of the *Shiji*, dealing with the rites and music, astronomy and the calendar, sacrifices, the Five Phases and geography, and including a bibliographical treatise;
- seventy biographies and monographs on foreign peoples *(liezhuan)*, this last part occupying nearly half the work.

Thus the history of the period is approached from four different angles, each throwing a complementary light on the subject. For the second century B.C. Ban Gu made copious use of the *Shiji* and, for the second half of the Former Han, of works that are now lost but some of which formed a continuation of the *Records of the Historian*. He also used documents of all kinds from the imperial archives, including administrative and political texts, reports, financial proceedings, petitions, edicts, decrees, reports to the throne, and also works of the great scholars and poets of the time. Like the *Shiji,* many passages of the *Hanshu* consist of excerpts from earlier writings, selected and carefully compiled to form an anthology of old texts; these include official and private documents, verse and speeches.

Ban was more interested in contemporary affairs than Sima Qian had been; he was less polemical, more at ease within the framework of orthodox Confucianism. His main innovation was the treatises, the most successful of these being the treatise on bibliography *(yiwenzhi),* which affords a complete picture of the literature known then.

The *Hanshu,* on which Ban Gu worked for twenty years, is the work of one who was both a historian and a writer, and it was already considered by his contemporaries to be of inestimable value; it is both a political history of the ruling house of Liu at the time of the Former Han and an encyclopaedia of the Chinese world during the last two centuries before the Christian era.

The Luoyang historians did not confine themselves to the study of the past. The *Dongguan Hanji,* the official history of the Latter Han, was begun in the reign of Mingdi and continued to that of Lingdi. It was a work of collaboration, for which Ban Gu wrote the earliest parts, and described contemporary or recent events in which the authors had sometimes been involved. Part of the *Dongguan Hanji* was lost when Luoyang was sacked in 190, but it served as a source for later histories of the period.

From Court Poetry to Lyric Poetry

The Fu

The art of the *fu,* which had been given its cachet by Sima Xiangru (c. 179–117 B.C.), continued to dominate literary life. Yang Xiong (53 B.C.–A.D. 18), the first to admire and emulate the master of Wudi's court, followed in his footsteps. Sima Xiangru's influence is very much in evidence in the *Fu of the Two Capitals (Liangdu fu)* by Ban Gu (32–92), the subject of which was provided by an immediate political problem, namely the choice of a capital. Using this theme and the form of an oratorical contest between two protagonists, one a citizen of Chang'an and the other of Luoyang, Ban Gu gives a brilliant description of the two cities and life at their courts. Luoyang naturally gains the final advantage, and the author uses his description as a device for praising moral strictness and austerity. Zhang Heng (78–139) in the second century tried to rival Ban Gu on the same subject, while Ma Rong (79–166) used the theme of the imperial hunts to express indirect criticism and to try to influence imperial policy, as Sima Xiangru and Yang Xiong had done before him.

Despite the success of these verses, the *fu* had become somewhat sterile under the Latter Han, having lost its fantasy and exuberance to a rather narrow morality, some pedantry and an often servile imitation of earlier works.

The Narrative Verse of the Yuefu

The dissolution of the Bureau of Music *(Yuefu)* in 7 B.C. sounded the death-knell neither of musical entertainments nor of the work of the Bureau. Both the *fu* and the musical poem contributed to the brilliance of the court, and that the Han enjoyed light music of the kind that accompanied banquets is amply confirmed by the burial decorations of the period. Instrumentalists, dancers and acrobats brought life and gaiety to the banquets. Dances were performed to music, sometimes to a simple rhythmic accompaniment, sometimes to a poem or song. The narrative and lyric poetry of the time (the *Yuefu*) was associated with music, dance and variety entertainments. The emotions and universal aspirations that it expressed, the suppleness, even the freedom, of its composition must have enhanced the sinuosity of the melodic line and the variations of the dance.[5]

One poem describes a case of abduction, telling of the ransom that had been demanded (lines 5–6), of the calf that would have to be sold to raise it (line 12), and of the fear that the abductors might kill their prisoner (line 9):

> East of the Pingling tomb,
>   Among the pines, the cypresses, the *wutong* trees,
> I don't know who abducted our True Lord.
>
> They abducted our True Lord
> To the Magistracy
> For a ransom of a million cash and two swift horses.
>
> Two swift horses
> Are hard indeed to get.
> I look at the extorting constables, my heart is full of pain.
>
> My heart is full of pain,
> My blood is draining out.
> Now back to tell my family to sell the brown calf.[6]

Here is feeling, sincere and unadorned. Simplicity, concision, straight-forwardness of tone and form derived from popular song and speech—these are the qualities that go to make the charm of the surviving *Yuefu,* which were composed by court song-writers, mostly under the Latter Han. Popular inspiration in all its freshness, refined and often reduced to formulae, must have come as a relief after the pomp of the *fu*. The organizers of banquets, the entertainers and song-writers who composed these poems thus presented the writers of the first and second centuries A.D. with a source of revitalization for poetry that was to result in the perfect form of the *Nineteen Old Songs (Gushi shijiushou)*.

The Nineteen Old Songs

These anonymous poems in five-foot metre written in a popular vein but with consummate artistry are the finest of Han verse. They probably date from the period A.D. 50–150.[7] Strongly influenced by the narrative verse of the *Yuefu,* by folklore and by the earlier tradition of the *Shijing* and the *Songs of Chu,* they are the work of scholars. The precision and harmony of their construction and the authority of the argument show that they are not fortuitous products of popular inspiration or of entertainers' arrangements.

The authors of the *Gushi* have evolved a sort of synthesis of the different elements; they have adapted and organized the poetic language—we know that scholars such as Ban Gu and Zhang Heng had attempted this—returned to and rethought the themes.

Two topics form the subject-matter of the *Nineteen Old Songs:* separation and death, which, as J. P. Diény says,[8] become one in the end through the repeated association of the themes of solitude, the passage of time, love and death. Sorrow lies at the heart of the anthology; here, again, is Han pessimism, that sense of the brevity of life and the caprice of an inscrutable fate, of which man is the plaything.

> In the courtyard is a marvellous tree,
>   Flowers in profusion start from the green leaves.
> I pull down the branches, I gather their splendour,
>   I will do homage with them to the friend of my heart.
>
> Their fragrant scent fills my breast, my sleeves,
>   The road is long, and no way of sending them...
> The thing in itself is not worth giving you,
>   All that affects me is time which passes and keeps us apart.[9]

She gathers flowers for a distant lover, but the impossibility of sending them merely sharpens the grief of separation. This poetry, which suggests more than the words say, illuminates objects—in this case, flowers—background, and incidentals, and veils in mystery the essential element, which is feeling. It is an admirably reticent style of writing, with its controlled emotion and dignity in suffering.

The Pleiad of the Jian'an Era (196–220)

With the disorder that preceded the fall of the Han dynasty, verse became freer in both form and spirit. The seven poets of the Jian'an era and their patrons, Cao Cao (155–220), Cao Pi (187–226), Emperor Wen of the Wei dynasty, and Cao Zhi (192–232), retained the vigour and simplicity of the popular themes of the *Yuefu* and the elegance of the *Gushi*. But in their very personal verse they abandoned the restraint of the *Nineteen Old Songs* for a free play of the emotions.

Dramatic descriptions of the misfortunes of the time, the rough existence of the warrior, separation, the fragility of life, the illusions fostered by wine and drunkenness, dreams of joining the Immortals—such are the major themes of these poems; they are written in lines of five or seven syllables and are longer than the songs of the *Gushi*; they are sometimes impetuous, sometimes nostalgic, but always grief-stricken and always inspired.

The following poem by Wang Can (177–217), the first of a series entitled *The Seven Sorrows*, describes the crumbling of the dynasty and the wretchedness of people driven from their homes.

> The great-city of the West [Chang'an] sinks into chaos.
>   Tigers and wolves, the ravagers have arrived…
> Exile again, we must leave China,
>   And submit to the yoke, in the land of the Barbarians.
>
> My parents look with tearful eyes into mine;
>   My friends' hands clutch my hands…
> I leave our house. No living soul;
>   Only whitened bones strew the plain.
>
> On the road, driven by hunger, a woman
>   Carries away a new-born child, and leaves it in a field.
> The child cries and yells; on the alert, the mother listens
>   But turns away, drying her tears.
>
> 'I do not even know where death will seize me:
>   How could I possibly save our two lives?'
> I lash my horse on, and leave her far behind;
>   I cannot bear to listen to that voice.
>
> I have climbed due south up the Baling ridge.
>   When I look back, seeing Chang'an again,
> I think of all my dead, at the edge of the Yellow Springs;
>   And deep sighs rend my heart.[10]

Part V

Legacies of the Han Civilization:
Literature, Science and Art

Chapter I

The Spiritual and Cultural Landscape

Conception of the Universe and Syncretic Confucianism

The *Yin-Yang* theory and the theory of the Five Phases *(Yin Yang wuxing shuo)* dominated the whole of Han thought from the second century B.C. It evolved from the reflective thinking of the fourth and third centuries, the belief in an immanent world-order, and was based essentially on the identity and interaction of the cosmic and human spheres, the physical and moral worlds. Thus everything in the natural and human world is divided between *Yin* and *Yang* and related to one of the Five Phases. In other words, Heaven, Earth and man are governed by the principles of *Yin* and *Yang* operating through the Five Phases. These categories and their relationships weave a dense network between nature and man, who is himself conceived as a microcosm made in the image of the macrocosm.

The Han vision of the world, then, is closely structured and highly dynamic, a world that is ceaselessly reforming in an eternal cycle. In this perspective, ideas of integration, harmony and centre are as essential as those of totality and rhythm. Natural phenomena are seen as manifestations and signs referring to a cosmic order that any error may endanger. Man, and in particular the emperor, the Son of Heaven, is in some way responsible for the harmony of the universe. In this context the science of presages and anomalies, the rôle of sympathetic magic, the innumerable superstitions, all become intelligible, as does the impor-

tance attached to ritual—for correct celebration of the rites was considered the best regulator of natural harmony. It was also for the sake of integration and harmony that man created round himself, at all levels, space-time microcosms, such as *mingtang,* capitals, carefully sited and defended dwelling-places and tombs, TLV mirrors, *shipan* astrological instruments, *liubo* games and talismans, and at the heart of all these he replaced himself in a correct position at the heart of the universe.

In conformity with this organicist conception of the universe, the official ideology—called Confucianism for convenience—gradually established a political and moral order capable of governing human society. In fact, Han official ideology was a synthesis of ideas and systems of thought some of which were alien to primitive Confucianism; it assimilated Legalist concepts and practices as well as many magical ideas—such as soothsaying, auspicious and inauspicious days—and regional traditions.

The main channel through which this ideology was disseminated was education, in this case the Grand School, the custodian of orthodox literature and thought and the formative influence on the future administrators of the State. The Grand School thus moulded and unified Confucian society round a few ethical and social values, such as filial piety and respect for authority and age. The great achievement of Han Confucianism was therefore pedagogic; in an age obsessed by, among other things, the problem of knowing how to judge men, Confucianism established the foundations of the system of examinations that opened the way to the highest office for the ablest. In fact the movement was only just beginning in the Han period, for birth and family remained important factors in social advancement. The scholarly class that was taking shape at the period within the sphere of the official ideology struggled throughout the dynasty to gain status and play a definite part, to become the governing class of Chinese society. In large measure and in the long term it succeeded, but lost its independence in the process. It became a bureaucracy with its destiny ever more closely linked to that of central government.

The symbiosis of cosmological theory and moral ideas produced the Han vision of the world with man at its centre. As we shall see, the natural world was of interest only in so far as it was seen to be connected with mankind, and the man who is at the centre of the official ideology is man in society, the collective being, not the individual. The individual interested the Confucian only to the extent that he might one day be appointed to a share of authority. Confucianism had no satisfactory reply to those who strove after a personal religion and were curious about problems of justice and destiny.[1] By contrast, Taoism offered them a path of personal salvation in the form of physical immortality. No wonder that to many scholars the two ways, the two formulae *(dao)* appeared complementary. Many Confucians—Sima Qian, Yang Xiong, Huan Tan, Wang Chong and Ma Rong, to name but a few—were influenced by Taoism, and in many spheres of Han thought there was real interpenetration between Confucianism and Taoism.

The official ideology and its global vision of the world was to prevail for as long as the Han empire lasted; it did not survive the political and social disorder that engulfed China from the end of the second century. From then onwards men turned to mysticism, escape and the sheltered life of religious communities, both Taoist and Buddhist.

China as the Cultural Centre of the World

With Chinese expansion and descriptions of distant lands, especially those of the west, miraculous countries, long associated with Paradise, were imagined beyond the frontiers. The old ideas of Mount Kunlun in the west, the domain of Xi-

wangmu, and of the islands of the Immortals in the East Sea had been popular before the belief in Da Qin [Rome] as utopia became widespread. But these countries at the end of the world remained figments of the imagination. As B. Watson[2] stresses, the Chinese were less fortunate than the Greeks and Romans, who were surrounded by neighbours belonging to ancient and advanced civilizations. Even struggles against the Xiongnu, the peoples of the south and the oasis civilizations could not shake the formidable confidence in himself and in the worth of his own civilization that was a specific feature of a cultivated Chinese around the beginning of the Christian era. The meeting of east and west in Central Asia remained difficult, and perhaps China's only acquisition in the foreign marketplace of ideas was Buddhism.

Han belief in its own superiority was based essentially on culture. As He Xiu wrote in the second century: 'what distinguishes the people of the Empire of the Centre is that it is capable of honouring what deserves to be honoured'.[3] This sense of the superiority of the rites, of the ethical values of the Han 'way of life' asserted itself once the empire had become unified and was expanding. It was then combined with a civilizing mission that was much stronger and more enduring than was the cultural hold of Greece on the east during the Hellenistic period. In this sense Han China gave much, even if she also destroyed much. But the sense of superiority and the belief that China was the centre of the world remained one of the most deeply held of Chinese convictions for centuries, indeed, for as long as China possessed no yardstick other than her own to measure the lastingness and stature of her civilization.

Exegesis, History and Poetry

Han philosphical values were rooted in the thought prevailing towards the end of the Zhou dynasty more firmly even than those of Rome were rooted in Greek thought; indeed, Zhou literature assumed the status of canonical literature under the Han. The scholars of the time were wholly convinced of the authority of the Classics and displayed a spirit of violent controversy over the authenticity, meaning and importance of each text. A liking for discussion and debate is characteristic of the period. These debates began with questions concerning textual variations, moved to philosophical interpretation and finally to problems of transmission and textual criticism. Cosmology long remained the major element in interpretation, and the holistic vision of the *Yin Yang wuxing shuo* was applied to its utmost limits in the apocryphal texts *(weishu)*, which seek to weld all the phenomena of the physical and human world into one coherent system. The intellectual life of the whole period is thus marked by reflexions prompted by the ancient texts and by disputes between schools and different philosophical and philological traditions. The great works of exposition that came out of this ongoing debate—the collation, history, discussion and commentary on the texts—constitute the major contribution of the Han, especially the Latter Han, to later scholarship. The merit of scholars like Ma Rong and Zheng Xuan is to have established the great recensions of the Classics, comprising the original texts with commentaries, and in the process to have evolved a technique of critical philology that the Chinese were to develop much further during the centuries that followed.

Another field to which the Han made a major contribution is that of historical knowledge. Sima Qian, perhaps the greatest of Chinese historians, was the first to conceive the plan of a general history of China, a synthesis of all the historiographical traditions of antiquity, a moralizing and didactic work rather than a simple chronicle of events. Sima's plan was adapted by Ban Gu and became the inspiration of the twenty-six dynastic histories written up to the twentieth century, each dynasty publishing the history of the dynasty that it had overthrown, using documents prepared during the latter's reign. The *Shiji* of Sima Qian and the *Hanshu* of Ban Gu are thus the prototypes of an unbroken sequence covering two thousand years and testifying to the extraordinary sense of historical continuity that is peculiar to the Chinese.

Reflexions on man and politics formed the whole substance of Han intellectual life—at least of its official face—including poetry and other forms of literature. Thus the *fu* was rarely an objective description; it had a practical purpose. The genre was both brilliant and moralizing, and sometimes satirical; *fu* were written by scholars at the imperial court, or at a princely court. When all is said and done, their major virtue was eloquence; they set out to persuade but also to dazzle, so much so that verbal decoration and the love of grandeur often obscured the moral message. Behind the themes of hunting, ceremonies and the pleasures of the court, indirect criticism, exhortation and sometimes a straightforward desire to please are addressed exclusively to the sovereign, his ministers and courtiers. This is one more example of the Han scholar's constant concern for his place at the heart of government and for his relationship with the ruler.

But with no didactic purpose and no thirst for power, used simply to enhance the attractions of banquets, the expressive means of popular lyrics found their way into the court and played a part in the creation of a personal mode of art and the formation of classical poetry. While Han poetical language owes some of its descriptive richness to the creative daring of Sima Xiangru, the rhythm and tonality of lyric poetry stem from many centuries of collaboration between minstrels and musicians. Poets and musicians worked in concert for the courts, principally the imperial court, where the commissions and musical cosmopolitanism were a perpetual spur to emulation. The case of Wudi was no exception: he liked to surround himself with musicians, singers and dancers—his second empress, Wei Zifu, had been a member of the chorus, and his favourite concubine, Li Furen, sister of the musician Li Yannian, was a superb dancer.

This poetry, sung as it was to accompany wine-drinking in beautiful surroundings, also expresses the confusions of a society tormented by its obsession with death. The passage of time, a sense of the brevity of life that no pleasure can efface, recur repeatedly in the *Gushi* and the work of the poets of the early third century:

> Over wine in the presence of song:
> How long does human life last?
> It is comparable to morning dew.
> Bitterly many are the days that have passed![4]

Epicureanism may have been a palliative, for some it was epicureanism of the moment, for others the Taoists' search for longevity and immortality. But the melancholy and anguish remained. Real enough though often hidden, this was the darker side of a period that was otherwise intensely dynamic.

Chapter II

The Beginnings of Science[1]

Medicine and Alchemy

The whole of Han medical theory was still permeated by the idea of universal balance and correspondences between man, Heaven and Earth. The human body was regarded as an exact replica of the macrocosm, and medical art sought to maintain the equilibrium between *Yin* and *Yang* within the organism.

Physiology was based on three essential points that reflected the cosmology theory: *Yin* and *Yang* alternate and complement one another; the five entrails (liver, heart, spleen, lungs, kidneys) correspond with the Five Phases (wood, fire, earth, metal, water) and with the seasons, tastes, colours, etc.; there is an energy or vital breath *(qi)* that circulates through the cavities or ducts *(jingmai)*.

Man must remain in the middle, the centre, and any excess creates imbalance between the principles of *Yin* and *Yang* and provokes disease. But this happy medium is not a stable state; it oscillates between the *Yang* maximum and the *Yin* maximum according to a complex movement, which corresponds to the cosmic rhythm. A healthy man is thus an equilibrium—modified by the exterior world—between his *Yin* interior-medium (damp, warm and dark) and the exterior-medium, which is *Yang* (dry, hot and bright). Han medicine also centred round the concept of the vital breath. By good use of the breath health is preserved and longevity achieved. Inside the body the breath, *Yin, Yang* and the blood should circulate freely and all in the same direction within the cavities, in a cycle similar to that of the stars in Heaven.

These principles were firmly established by the second century B.C., and medicine had by then already become a very complex art, embracing the taking of the pulse, knowledge of the key points for acupuncture, and complicated therapy. The medical texts discovered in Mawangdui tomb No. 3 contain hundreds of prescriptions with comments on the causes and symptoms of the diseases to be treated. The idea of the syndrome also made its appearance at this time. A little later—at the end of the first century B.C. or the beginning of the first century A.D.—the notions of the six viscera-receptacles *(fu)* appeared side by side with the five entrails *(zang)*. They were, respectively, the stomach, gall-bladder, bladder, small and large intestines, and the 'three burners': the oesophagus, the internal cavity of the stomach and the urethra. The first official dissection was carried out in the year A.D. 16 by order of Wang Mang. This operation on the body of a criminal consisted in 'weighing and measuring the five entrails and following the course of the cavities with the aid of a bamboo stylet to see where they begin and end, observations that would make it possible to cure diseases'.[2] There is no other mention of official dissection in the texts until 1106.

The essential elements of Han therapy were vegetable and mineral medicines, acupuncture and moxibustion, dietetics, gymnastics, massage, plasters, lancing and puncturing.

Plants were macerated or infused in fermented beverages. Minerals used for treating diseases included cinnabar (mercuric sulphide), orpiment or realgar (bisulphide of arsenic) and alum (basic sulphate of aluminium).

This very comprehensive pharmacopeia based on medicinal herbs and minerals undoubtedly benefited from the researches and experiments of those adepts of immortality, the alchemists. In the same way, Taoist dietetics, breathing techniques and physical culture certainly influenced the course of Chinese therapy.

In their search for bodily immortality the Chinese, from the time of the Former Han onwards, bent their efforts to preparing a pharmaceutical gold that could be swallowed and would eventually transform the body that absorbed it. This artificial gold was prepared by the processes of alchemical sublimation and transmutation, using mercuric sulphide (cinnabar) as the basis. Other ways of gaining immortality by transubstantiation were tried, including the effects of absorbing small doses of other metals such as gold, arsenic and lead over long periods. Similarly, cranes' eggs, and tortoise-shell—both beasts were symbols of immortality—the herb *zhi,* pine, cypress, peach, cinnamon, leek, aconite, sunflower and many other plants and substances increased vitality and longevity.

Besides these elixirs, which were absorbed, the Han thought that the use of dishes made of alchemical gold might prolong life indefinitely.

All these alchemical procedures for ensuring longevity were connected with the techniques for preserving bodies, which were also much favoured during the Han period. These included the traditions of preserving cadavers as found in the former kingdom of Chu, e.g. at Mawangdui, and the much less efficacious protection by jade shrouds and the placing of jade stoppers in the deceased's nine orifices.

Research into minerals and plants, which were closely linked with cosmology, Taoism and ideas about the next world, formed part of a whole medical art of immortality at the Han period.

Astronomy and the Observational Sciences

In Needham's opinion, the Chinese were the most patient and accurate of all pre-Renaissance observers. Although the geometric planetary theory was unknown to them, they devised a rational cosmology, established a celestial map that uses our modern coordinates, and compiled lists of eclipses, comets, novas and meteors that are still usable today.[3]

Astronomy during the Han period had three purposes:
- to study the sun, the moon and the Five Planets with a view to establishing the calendar. The calendar was lunar-solar; it was therefore necessary from time to time to harmonize the period of twelve lunar months (355 days) with the solar year (365 days) by inserting an extra lunar month. The civil calendar drawn up by the astronomers also had political aims and was intended to express the magical powers represented by the dynasty;
- to study the stations of the moon and the Celestial Palaces with a view to determining the twenty-four divisions of the year;
- to study meteorology.

Astronomy, astrology and meteorology were closely linked to politics. Astronomers were regarded as interpreters of the celestial signs. Exploiting the resonances between the natural and political worlds, they read the destiny of the empire in the Heavens by observing the stars, the course of the Five Planets and their transits through the twenty-eight stations of the moon, etc. In fact, Han astronomy failed to break free of astrology and divination. But this bias did not detract from the quality of the observations. Thus the astronomical text found in Mawangdui tomb No. 3 (168 B.C.) lists with great precision observations relating to the movement of the Five Planets during the period 246 to 177 B.C.: a complete passage of Saturn through the sky was reckoned to take 30 years, a figure close to the 29.46 years calculated by modern astronomers. Sun-spots were being observed and listed by the first century B.C.

Astronomical instruments developed to a remarkable degree in Han China. Chinese astronomical measurements were always equatorial. The Han divided the celestial equator into 365¼ divisions, more or less corresponding to the 365 days and 5 hours of the year; the sun was thought to move through one division a day. The use of the gnomon and its refinements and, from the time of the Former Han at latest, of the hydraulic clock, made measurement easier. Indeed, by giving the exact time, the water-clock enabled astronomers to measure the movement of the stars accurately. The equatorial armilla presented to the emperor by Geng Shouchang in 52 B.C. marked a further advance. But the astronomers related the paths of the sun, moon and planets that moved on the ecliptic to the twenty-eight stations of the moon *(xiu)* measured at the equator. The scientists of the first century A.D. applied their minds to the problems of observation and measurement on the ecliptic. In the second half of the century, Fu An established the duration of the twenty-eight stations of the moon on the ecliptic and probably invented the ecliptic armilla that Jia Kui was authorized to make. Some twenty years later Zhang Heng (78–139) hit on the idea of representing the whole celestial globe schematically; he added two circles, the equatorial and ecliptic, and two other graduated rings bisecting one another at right angles: one horizontal, the other marking the meridian plane. This armillary sphere was made in bronze in 124 and performed the diurnal revolutions under hydraulic power. Zhang Heng's armillary sphere was the quintessential Chinese astronomical instrument, and refinements followed from century to century. It was used to determine the degree of graduation on the ecliptic corresponding to a given degree on the equator.

Zhang Heng was an extraordinary man; he was an eminent mathematician, an astronomer, Grand Astrologer under Andi and Shundi, and a poet and painter as well. He left a treatise on astronomy that contains important findings, such as the fact that the sun is the source of the moon's light and that a solar eclipse occurs when the moon obscures the sun. Some other observations had already been set down by earlier writers; for example Wang Chong (A.D. 27–*c.* 100) noted in his *Lunheng* that the tides depend on the phases of the moon, that rain comes not from the sky but is the humidity of the soil condensed in the form of mist and cloud and reprecipitated, giving rain and dew in summer and snow and ice in winter.

Zhang Heng is further credited with having invented an instrument for measuring distance (a sort of hodometer) and one for indicating the south. But, besides the armillary sphere, his great claim to fame was the seismograph. The instrument that he devised in 132 for locating the sites of

earthquakes—signs that nature was out of harmony—took the form of a great bronze alcohol jar (8 *chi* = 1.84 m in diameter) with a domed cover. The outside was decorated with archaic characters, mountains, tortoises and other animals, while a relief depicting eight dragons each with a bronze ball in its mouth encircled the body. On the base of the vessel, below each dragon, was an open-mouthed frog. The internal mechanism, the details of which are still controversial, consisted of a central column that moved along eight grooves, each ending in the head of one of the dragons. In each groove was a kind of trigger, which opened the mouth of one of the dragons when touched by the pendulum movement of the central column. The mechanism reacted to the shock of an earthquake by making the ball drop from the mouth of one of the dragons into that of the frog below it. The dragons were spaced at equal intervals and, since each pointed to an azimuth, the direction of the earthquake could be ascertained. Zhang Heng's seismograph was enormously successful at court and is said to have located an earthquake that occurred in Gansu province.

Cartography

The importance of geographical maps at the time of the Former Han, and before, is well attested by texts, which include maps of the provinces and kingdoms of the empire, the frontier regions, mineral deposits and military plans. The maps were painted on silk and stored in boxes. Jing Ke concealed the dagger with which he intended to assassinate the future Qin Shi Huangdi in a folded map 120 in a box. However, until the discovery in 1973 of Mawangdui tomb No. 3 (168 B.C.), no map of the period had been known. The three documents then unearthed—two maps and a town plan— are thus the earliest known maps not only in China but in the world.

The two maps are painted on silk. One is topographical (96×96 cm) with a scale of about 1:180,000; the other is military (78×98 cm) with a scale of 1:80,000–100,000. They are graphic representations of the region of the upper Xiao *shui,* in the south of Hunan province, north of Guangxi province and north-west of Guangdong province. In conformity with Chinese cosmology, the south is shown at the top and the north at the bottom. The maps show the relief, the rivers and roads as well as towns; place-names are inscribed within the symbols. The lines of the rivers become thicker with the widening of the rivers towards the mouth.

29   The military map shows the defensive positions of the kingdom of Changsha during the war that followed the invasion of the kingdom by the king of Nan Yue in 183 B.C. On the topographical map mountains are indicated by a double irregular wavy line: here they are delineated by a single fine line terminating in a loop or a lanceolate shape; each summit is represented by a trilobed and hatched symbol reminiscent of the character *shan* ('mountain'); a black dot corresponds to the trefoil 16–17, 19   on the other side of the line. The whole effect is reminiscent of the spiral ornament on contemporary lacquers and textiles. Garrisons are represented by toothed rectangles with the name of the camp commandant and his title inside. In the centre of the defensive position the headquarters, a 29   five-towered fortress, is indicated by a triangle underlined in red and black. The fortress is connected to the garrisons by roads (in dotted lines) and especially by rivers, which formed a network serving the transport of troops and provisions. Villages are symbolized by a red circle; the map gives the name, the number of inhabitants or the state of the place as a result of the war, e.g. '35 families, all have left' or 'now uninhabited'.

The accuracy and quality of these maps would appear to have remained unsurpassed during the Han period, at least until the second or third century A.D., when the grid system of map-making was adopted.

The great merit of the Han scientists is to have observed, listed and classified natural phenomena with a rigour and determination encouraged by official patronage, and to have invented scientific instruments that were remarkably accurate for the time. The relatively official character of science, pure and applied, remained a specifically Chinese feature. The Han astronomer was an official who came under one of the government departments; most engineers and most artisans belonged to the bureaucracy or the imperial workshops and arsenals. Although many inventions and improvements were undertaken by private initiative, they needed the patronage of the great if they were to circulate widely, and vast projects were most often realized within the framework of the State.

Patronage was one of the elements, though not the only one, which led to priority being given to practical schemes, i.e. innovations and techniques that would improve production, the administration of the empire or the standard of life. To conclude, the following were the main technological inventions made under the Han: the cog-wheel, crank, hodometer, water mill, calliper rule with decimal scale (used by Chinese artisans from the beginning of the first century A.D. at the latest), paper, the wheelbarrow, sternpost, mechanical seeder and the winnower with rotary wings. Besides these inventions, advances were made in older techniques, unknown outside China at the time, like silk and lacquer work, bronze casting and the production of steel, not to mention the crossbow and breast harness, which were exclusively Han.

Chapter III

The Diversity of Han Art

An attempt has been made to identify some of the values, beliefs and traditions that sustained and determined Han art during the four centuries of its history. Little more will be said here about the themes and leitmotivs—the mythical images, the symbolism of the *Yin Yang wuxing shuo,* the evocation of the pleasures of life and aspirations to immortality—or about the social and religious function of this art. Remarks will also be restricted to its purely Chinese manifestations, leaving aside the artefacts of the subject peoples (Dian, Yue, Xiongnu, etc.). Instead, an attempt will be made to indicate the form and the specific character of Han artistic expression, its choices and its main achievements. The task is a difficult one because our vision remains fragmentary. Only a small proportion of the work of the Han artists has survived. We have many objects of everyday and funerary use, some of exceptional quality but most of them modest and lacking any serious aesthetic pretension, decorated tombs but no palace paintings, depictions and models of buildings but no monument, no actual structures. The other difficulty lies in the fact that the period was a turning-point. Indeed, these four centuries during which the freshest imagination and the most total conventionality developed side by side, drew deeply from the springs of the past—especially the Period of the Warring States—and carried within them the germ of all that was to be realized in the next period, from Buddhist architecture and sculpture to calligraphy, painting and ceramics.

In Han art figurative images that are essentially human and alive in character are combined with a fondness for ornament transposed into a play of curves and spirals that is virtually abstract. Although it displays astonishing vigour and expressiveness when depicting human activities and the animal world, it shows little interest in nature itself, except in connection with man. When it appears, landscape is never other than a background 40, 58–9, and is treated only in terms of a statement of which 69, 83, 96 it is not the subject. This was not a mark of inability—certain bricks from Sichuan province show a very sensitive observation of landscape—but was 7, 127 deliberate.

The dynamism of the period is embodied in its plastic arts more markedly even than in its literature; it is expressed in a fondness for modulated 16–17, 25, lines in perpetual motion, for taut curves, savage 27–8, 57–8, energy, rhythm, speed, expressive postures and 67, 72–3, 75, *horror vacui.* These characteristics are as pro- 97,109,119, nounced in the figural themes (warfare, hunting, 144–5, 149, dance, etc.) as in geometric decoration. Moreover, 154 it is the calligraphic expression of rhythm and movement, in which every line is matched by a 25, 27 counter-line, that gives Han decorative art its undeniable unity, from lacquerware, to embroidery, 11, 16–17, bronzes and painted ceramics. With the flexibility 19, 68 of its painted motifs the art of lacquer seems to have set the tone and influenced the other graphic 30, 56–7, 75, arts. 140, 150

Painting

Modulated, fluid lines and motifs made up of rounded curves reappear at the beginning of the

dynasty in painting on silk and lacquer. In this context, a study of the banner and the coffins from
Mawangdui tomb No. 1 illustrates all that painting
in the first half of the second century owed to the
art of lacquer. The remarks that follow will deal
only with the banner, perhaps the most accomplished of surviving Han paintings.

23   The banner divides into two sections: an upper,
horizontal, and a lower, vertical, one, each composed of two perfectly symmetrical halves on
either side of a central axis. The upper section
(Heaven) is fairly open, orchestrated round and
based on elements—the moon, the central divinity,
the sun and the two guardians of the gateway—that
form points of convergence and stability. The
composition of the vertical section is denser, with
more intertwining variations, the nodal point of
the interlacements being the two dragons that pass
through the central *bi* ring. The play of rings and
curves defines two fields, an upper and a lower;
this separation is counterbalanced by the complete
symmetry of the movement and elements on either
side of the central axis.

    The whole rhythm of the design can be ex-
plained in terms of an alternation between passages
dominated by movement, undulating and soaring
motifs, accentuated by the elongated and stretched
motifs of the dragons and the fish, and points of repose and stability. In the celestial zone the movement represented by the dragons and Immortals on
horseback comes between the four stable points,
whereas in the vertical section it surrounds and in-
tersects the two scenes of sacrifice and homage,
which are the only passages dominated by straight
lines—i.e. the vertical lines of the figures and vases
and the horizontal lines of the platforms and tables.
These two anchoring points are also the focal
21   points of the vertical zone, the principal zone, cen-
tring round the standing figure of the deceased,
who stands out against the empty space above her.
Round these two scenes, the long undulating
motifs, all the symbols of movement and journey-
ing, form the links and transitions from one part to
another.

    In order to highlight the whites, before the silk
was painted, it was dyed a rather warm terra-cotta
red, which has darkened further and turned brown
with time. A sketch was then drawn on the silk in
pale ink; next, colour was applied, before the

motifs were further defined by the addition of an
outline. Some features, such as the suns, the crown
and the dragons' tongues, were left unoutlined as
simple, flat areas of colour.

    Colours include vermilion (for the suns, tongues
and certain parts of the fabulous beasts), brown
ochre (for the faces of the figures and the heads and
paws of the dragons), silver powder (for shading,
for some of the outlines and to lend brilliance to
other colours), indigo (for the blue of the *fusang*
tree, birds' wings, etc.), sometimes mixed with
oyster-white, gamboge yellow in conjunction
with other colours (on the *bi* ring and the heads and
paws of dragons) and oyster-white alone (for the
platforms), or mixed. Thus colours are for the
most part laid on flat, though they are sometimes
superimposed for shading or to give effects of relief, depth or transparency. This shading or tonal
modulation, which also occurs on the cloud scrolls
on the coffin with paintings on a black ground 27, 30
from the same tomb, is the earliest known example
of this type of experiment in Chinese painting.

    The brushwork is equally varied: human fig-
ures are drawn in very fine, fluid lines; thicker but
modulated strokes are used for fabulous beasts and
objects, while inflexions help to give the effect of
relief. Although the choice of colours conforms to
traditional iconography and symbolism, it also
matches the rhythm of the composition. The same
applies to the brushwork. The inflexions of the
strokes and the shading of the colours give the various components of the painting a vigour and a
sculptural quality that counterbalance the calligraphic nature of the undulating interlacements and
elongated motifs. This sculptural character reminds one a little of the lacquered wood carvings
of the kingdom of Chu.

    There can be no doubt that the sense of move-
ment and the prominence of colours that stand out
against a fairly strongly coloured ground owe
much to the decoration of lacquerware, and one
may wonder whether at the beginning of the Han
the distinction between painters on silk and on lacquer was sharp as it is thought to have been.

    The style of the banner is also characterized by
the contrast between realism and fantasy. Realism
prevails in the two main scenes of the vertical field,
especially round the portrait of the deceased woman, with her bowed head, slightly curved back

and plump body. The realism of the treatment of the human world is expressed in a very fine line and minute brushwork; by contrast, the artist has interpreted the mythical universe in broader strokes and in a movement that is in itself remarkably observed, e.g. in the leopards, the flight of the birds and the Immortals on horseback.

Some considerable space has been devoted to this painting because, with its complex, structured composition, its technique and style, it represents a kind of culmination. The keenness of observation and the art of portraiture achieve a perfection here that invites reconsideration of judgments asserting the inability of Han painters to master the art of capturing likenesses. This painting, which dates from the beginning of the dynasty and is still strongly influenced by Chu art, stands alone. No other painting on silk has survived from the Han period, and we are obliged to trace the development of painting through works that employ other techniques and, especially, are the outcome of far more modest commissions. The choice of themes also changed at a fairly early date. The imaginary world was gradually codified and humanized and was increasingly replaced by scenes of everyday life, and by legendary and historical scenes. This choice is evident in the surviving wall paintings, impressed bricks and engraved stones, all of which were inspired by contemporary paintings.

83, 87–9, 116, 122, 82, 127, 95–6, 118, 120

The decorated tombs in the region of Luoyang dating from the end of the Former Han provide a good example of such paintings as must have adorned not only the tombs but also the houses of the rich. The bricks were lime-washed and the painted decoration stands out against the white-lime ground. Colours are applied flat and shapes are outlined with black brush strokes of varying thickness. Certain details are rendered in black lines and touches painted over the colour. Experiments in shading by means of superimposed washes, as at Mawangdui, have sometimes been attempted here; on the end wall of tomb No. 61, purple shading inside the contours of the mountains gives an impression of volume and depth.

83

Figures are usually depicted in three-quarter view, isolated from one another, in a purely linear style with no modelling. Garments are puffed out to suggest volume, but there is no attempt to make the folds follow the form of the body or to hint at

83, 87, 89

the body beneath the drapery. The most interesting characterization concerns the faces, those of civilians being more bland, those of warriors and fighters more vigorous. Though the means employed are very simple, these faces are meant as portraits, and we know from the texts that portraiture had an important rôle during the Han period. But the realism as conceived here is far removed from the individualization associated in the west with the idea of a portrait. It is rather that a type of man or character is suggested by what has already become something of a formula. The realism therefore consists in bringing a face or posture to life by making it conform to the type the artist wished to portray, in using visual notations—a particular oval or a particular form of arched eyebrow or nose—to embody the essence of a person's character.

89 83

Since there is no modelling or depth, it is the graphic quality that strikes one in these paintings. The outline, on which the movement and life of the work depends, is extremely free and nervous in its modulations. This graphic quality, which is so pronounced in the Boston tiles in the elegance, elongation and static posture of the figures, is one of the characteristics of Han painting and, since the colours are relatively faded on many of the wall paintings, might make us forget that these images were also—and perhaps primarily—admired for their bright colours. The Han liked warm, brilliant colours, and it is more than probable that the engraved stone slabs and impressed bricks, on which only the drawing survives, were originally heightened with colour. Moreover, painting of the period is often designated by the term *danqing,* 'the reds and blues'. Nevertheless, the graphic quality becomes important again at the period of the Latter Han, in the paintings of the Helingeer and Wangdu tombs, on the impressed bricks of Sichuan province and on the engraved stone slabs of Henan, Shandong and Sichuan provinces. Here again, figures, carriages and horses are rendered in silhouette, isolated from one another, and, as at Luoyang, relationships between the figures are indicated by posture or gesture alone. The silhouettes stand out against a ground that is often plain and empty. This tradition was long-lived and is found again, for example, on the painted screen from the tomb of Sima Jinlong at the end of the fifth cen-

89 72, 110 116, 122, 127, 141, 143 95, 127, 143 95–6, 117 109 89, 119, 121, 126, 138 123

tury. During the Han period the idea of space and depth was rendered by a simple vertical juxtaposition of motifs, by effects of diagonals, or more rarely by overlapping planes.

These paintings, which, at the same time, form invaluable records of material life and beliefs, are undoubtedly mere pale reflections of the palace decorations of painted plaster, lacquer and silk. The banner of the Marchioness of Dai from Mawangdui, at the beginning of the dynasty, is perhaps the unique example of a painting approaching the quality of the best works of the period.

From Writing to Calligraphy

The Han period was one of exceptional inventiveness in the sphere of handwriting, and it is probably true to say that, by the end of the dynasty, the main characteristics of all the forms that the art of calligraphy would perfect at a later date were already established. Indeed, from the third century B.C. to the second century A.D. all efforts were directed towards the two essential qualities of simplicity and speed of execution.

As early as the Qin period, the adoption of the scribal hand *(lishu),* a simplified form of the small-seal hand *(xiaozhuan),* marked a major turning point, for as we shall see, all modern types of writing derive from *lishu.*

The early hands, including *xiaozhuan,* which were perfectly suitable for inscriptions on bronze and stone, were characterized by firm strokes of equal thickness with rounded angles.[1] By making much fuller use of the brush's potential for suppleness and articulation, *lishu* modulated the strokes and angles, which now became straight.[2] From the beginning of the Han dynasty, *lishu* became the ordinary handwriting. Thus most of the writing on wooden or bamboo slips is in *lishu,* as are letters, inscriptions on wall paintings, on painted lacquers and on engraved stone slabs. But *xiaozhuan* did not disappear; it was still used for inscriptions on coins, seals, tiles and on some mirrors. It also continued for some time to influence the scribal hand; at the beginning of the Han dynasty, many writings and inscriptions were executed in a hybrid style of *lishu*

and *xiaozhuan* or in a combination of the characters of both hands. In fact, the contamination worked in both directions, for the Han *xiaozhuan* often lost its elongated and rounded form and came more to resemble the compact, angular appearance of *lishu.*

Thus *lishu* spread by degrees, and it took three centuries for the official script to reach its point of equilibrium and perfection. At first, and in contrast to the rigidity of the early hands, *lishu* writers sought no symmetry or balance in the arrangement of the strokes. The aim was for a simple, practical hand without a hint of aestheticism. But gradually a desire for harmony became apparent in these heavy characters that are wider than they are tall, and this desire culminated in the classicism reached at the end of the Han dynasty. The great calligraphic achievements of the dynasty are the monumental inscriptions on stone. Stelae *(bei)* were put up to commemorate a historical event, to perpetuate the memory of an individual and to record facts that needed to be passed on to posterity. They were erected in public places or in front of burial mounds and varied in height between 1 and 6 metres. The golden age of Han stelae was the second century A.D., and one of the finest examples is the *Kongmiao liqi bei,* dating from 156. The text relates to the temple of Confucius at Qufu, its restoration, the gift of ritual objects to the temple and the granting of privileges to the master's descendants. Each character of the stela—they are still fairly broad—occupies an imaginary square; the squares are equal and regularly spaced and, taken together, form a grid of horizontal and vertical columns into which the characters are fitted. Each stroke is executed with a firm brush, in one movement, independently, and almost without modulation, except for the triangular finial of the right-hand stroke, which alone suggests the elasticity of the brush-point. This broadening of the right basal stroke gives the somewhat static and austere art of *lishu* its elegance.

In its angular stability *lishu* was the official writing of the Han period. But very soon, even before the Han, there were those who sought to create an even more rapid script for their personal use, such as letter-writing and rough work. Their experiments, which had no artistic pretensions, were the origin of the cursive or scribbling hand known as *caoshu.* The simplification was based on the elimi-

214

nation of some strokes, the invention of symbols to express certain concepts more rapidly and on ligatures between the strokes. This rounder, abbreviated, cursive hand was very soon combined with *lishu* or replaced it in everyday writing.

Created out of a need for a shortened form, *caoshu* also became a personal hand through which the writer could give free rein to his inspiration, spontaneity and impetuosity. At the same time, during the first, and especially the second, centuries A.D., appreciation of calligraphy grew. Stelae began to be signed and biographies of scholars mention their calligraphic or even their painterly talents. Zhang Heng (78–139), Cui Yuan (77–142), Cai Yong (133–92), Zhang Zhi (died *c.* 190–4) were

looked upon as masters of a noble art, not as craftsmen. The art of calligraphy would seem to have originated at the same moment and in the same setting as lyric poetry. The scholar used his brush to evoke images or express the ardour of his feelings. Sustained by the sensibility and intelligence of the writer, by the breath of his inner life, writing too acquired an inner power of its own.

157
Tomb of General Huo Qubing (140–117 B.C.), near the tumulus of Wudi, district of Xingping, Shaanxi.
Grey granite, H. 1.40 m, (foreground) a statue of a horse trampling a Xiongnu.

Every scholar now practised both *lishu,* which was the only hand permitted in the examinations and in official documents, and *caoshu,* which held for him the charm of dynamism, spontaneity and naturalness, an almost abstract game that was intelligible only to the initiate.

In their continuing pursuit of convenience and ease, the calligraphers of the end of the Han dynasty invented other hands derived from *lishu.* The first was *kaishu* or 'regular writing', which was to replace *lishu* at the time of the Six Dynasties (221–581). The strokes were more regular and standardized than in *lishu* and some were joined; the characters were less thickset, more harmonious, with a controlled balance between verticals and horizontals. The second hand derived from *lishu* was the 'semi-cursive' *xingshu,* slightly speedier and more abbreviated than *kaishu,* but more legible than *caoshu. Kaishu, xingshu* and *caoshu* were definitively formulated during the Six Dynasties period, but it was under the Han dynasty, within the field of cursive hands, that the aesthetic dimension of handwriting was first explored.

Sculpture

Most surviving Han sculpture is connected with burial and consists of statuettes of clay, bronze and wood, which were placed in the tombs, stone slabs decorated with engraved or relief ornament, which adorned tombs and sacrificial chambers, and columns and stone statues, which were set up at the entrance to burials. Here again the tomb was one of the quintessential manifestations of Han civilization. The main characteristics of Han sculpture, for which all techniques were tried, were its monumentality, realism and the vigour with which movement was captured.

The first two qualities had already been brilliantly exemplified in Qin sculpture. It was a monumental, rugged art, and an astonishing gallery of portraits in the case of the warriors and maidservants unearthed near Qin Shi Huangdi's mausoleum. Each statue was modelled in coarse grey clay, with hollow body and solid legs. When the different parts had been assembled and details modelled separately had been placed in position, the statue was coated with fine clay slip and fired at a high temperature. Hands, human heads and the tails and forelocks of horses were fired separately and fitted to the body afterwards. Finally, statues were painted in bright colours—red, green, purple, blue, brown, yellow, black and white—and armed with real weapons.

With only a small gap between the body and the arms, and stiff, podgy limbs, these statues were designed to be viewed as a group, *en masse,* from front or back, in rows, and in repose. As the sides, which are not highly finished, show, the spectator was not meant to walk round such sculpture. The bodies, garments and some of the faces would seem to have been worked with a knife, sharply and vigorously; similarly, despite a few details, bodies are barely perceptible beneath the garments, which accentuate the frontal and rather stiff appearance of the statues. The modellers' talents were focussed mainly on the faces, also on the headdresses and weapons, which are treated with extraordinary verve and concern for detail. Faces are square, foreheads broad, arched eyebrows prominent. Mouths are wide, accented by thick lips and emphasized by moustaches. In their very realism these faces remain idealized. More even than portraits of individuals, they are human beings of overwhelming presence and verisimilitude.

This superb art, so vigorous in its static rigidity, was a considerable influence on the sculpture of the beginning of the Han, from the Yangjiawan statuettes to the lamp from Changxin Palace. One need only compare the gilt bronze lamp-bearer with the maidservant and the Qin warriors to be struck by the similarities: here are the same drapery folds cut with the knife, the same rudimentary treatment of the arms, the same idealized facial conventions, with arched eyebrows and hair tapering down to the temples, but now there is a gentleness and sensitivity in the modelling, that indicates

158
Horse.
Earthenware, painted, L. 39 cm, between second century B.C. and second century A.D.
Private collection, Tokyo.

a far more highly evolved art. The same canon of beauty and freshness is found in less ambitious 84 statuettes of the period.

Although the colossal bronze statues set up by Qin Shi Huangdi have been lost, the monumental sculpture of the Former Han survives in sixteen grey granite statues discovered in front of the tomb of Huo Qubing (140–17 B.C.), near the mausoleum of Wudi. The most accomplished of these, which 157 represents a horse trampling a Xiongnu (1.40 m), has been admirably described by Victor Segalen: 'the horse, unsaddled and unbridled, with its heavy forms and short legs symmetrically arranged, firmly planted on a massive tail, which reaches to the ground, crushes the man struggling under him, belly to belly'.³ The group, 'a mixture of animal nobility and human contortion', possesses an air of immense power. This archaic art, so very expressive despite its crudity, is the ancestor of the great burial statuary of the periods of the Latter Han and 108 the Six Dynasties. Sculpted in sandstone, which is more tractable than the heavy granite of the Huo Qubing sculptures, the Han felines are no longer captive within the block. They exist in space, with their hindquarters drawn up and their swelling chests accentuated by manes and great square jaws. There is movement in these figures, concentrated and collected.

This feeling for volume characterizes the whole of Han sculpture. It is often expressed in geometri-42, 149, 151 cally constructed figures carved in clean-cut planes 63, 90 or by full, rounded forms, from which details are virtually excluded. Deliberate schematization em-142 phasizes the three-dimensional quality, the prominent feature or attitude, the essence of a movement. It gives even a small object a surprising monumentality.

One of the most consummate achievements in sculpture of the end of the Han dynasty, the galloping horse from the tomb at Leitai, brings us back to 154 the problem of realism. Here again the dominant factor is the observation and expression of posture and speed, that is, the qualities peculiar to a charger, not the study of a particular horse. The extraordinary balance of the neighing animal caught at full gallop derives from the contrast between the strength and energy of the curve of the back, the tension of the head—which is small in relation to the body—the raised tail, and the lightness of the slender legs, one of which skims a flying swallow, itself a symbol of speed.

No more will be said here about the engraved burial slabs, which belong as properly to graphic art as to sculpture. Many techniques were avail- 95–7, 105, able; they included incised lines, lines in relief, or 117, 119–12 the whole motif could be brought out in low relief against a plain or hatched ground. Styles too varied greatly, from being somewhat severe, static and conventional in the rooms of the Wu family to the 120 often more dynamic, realistic and free styles of Henan, Jiangsu and Sichuan provinces.

This last province was certainly one of the major centres of sculptural art at the time of the Latter Han, remarkable for its clay burial statuettes, im- 145 pressed bricks and stone carving. In its power and its movement caught at the delicate point of bal- 7, 106–7, ance, the admirable red bird of the South is allied to 109, 127, 14 the galloping horse at Leitai. Naturalism, love of life, freedom of expression and execution combined with a keen sense of humour, a true love of landscape and a new sensitivity to space and at- 145 mosphere, these are qualities that the artists of 127 Sichuan province developed with unusual mastery.

Notes

Part I

CHAPTER I

1 Gernet, *Le Monde chinois,* p. 79
2 Vandeermeersch, *La formation du légisme,* p. 194
3 Tomb No. 11 at Shuihudi, district of Yumeng, Hubei province. Cf. articles in *Wenwu,* nos. 5–6, 8–9 (Peking, 1976); no. 7 (1977) and in *Kaogu xuebao,* no. 1 (Peking, 1977); no. 1 (1979); no. 1 (1980)
4 From Sima Qian, *Shiji,* ch. 6; translated into English from Chavannes, *Mémoires historiques,* Vol. 2, 1897, pp. 171–4
5 Cf. *Wenwu,* no. 11 (1975); no. 5 (1978) [translated by A.E. Dien in *Chinese Studies in Archaeology,* vol. 1, no. 1. New York: Sharpe, Summer, 1979]; no. 12 (1979)

CHAPTER II

1 Maspero and Balazs, *Histoire et Institutions de la Chine ancienne,* p. 66
2 Hulsewé, *Remnants of Han Law,* p. 225

CHAPTER III

1 *Kaogu xuebao,* no. 3 (1959)
2 Yangjiawan is to the north-east of modern Xianyang. *Wenwu,* no. 3 (1966); no. 10 (1977)
3 From Ban Gu, *Hanshu,* ch. 24A: 1132; translated into English from the author's French translation

CHAPTER IV

1 From Gaozudi, 'Song of the Great Wind'; translated into English from Hervouet in Demiéville, *Anthologie de la poésie chinoise classique,* p. 62
2 Ban Gu, *Hanshu,* ch. 94A

CHAPTER V

1 Besides the site report of tomb No. 1 in two volumes (see Bibliography), the contents of the three tombs have been studied in very numerous articles in Chinese archaeological journals: *Kaogu,* nos. 5–6 (Peking, 1972); nos. 1–2, 4 (1973); nos. 1, 4 (1974); nos 1, 6 (1975); no. 2 (1976); no. 4 (1978); nos. 2–3, 6 (1979); *Kaogu xuebao,* no. 1 (1974); *Wenwu,* no. 9 (1972); nos. 7, 9 (1973); nos. 7, 9–11 (1974); nos. 2, 4, 6, 9 (1975); no. 1 (1976); nos. 1, 8 (1977); no. 2 (1978); nos. 4, 6 (1979)
2 *Wenwu,* no. 2 (1963)
3 Idem.

4 *Wenwu,* no. 11 (1977)
5 *Wenwu,* no. 6 (1977)

Part II

CHAPTER I

1 Ban Gu, *Hanshu,* 65:2841; translated into English from the author's French translation

CHAPTER II

1 Poem by Wudi translated into English from Demiéville, *Anthologie de la poésie chinoise classique,* pp. 63–5
2 Gernet, *Le Monde chinois,* p. 67
3 Maspero and Balazs, *Histoire et Institutions de la Chine ancienne,* p. 77
4 From Wang Chong, *Lunheng,* k. 12/189; translated into English from the author's French translation

CHAPTER III

1 Numerous papers on the civilization of Dian have appeared in Chinese archaeological journals. For Shizhaishan, besides the site report (see Bibliography), see the bibliography in M. Pirazzoli-t'Serstevens, *La civilisation du royaume de Dian....* For discoveries after 1971, see in particular: *Wenwu,* no. 8 (1972); no. 1 (1974); no. 10 (1978); no. 9 (1980); *Kaogu,* no. 1 (1979); *Kaogu xuebao,* no. 2 (1972); no. 2 (1978); no. 4 (1980); *Wenwu Ziliao congkan,* no. 3 (1980)
2 See *Kaogu,* no. 2 (1978)
3 From a poem by Liu Xijun, translated into English from Hervouet in Demiéville, *Anthologie de la poésie chinoise classique,* p. 69

CHAPTER IV

1 See *Wenwu,* no. 11 (1976). For digs at Chang'an under the Han: *Kaogu tongxun,* no. 5 (1957); no. 4 (1958); *Kaogu* no. 9 (1963); *Kaogu xuebao,* no. 2 (1959); *Wenwu,* no. 1 (1981)
2 From Ban Gu, *Hanshu,* ch. 65: 2849–50; translated into English from the author's French translation
3 See *Wenwu,* no. 11 (1976)
4 Diény, 'Le système des images dans la poésie classique', p. 1153
5 Maspero and Balazs, *Histoire et Institutions de la Chine ancienne,* p. 57

[6] From Ban Gu, *Hanshu*, ch. 22; translated into English from Kaltenmark, 'Les danses sacrées en Chine', p. 427

[7] Letter from Sima Qian to Ren An, in Ban Gu, *Hanshu*, ch. 62; translated into English from Chavannes, *Mémoires historiques*, vol. 1, 1895, p. CCXXXII

[8] Idem

[9] From Sima Xiangru, *Shanglin fu*; translated into English from Hervouet, *Le chapitre 117 de* Che-ki, pp. 101–3

[10] Idem, p. 119

[11] Diény, 'Les dix-neuf poèmes anciens', p. 72

[12] See *Kaogu*, nos. 1–2, 5 (1972); no. 1 (1974); no. 1 (1981); *Mancheng Han mu*, Peking, 1978; *Mancheng Han mu pajue baokao*, Peking, 1980

Part III
CHAPTER I

[1] Loewe, *Crisis and Conflict in Han China*, pp. 91 ff.

CHAPTER II

[1] Yü Ying-shih, *Trade and Expansion in Han China*, p. 64

[2] Yunnan sheng bowuguan, *Yunnan Jinning... baogao*, vol. 2, p. 107/4

[3] *Wenwu*, no. 1 (1978)

[4] Letter by Officer Zheng, translated into English from Chavannes, *Les documents chinois découverts par Aurel Stein...*, p. 89, no. 398

CHAPTER III

[1] Maspero, *Le taoïsme et les religions chinoises*, p. 73

[2] Ngo Van Xuyet, *Divination, magie et politique...*, p. 177

[3] From Ban Gu, *Hanshu*, ch. 75; translated into English from Ngo Van Xuyet, *Divination, magie et politique...*, pp. 90–1

[4] Tomb of Bu Qianqiu at Luoyang: see *Wenwu*, no. 6 (1977); no. 11 (1979). Tomb of Xintongqiao at Zhengzhou: see *Wenwu*, no. 10 (1972)

[5] The so-called *sishen*, see the table on p. 99

CHAPTER IV

[1] From Ban Gu, *Hanshu*, ch. 66: 2896; translated into English from the author's French translation

[2] See *Wenwu*, no. 1 (1972); no. 5 (1975); *Kaogu*, no. 1 (1972)

[3] From Ban Xuan, *Hanshu*, ch. 72: 3087; translated into English from the author's French translation

[4] Idem, ch. 27:2; translated into English from Schipper, 'Millénarismes et messianismes dans la Chine ancienne', p. 33

CHAPTER V

[1] Bielenstein, 'The Restoration of the Han Dynasty', 1954, p. 83

[2] Idem

Part IV
CHAPTER I

[1] Cartier and Will, 'Démographie et institutions en Chine...', p. 171

CHAPTER II

[1] From Ban Biao, *Hou Hanshu*, ch. 117: 3184; translated into English from the author's French translation

[2] Excavation of J. Hackin, 1936–40

[3] *Wenwu*, no. 4 (1977): 1–22

[4] Excerpt from the *Yantielun* translated into English from Baudry, *Dispute sur le Sel et le Fer*, p. 236

[5] *Wenwu*, no. 7 (1981): 1–20

CHAPTER III

[1] As in the Helingeer tomb in Inner Mongolia: see site report and *Wenwu*, nos. 1, 3, 11 (1974); or the Wangdu tomb No. 2 in Hebei province and the Leitai tomb in Gansu province: see *Wenwu*, no. 2 (1972); *Kaogu xuebao*, no. 12 (1974); *Kaogu*, no. 6 (1979)

[2] From Ban Zhao, *Nüjie*; see Swann, *Pan Chao: Foremost Woman Scholar of China*, p. 85

CHAPTER IV

[1] Bielenstein, 'Lo-yang in the Later Han Times', p. 21

[2] Translated into English from Diény, 'Les dix-neuf poèmes anciens', p. 13, No. 3

[3] From Wang Chong, *Lunheng*, 29, II: 444; translated into English from the author's French translation

[4] Maspero, *Le taoïsme et les religions chinoises*, p. 358

[5] See Diény, *Aux origines de la poésie classique en Chine...*, pp. 79–80

[6] From Frankel, '...Three Early Chinese Ballads', p. 7

[7] Diény, 'Les dix-neuf poèmes anciens', p. 187

[8] Idem, p. 163

[9] Translated from Idem, p. 25, No. 9

[10] Poem by Wang Can translated into English from Diény in Demiéville, *Anthologie de la poésie chinoise classique*, p. 123

Part V
CHAPTER I

[1] Maspero, *Le taoïsme et les religions chinoises*, p. 283

[2] B. Watson, *Ssu-ma Ch'ien...*, pp. 10–12

[3] Idem, p. 10

[4] Cao Cao, *Duangexing*, translated by Steinen, 'Poems of Ts'ao Ts'ao', p. 147

CHAPTER II

[1] Several articles on the development of science and technology in the light of recent archaeological finds have been published lately. See *Kaogu*, no. 2 (1977); *Wenwu*, no. 12 (1973); no. 11 (1974); no. 2 (1975); no. 1 (1976); nos. 1–2 (1978) [translated by D. J. Harper in *Chinese Studies in Archaeology*, vol. 1, no. 1, New York: Sharpe, Summer, 1979]; no. 5 (1981); *Zhongguo lishi bowuguan guankan*, no. 2 (1980). The standard work in English is by Joseph Needham (see Bibliography).

[2] From Ban Gu, *Hanshu*, ch. 99b: 4145–6

[3] See Needham, *La science chinoise...*, p. 11

CHAPTER III

[1] Pl. 155, the two first rows of each register of three characters starting from the top

[2] Pl. 155, third row of each register

[3] Segalen, Voisins, and Lartigue, *Mission archéologique en Chine (1914)*, vol. 1, pp. 35–6

Provinces of Modern China, Showing Archaeological Sites of the Han Period

(Only the sites mentioned in the text are named.)

State frontiers

provincial boundaries

lakes

0 300 600
km

1 – Lintong
2 – Xi'an
3 – Yangjiawan
4 – Luoyang
5 – Nanyang
6 – Dengxian
7 – Gongxian
8 – Zhengzhou
9 – Yunmeng
10 – Jiangling
11 – Shouxian
12 – Xuzhou
13 – Lianyungang
14 – Shaoxing

15 – Changsha
16 – *Xiao River*
17 – Canton
18 – Hepu
19 – Jinning (sites at Shizhaishan, Taijishan, Lijiashan, and Chenggong)
20 – Dapona (Xiangyun district)
21 – Wanjiaba (Chuxiong district)
22 – Chengdu
23 – Wuwei
24 – Dunhuang
25 – Helingeer
26 – Datong

27 – Tianjin
28 – Dingxian
29 – Mancheng
30 – Wangdu
31 – Jinan
32 – Jiaxiang
33 – Jining
34 – Qufu
35 – Linyi
36 – Yinan
37 – Xiaotangshan (Feicheng district)
38 – Noïn Ula
39 – Lelang

Han Administrative Divisions, Han Towns and Sites

(excluding Central Asia, as in second and first centuries B.C.)   Only the names mentioned in the text are listed.

— Administrative divisions are in italics.
— Names of non-Chinese peoples (Xiongnu, Xianbei, Dian, Nan Yue) are in parentheses, e.g. (DIAN).

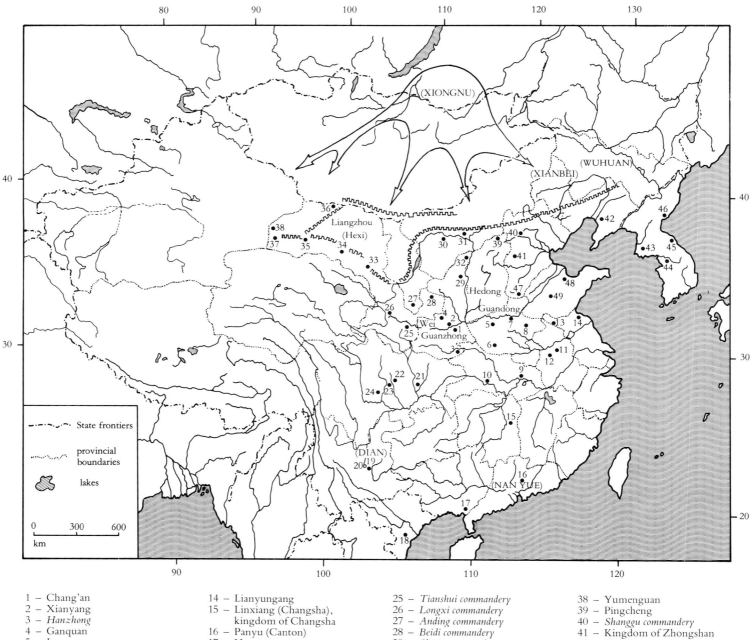

1 – Chang'an
2 – Xianyang
3 – *Hanzhong*
4 – Ganquan
5 – Luoyang
6 – Wan (Nanyang)
7 – Fanyang
8 – Xiangyi (Suixian)
9 – *Jiangxia (commandery)*
10 – *Nan commandery* (Jiangling)
11 – Kingdom of Huainan
12 – Shouchun (Shouxian)
13 – Pengcheng

14 – Lianyungang
15 – Linxiang (Changsha),
   kingdom of Changsha
16 – Panyu (Canton)
17 – Hepu
18 – *Jiaozhi (commandery)*
19 – *Yizhou commandery*
20 – Lake Dian
21 – *Ba commandery*
22 – *Shu commandery*
   (capital: Chengdu)
23 – *Guanghan commandery*
24 – Linqiong

25 – *Tianshui commandery*
26 – *Longxi commandery*
27 – *Anding commandery*
28 – *Beidi commandery*
29 – *Shang commandery*
30 – *Shuofang commandery*
31 – *Wuyuan commandery*
32 – *Xihe commandery*
33 – *Wuwei commandery*
34 – *Zhangye commandery*
35 – *Jiuquan commandery*
36 – Juyan (Etsin-gol)
37 – *Dunhuang commandery*

38 – Yumenguan
39 – Pingcheng
40 – *Shanggu commandery*
41 – Kingdom of Zhongshan
42 – *Liaodong commandery*
43 – *Lelang commandery*
44 – *Zhenfan commandery*
45 – *Lintun commandery*
46 – *Xuantu commandery*
47 – Handan
48 – Linzi
49 – Taishan

Routes of the Silk Road

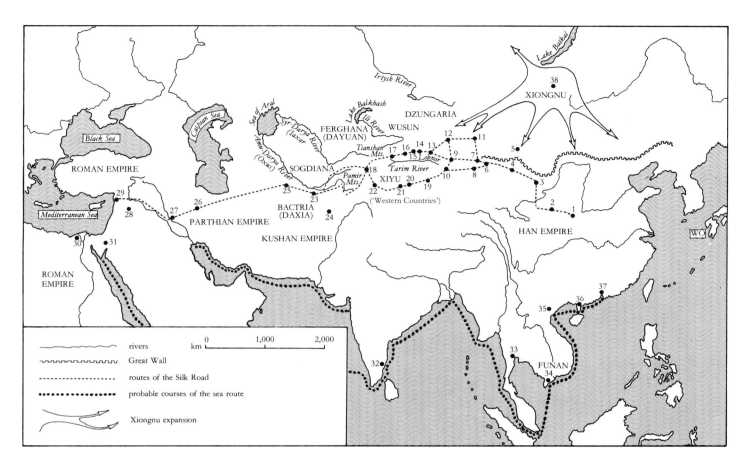

1 – Chang'an
2 – Tianshui
3 – Wuwei
4 – Jiuquan
5 – Juyan
6 – Dunhuang
7 – Yumenguan
8 – Yangguan
9 – Loulan
10 – Shanshan and Mirān
11 – Yiwu (Hami)
12 – Turfan (former kingdom of Jushi)

13 – Karashahr (Yanqi)
14 – Wulei
15 – Luntai
16 – Kuchâ (Jiuci)
17 – Gumo (Aksu)
18 – Kashgar (Sule)
19 – Jumo
20 – Niya
21 – Khotan (Yutian)
22 – Yarkand (Suoju)
23 – Bactres (Balkh)
24 – Begram
25 – Merv

26 – Ecbatana
27 – Ctesiphon
28 – Palmyra
29 – Antioch
30 – Alexandria
31 – Petra
32 – Virapatnam
33 – P'ong-tük
34 – Oc-eo
35 – Jiaozhi
36 – Hepu
37 – Canton (Panyu)
38 – Noïn-Ula

Plan of Chang'an, Capital of the Former Han and of Wang Mang

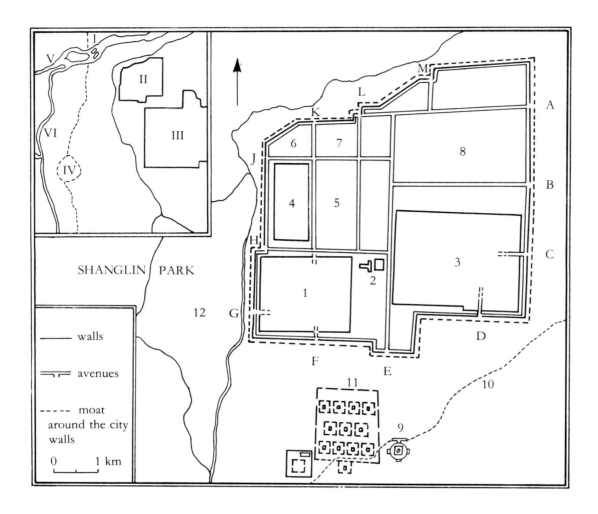

I – Xianyang of the Qin
II – Chang'an of the Han
III – Chang'an of the Tang
IV – Lake Kunming
V – Wei River
VI – Feng River

A – Xuanping men
B – Qinming men
C – Bacheng men
D – Fu'ang men
E – An men
F – Xi'an men
G – Zhang men
H – Zicheng men
J – Yong men
K – Heng men

L – Chucheng men
M – Luocheng men

1 – Weiyang Palace
2 – Arsenal
3 – Changle Palace
4 – Gui Palace
5 – Northern Palace
6 – Western market
7 – Eastern market
8 – Mingguang Palace
9 – *mingtang* and *biyong* built
   in A.D. 4
10 – Canal (course partially
   reconstructed)
11 – Cultural ensemble built
   by Wang Mang
12 – Jianzhang Palace

Plan of Luoyang, Capital of the Latter Han

after Bielenstein, 'Lo-yang', p. 124

Shaded area represents Greater Luoyang
(the city within the walls and suburbs)

A – Southern Palace
B – Northern Palace
C – Arsenal, great granary
D – Dynastic temple of the ancestors
    (Zongmiao), altar of the gods
    of the soil and grain (Sheji)
E – City market
F – Stone bridge
G – lingtai ('transcendant terrace')
H – mingtang ('sacred hall')
J – biyong ('palace of the
    encircling moat')
K – taixue ('Grand School')
L – Altar of Heaven
M – Altar of Earth
N – Altar of the suburb
    of the centre

1 – Guanyang men
2 – Yong men
3 – Shangxi men
4 – Xia men
5 – Gu men
6 – Shangdong men
7 – Zhongdong men
8 – Hao men
9 – Kaiyang men
10 – Pingcheng men
11 – Xiaoyuan men
12 – Jincheng men

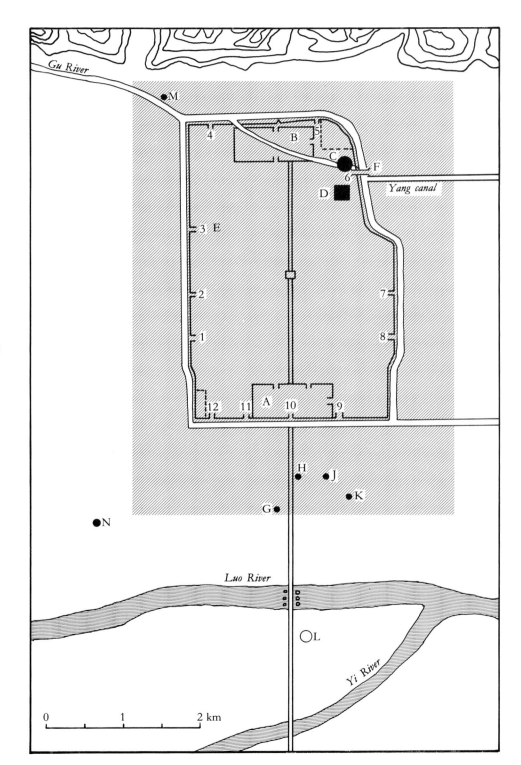

Cross-section of Tomb No. 1 at Mawangdui, Changsha

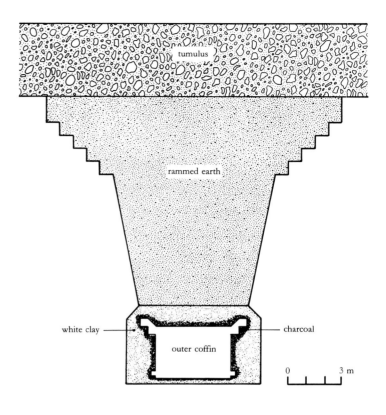

tumulus

rammed earth

white clay — — charcoal

outer coffin

0   3 m

Weights and Measures in the Han Period[1]

Measures of Length
1 *fen* 分 = 2.30 mm
10 *fen* = 1 *cun* 寸 = 2.30 cm
10 *cun* = 1 *chi* 尺 (foot) = 23 cm
6 *chi* = 1 *bu* 步 (pace) = 1.38 m
10 *chi* = 1 *zhang* 丈 = 2.30 m
10 *zhang* = 1 *yin* 引 = 23 m
1,800 *chi* = 300 *bu* = 1 *li* 里 = 414 m

Measures of Weight
1 *shu* 銖 = 6 *dou* 豆 = 0.64 grams
24 *shu* = 1 *liang* 兩 = 15.25 g
16 *liang* = 1 *jin* 斤 = 244 g
30 *jin* = 1 *jun* 鈞 = 7.32 g
4 *jun* = 1 *shi* 石 = 29.3 kg

Square Measures
1 bu^2 步 = 1.90 m²
240 bu^2 = 1 *mu* 畝 = 457 m²
100 *mu* = 1 *qing* 頃 = 4.57 ha

Liquid Measures
2 *yue* 龠 = 1 *ge* 合 = 19.96 cm³
10 *ge* = 1 *sheng* 升 = 199.68 cm³
10 *sheng* = 1 *dou* 斗 = 1,996.87 cm³ = 2 litres
10 *dou* = 1 *shi* 石 or *hu* 斛 [2] = about 20 l [3]
1 *zhong* 鍾 contained 10 *dou*

[1] These measures varied slightly throughout the dynasty ; the above figures are given as indications and need to be adjusted depending on the period under consideration :

    e.g. *1 jin* = between 244 and 250 g, from 206 to 87 B. C.
                between 250 and 264 g, from 86 B. C. to A. D. 8
                between 240 and 244 g, from A. D. 9-23
                250 g, from A. D. 25 to 220

[2] Introduced in the reign of Wang Mang

[3] Of hulled grain

Bibliography

Adachi, K. *Chang'an shiji kao*. Trans. by Yang Lian. Shanghai: Shangwu yinshuguan, 1935.

Balazs, E. *La Bureaucratie céleste*. Paris: Gallimard, 1968.

Ban Gu. *Hanshu*. Shanghai: Zhonghua shuju, 1964.

Barnard, N. (Ed.) *Early Chinese Art and Its Possible Influence in the Pacific Basin*. New York: Intercultural Press, 1972.

Baudry, D. and P. *Dispute sur le Sel et le Fer*. Trans. by J. Levi. Paris: Lanzmann et Seghers, 1978.

Bielenstein, H. 'The Census of China during the Period A.D. 2–742.' *Bulletin of the Museum of Far Eastern Antiquities*, no. 19 (Stockholm, 1947): 125–63.

—— 'The Restoration of the Han Dynasty.' *Bulletin of the Museum of Far Eastern Antiquities*, no. 26 (Stockholm, 1954): 1–209; no. 31 (1959): 1–287; no. 39 (1967): 1–198; no. 51 (1970): 3–300.

—— 'Lo-yang in the Later Han Times.' *Bulletin of the Museum of Far Eastern Antiquities*, no. 48 (Stockholm, 1976): 3–142.

—— *The Bureaucracy of Han Times*. Cambridge: Cambridge University Press, 1980.

Bodde, D. *China's First Unifier: A Study of the Ch'in Dynasty as Seen in the Life of Li Ssu (280?–208 B.C.)*. Leiden: Brill, 1938.

—— *Festivals in Classical China*. Princeton: Princeton University Press, 1975.

Bray, F. 'Agricultural Technology and Agrarian Change in Han China.' *Early China* 5 (Berkeley, 1979–80): 3–13.

Bridgman, R.F. 'La Médecine dans la Chine antique, d'après les biographies de Pien-ts'io et de Chouen-yu Yi (chap. 105 des *Mémoires Historiques* de Sseu-ma Ts'ien).' *Mélanges chinois et bouddhiques* 10 (Brussels, 1955): 1–213.

Brinker, H. and Goepper, R. *Kunstschätze aus China*. Zurich: Kunsthaus, 1980–1.

Bulling, A.G. 'The Decoration of Mirrors of the Han Period: A Chronology.' *Artibus Asiae*, suppl. XX (Ascona, 1960).

—— 'A Landscape Representation of the Western Han Period.' *Artibus Asiae*, no. 4, XXV (Ascona, 1962): 293–317.

—— 'Ancient Chinese Maps—Two Maps Discovered in a Han Dynasty Tomb from the Second Century B.C.' *Expedition* (Philadelphia, Summer, 1978): 16–25.

Bunker, E. C.; Chatwin, C. B.; and Farkas, A. R. *Animal Style Art, from East to West*. New York: The Asia Society, 1979.

Cartier, M. and Will, P. E. 'Démographie et institutions en Chine: Contribution à l'analyse des recensements de l'époque impériale (2 ap. J.-C.–1750).' *Annales de démographie historique* (Paris: Mouton, 1971): 161–245.

Ceng Zhaoyu et al. *Yinan gu huaxiangshi mu fajue baogao*. Shanghai: Wenhua bu wenwu guanliju, 1956.

Chang Kwang-chih (Ed.) *Food in Chinese Culture, Anthropological and Historical Perspectives*. New Haven: Yale University Press, 1977.

Chavannes, E. *Les Mémoires historiques de Se-ma Ts'ien*. 6 vols. Angers: Imprimerie orientale, 1895–1905; Paris: Maisonneuve, 1969.

—— 'Les pays d'Occident d'après le *Heou Han chou*.' *T'oung Pao*, 2nd series, 8 (Leiden, 1907): 149–234.

—— *Mission archéologique dans la Chine septentrionale*. Paris: E. Leroux et Imprimerie Nationale, 1909–15.

—— *Les documents chinois découverts par Aurel Stein dans les sables du Turkestan oriental*. Oxford: Clarendon, Press, 1913.

Chen Mengjia. *Han jian zhuishu*. Peking: Zhonghua shuju, 1980.

Cheng Te-k'un. 'Ch'in-Han Architectural Remains.' *The Journal of the Institute of Chinese Studies of the Chinese University of Hong Kong*, no. 2, IX (1978): 1–80.

—— 'Ch'in-Han Mortuary Architecture.' *The Journal of the Institute of Chinese Studies of the Chinese University of Hong Kong* XI (1980): 193–270.

Chūka Jimmin Kyōwakoku Kan Tō hekiga ten (ex. cat.). Tokyo, 1975.

Chūka Jimmin Kyōwakoku shutsudo bumbutsu ten (ex. cat.). Tokyo and Kyoto, 1973.

Ch'ü T'ung-tsu. *Han Social Structure*. Seattle: University of Washington Press, 1972.

Corpus des pierres sculptées Han. 2 vols. Peking: Centre d'études sinologiques, 1950.

Crespigny, R. de. Official Titles of the Former Han Dynasty, as Translated and Transcribed by H. H. Dubs: An Index. Canberra: Australian National University, 1967.

Demiéville, P. Anthologie de la poésie chinoise classique. Paris: Gallimard, 1962.

Dewall, M. von. 'Die Tien-Kultur und ihre Totenausstattung.' Beiträge zur allgemeinen und vergleichenden Archäologie I (Munich, 1979): 69–144. [Deutsches Archäologisches Institut.]

Diény, J. P. 'Les dix-neuf poèmes anciens.' Bulletin de la Maison franco-japonaise, new series, no. 4, VII (Paris: P.U.F., 1963).

—— Aux origines de la poésie classique en Chine: Etude sur la poésie lyrique à l'époque des Han. Leiden: Brill, 1968.

—— Pastourelles et Magnanarelles: Essai sur un thème littéraire chinois. Geneva: Droz, 1977.

—— 'Le système des images dans la poésie classique.' Annuaire 1977–8 (Paris: Ecole pratique des Hautes Etudes, IVe section, 1978): 1149–61. [Report on the communications for the years 1976–7.]

Dubs, H. H. 'The Victory of Han Confucianism.' Journal of the American Oriental Society 58 (New Haven, 1938): 435–49.

—— The History of the Former Han Dynasty. 3 vols. Baltimore: Waverly Press. 1938–55.

Ebrey, P. 'Estate and Family Management in the Later Han as Seen in the "Monthly Instructions for the Four Classes of People".' Journal of the Economic and Social History of the Orient, part 2, 17 (Leiden, May, 1974): 173–205.

Elisseeff, V. Trésors d'art chinois. Paris: Petit Palais, 1973.

Fairbank, W. Adventures in Retrieval. Vol. XXVIII. Cambridge, MA: Harvard-Yenching Institute Studies, 1972.

Fan Ye. Hou Hanshu. Peking: Shangwu yinshuguan, 1959.

Finsterbusch, K. Verzeichnis und Motivindex der Han-Darstellungen. 2 vols. Wiesbaden, 1966; 1971.

Fontein, J. and Tung Wu. Unearthing China's Past. Boston: Museum of Fine Arts, 1973.

Forke, A. Lun-Heng: Weng Ch'ung's Essays. New ed., 2 vols. New York: Paragon Book Gallery, 1962.

Frankel, H. H. 'The Abduction, the War, and the Desperate Husband: Three Early Chinese Ballads.' Ventures, no. 1, V (New Haven, 1965): 6–14.

—— The Flowering Plum and the Palace Lady. New Haven: Yale University Press, 1976.

Fujieda, A. Monji no bunkashi. 4th ed. Tokyo: Iwanami shoten, 1975.

Gale, E. M. Discourses on Salt and Iron: A Debate on State Control of Commerce and Industry in Ancient China. Taipei, 1967; new ed.: Ch'eng-wen Publishing Company, 1973.

Gernet, J. Le Monde chinois. Paris: A. Colin, 1972.

Han Tang bihua. Peking: Waiwen chubanshe, 1974.

Harada, Y. Kan Rikuchō no fukushoku. Vol. 23. Tokyo: Tōyōbunko, 1937.

Hayashi, M. 'Kandai no inshoku.' Tōhōgakuhō 48 (Kyoto, 1975): 1–98.

—— Kandai no bumbutsu. Kyoto: Kyoto University, Research Institute for Humanistic Studies, 1976.

Hebei sheng wenhuaju wenwu gongzuodui. Wangdu erhao Han mu. Peking: Wenwu chubanshe, 1959.

Hervouet, Y. Un poète de cour sous les Han: Sseu-ma Siang-jou. Paris: Institut des Hautes Etudes chinoises, P.U.F., 1964.

—— Le chapitre 117 du Che-ki (Biographie de Sseu-ma Siang-jou). Paris: Institut des Hautes Etudes chinoises, P.U.F., 1972.

Hou Ching-lang. 'La sculpture des Ts'in.' Arts Asiatiques XXXIII (Paris, 1977): 133–81.

Hsio-yen Shih. 'I-Nan and Related Tombs.' Artibus Asiae XXII (Ascona, 1959): 277–312.

—— 'Han Stone Reliefs from Shensi Province.' Archives of the Chinese Art Society of America XIV (New York, 1960): 49–64.

Hughes, E. R. Two Chinese Poets: Vignettes of Han Life and Thought. Princeton: Princeton University Press, 1960.

Hulsewé, A. F. P. Remnants of Han Law. Vol. 1. Leiden: Brill, 1955.

—— 'Quelques considérations sur le commerce de la soie au temps de la dynastie des Han.' Mélanges de Sinologie offerts à Monsieur Paul Demiéville. Vol. 2. Paris: Institut des Hautes Etudes chinoises, 1974, pp. 117–35.

Hunan sheng bowuguan, Zhongguo kexueyuan kaogu yanjiusuo. Changsha Mawangdui yihao Han mu. 2 vols. Peking: Wenwu chubanshe, 1973.

Hu Shih. 'The Establishment of Confucianism as a State Religion during the Han Dynasty.' Journal of the North-China Branch of the Royal Asiatic Society LX (1929): 20–41.

Jao Tsung-yi. 'Xinan wenhua.' Bulletin of the Institute of History and Philology, no. 1, XLVI (Taipei, 1974): 173–203. [Academia Sinica.]

Kaltenmark, M. Le 'Lie-sien tschouan'. Peking: Centre d'Etudes sinologiques, 1953.

—— 'Les danses sacrées en Chine.' Sources Orientales. Vol. 6: Les danses sacrées. Paris: Seuil, 1963.

Kierman, F. A. and Fairbank, J. K. (Ed.) Chinese Ways in Warfare. Cambridge, MA: Harvard University Press, 1974.

Knechtges, D. R. The Han Rhapsody: A Study of the Fu of Yang Hsiung (53 B.C.–A.D. 18). Cambridge: Cambridge University Press, 1976.

Koizumi, A. Rakurō saigyō tsuka. Seoul: Chōsen Kōseki Kenkyūkai, 1934.

Kroll, J. L. 'Toward a Study of the Economic Views of Sang Hungyang.' Early China 4 (Berkeley, 1978–9): 11–18.

Künstler, M. J. Ma Jong: Vie et Œuvre. Warsaw: Panstowe Wydawnictwo Naukowe, 1969.

Lao Kan. 'Population and Geography in the Two Han Dynasties.' in E-tu Zen Sun and Francis, J. de. Chinese Social History. Washington, D.C., 1956, pp. 83–102. [American Council of Learned Societies.]

—— Juyan Han jian kaoshi. Special issues, nos. 21, 40. Taipei: The Institute of History and Philology, 1957; 1960. [Academia Sinica.]

Li Zhong. 'Zhongguo fengjian shehui qianqi gangtie yelian

228

jishu fazhan de tantao.' *Kaogu xuebao,* no. 2 (Peking, 1975): 1–22

Liji. [Sibu beiyao]. Shanghai: Zhonghua shuju, 1936.

Liu Dunzhen et. al. *Zhongguo gudai jianzhu shi.* Peking: Zhongguo jianzhu gongye chubanshe, 1980.

Liu Xianzhou. *Zhongguo gudai nongye jixie faming shi.* Peking: Science Press, 1963.

Liu Zhiyuan. *Sichuan Han dai huaxiangzhuan yishu.* Peking: Zhongguo gudian yishu chubanshe, 1958.

Loewe, M. *Records of Han Administration.* 2 vols. Cambridge: Cambridge University Press, 1967.

—— 'Spices and Silk: Aspects of World Trade in the First Seven Centuries of the Christian Era.' *Journal of the Royal Asiatic Society,* no. 2 (London, 1971): 166–79.

—— *Crisis and Conflict in Han China.* London: George Allen and Unwin, 1974.

—— 'Man and Beast, the Hybrid in Early Chinese Art and Literature.' *Numen,* no. 2, XXV (Leiden, 1978): 97–117.

—— 'Manuscripts Found Recently in China: A Preliminary Survey.' *T'oung Pao,* nos. 2–3, LXIII (Leiden, 1978): 99–136.

—— *Ways to Paradise: The Chinese Quest for Immortality.* London: George Allen and Unwin, 1979.

Mancheng Han mu. Peking: Wenwu chubanshe, 1978.

Maspero, H. 'Les instruments astronomiques des Chinois au temps des Han.' *Mélanges chinois et bouddhiques.* (Brussels, 1939): 183–370.

—— *Mélanges posthumes sur les religions et l'histoire de la Chine.* Vol. 3: *Etudes historiques.* Paris: Musée Guimet, 1950.

—— *Le taoïsme et les religions chinoises.* Paris: Gallimard, 1971.

—— and Balazs, E. *Histoire et Institutions de la Chine ancienne.* Paris: P.U.F., 1967.

Miyasaki, I. 'Les villes en Chine à l'époque des Han.' *T'oung Pao,* nos. 4–5, 48 (Leiden, 1960): 376–92.

Nagahiro, T. et al. *Kandai gazō no kenkyū.* Tokyo: Chuokoron bijutsu shupan, 1965.

Needham, J. *La science chinoise et l'Occident (le grand titrage).* Paris: Seuil, 1973.

—— *Science and Civilisation in China.* 8 vols. [published.] Cambridge: Cambridge University Press, 1954–76.

Nei Menggu zizhiqu bowuguan wenwu gongzuodui. *Helingeer Han mu bihua.* Peking: Wenwu chubanshe, 1978.

Ngo Van Xuyet. *Divination, magie et politique dans la Chine ancienne: Essai suivi de la traduction des 'Biographies des magiciens' tirées de l'*Histoire des Han postérieurs. Paris: P.U.F., 1976.

Nguyen Van Huyēn and Hoang Vinh. *Nhung trōng dōng Dōng-son da phat hiēn o Viēt Nam.* Hanoi: Viēn ban tang lich-su Viēt Nam, 1975.

Pirazzoli-t'Serstevens, M. *La civilisation du royaume de Dian à l'époque Han.* Paris: Ecole française d'Extrême-Orient, 1974.

—— 'Le mobilier en Chine à l'époque Han.' *Journal des Savants* (Paris, 1977): 17–42.

Pokora, T. *Hsin-lun (New Treatise) and Other Writings by Huan T'an (43 B.C.–A.D. 28).* Ann Arbor, 1975.

Rawson, J. *Ancient China: Art and Archaeology.* London: British Museum, 1980.

Riboud, K. 'A Closer View of Early Chinese Silks.' in Gervers, V. (Ed.) *Studies in Textile History.* Toronto: Royal Ontario Museum, 1977, pp. 252–80.

Rudolph, R. C. and Wen You. *Han Tomb Art of West China.* Los Angeles: University of California Press, 1951.

Samolin, W. *East Turkestan to the Twelfth Century.* London: Mouton, 1964.

Schipper, K. M. 'Millénarismes et messianismes dans la Chine ancienne.' *XXVIth Conference of Chinese Studies* (Ortisei–St. Ulrich, Italy, Sept., 1978): 31–48.

Segalen, V.; Voisins, G. de; and Lartigue, J. *Mission archéologique en Chine (1914).* Vol. 1: *L'art funéraire à l'époque des Han.* Paris: Geuthner, 1935.

Seidel, A. *La divinisation de Lao-tseu dans le taoïsme des Han.* Paris: Ecole française d'Extrême-Orient, 1969.

Shaanxi sheng bowuguan et al. *Shaanbei dong Han huaxiang shike xuanji.* Peking: Wenwu chubanshe, 1959.

Shih Sheng-han. *On* Fan Sheng-chih shu, *An Agriculturist Book of China Written by Fan Sheng-chih in the First Century* B.C. Peking: Science Press, 1959.

Sichou zhi lu: Han Tang zhiwu. Peking: Wenwu chubanshe, 1972.

Sima Qian. *Shiji.* Shanghai: Zhonghua shuju, 1962.

Sivin, N. *Chinese Alchemy: Preliminary Studies.* Cambridge, MA: Harvard University Press, 1968.

Smith, R. B. and Watson, W. (Ed.) *Early South-East Asia: Essays in Archaeology, History and Historical Geography.* Oxford: O.U.P., 1979.

Sofukawa, H. 'Konron san to shōsen zu.' *Tōhō gakuhō,* no. 51 (Kyoto, March, 1979): 83–185.

Speiser, W.; Goepper, R.; and Fribourg, J. *Chinese Art.* Vol. 3: *Painting, Calligraphy, Stone Rubbing, Wood Engraving.* Trans. by Diana Imber. New York: Universe Books, 1964.

Stein, R. A. 'Remarques sur les mouvements du taoïsme politico-religieux au IIe s. ap. J.-C.' *T'oung Pao,* nos. 1–3, L (Leiden, 1963): 1–78.

Steinen, D. von den. 'Poems of Ts'ao Ts'ao.' *Monumenta Serica,* no. 1, IV (Tokyo, 1939).

Sullivan, M. *The Birth of Landscape Painting in China.* Berkeley: University of California Press, 1962.

Sun Ji. 'Cong xiongshi xijia fa dao antaoshi xijia fa.' *Kaogu,* no. 5 (Peking, 1980): 448–60.

Swann, N. L. *Pan Chao: Foremost Woman Scholar of China.* New York and London: Century, 1932.

—— *Food and Money in Ancient China.* Princeton: Princeton University Press, 1950.

Tian Shi. 'Xi Han duliangheng lüeshuo.' *Wenwu,* no. 12 (Peking, 1975): 79–89.

Tjan, T. S. *'Po hu t'ung': The Comprehensive Discussion in the White Tiger Hall.* 2 vols. Leiden: Brill, 1949; 1952.

Trésors d'art de la Chine. Brussels: Palais des Beaux-Arts, 1982.

Tsien, T. H. *Zhongguo gudai shu shi (A History of Writing and Writing Materials in Ancient China).* Hong Kong: The Chinese University, 1975.

Vandermeersch, L. *La formation du légisme*. Paris: Ecole française d'Extrême-Orient, 1965.

—— 'Le statut des terres en Chine à l'époque des Han.' in Lanciotti, L. (Ed.) *Il diritto in Cina*. Florence: L. S. Olschki, 1978, pp. 41–56.

Waley, A. *A Hundred and Seventy Chinese Poems*. London, 1918; rev. ed.: Constable and Co., 1962.

Wang Chong. *Lunheng*. Shanghai: Remin chubanshe, 1974.

Wang Yü-ch'üan. 'An Outline of the Central Government of the Former Han Dynasty.' *Harvard Journal of Asiatic Studies* XII (Cambridge, MA, 1949): 134–87.

Watson, B. *Ssu-ma Ch'ien: Grand Historian of China*. New York: Columbia University Press, 1958.

—— *Records of the Grand Historian of China*. 2 vols. New York: Columbia University Press, 1961.

—— *Chinese Rhyme-Prose: Poems in the Fu Form from the Han and Six Dynasties Periods*. New York: Columbia University Press, 1971.

—— *Courtier and Commoner in Ancient China: Selections from the History of the Former Han by Pan Ku*. New York: Columbia University Press, 1974.

Watson, W. *The Genius of China: An Exhibition of Archaeological Finds of the People's Republic of China*. London: Royal Academy, 1973.

Wen Fong. (Ed.) *The Great Bronze Age of China*. New York: The Metropolitan Museum of Art, 1980.

Wenhua dageming qijian chutu wenwu. Peking: Wenwu chubanshe, 1972.

Wiens, H. J. *Han Chinese Expansion in South China*. Hamden, CT: The Shoe String Press, 1967.

Wilbur, C.M. *Slavery in China during the Former Han Dynasty, 206 B.C.–A.D. 25*. Chicago: Field Museum of Natural History, 1943.

Wilhelm, H. 'The Scholar's Frustration: Notes on a Type of *Fu*.' in Fairbank, J. K. (Ed.) *Chinese Thought and Institutions*. Chicago: The University of Chicago Press, 1973, pp. 310–19.

Willetts, W. *Foundations of Chinese Art, from Neolithic Pottery to Modern Architecture*. London: Thames and Hudson, 1965.

Xi Han bohua. Peking: Wenwu chubanshe, 1972.

Xin Zhongguo chutu wenwu ('Historical Relics Unearthed in New China'). Peking: Waiwen chubanshe, 1972.

Xinjiang chutu wenwu. Peking: Wenwu chubanshe, 1975.

Yang Hong. 'Zhongguo gudai de jiazhou.' *Kaogu xuebao*, no. 1 (Peking, 1976): 19–46.

Yang, L. S. 'Great Families of Eastern Han.' in E-tu Zen Sun and Francis, J. de. *Chinese Social History*. Washington, D.C., 1956, pp. 103–34 [American Council of Learned Societies.]

Yü Ying-shih. 'Life and Immortality in the Mind of Han China.' *Harvard Journal of Asiatic Studies* 25 (Cambridge, MA, 1964–5): 80–122.

—— *Trade and Expansion in Han China*. Berkeley: University of California Press, 1967.

Yunnan sheng bowuguan. *Yunnan Jinning Shizhaishan gumu qun fajue baogao*. 2 vols. Peking: Wenwu chubanshe, 1959.

Zach, E. von. *Die chinesische Anthologie: Uebersetzungen aus dem Wen hsüan*. 2 vols. Cambridge, MA: Harvard University Press, 1958.

Zhang Chun-shu. 'The Han Colonists and Their Settlements on the Chü-yen Frontier.' *Ch'ing-hua hsüeh-pao*, no. 2, V (Taipei, 1966): 154–269.

Zhang Zhenxin. 'Han dai de niugeng.' *Wenwu*, no. 8 (Peking, 1977): 57–62.

Zhongguo kexueyuan kaogu yanjiusuo. *Luoyang Shaogou Han mu*. Peking: Kexue chubanshe, 1959.

—— *Xin Zhongguo de kaogu shouhuo*. Peking: Wenwu chubanshe, 1962.

Zhongguo shehui kexueyuan kaogu yanjiusuo. *Mancheng Han mu fajue baogao*. 2 vols. Peking: Wenwu chubanshe, 1980.

Zhonghua Renmin Gongheguo chutu wenwu xuan. Peking: Wenwu chubanshe, 1976.

Ziran kexueshi yanjiusuo. *Zhongguo gudai keji chengjiu*. Peking: Zhongguo quingnian chubanshe, 1978.

Photo Credits

The publisher wishes to thank the museums and institutions that provided the photographs reproduced in this book; without their cooperation it could not have been published. The numbers refer to plate numbers.

A.C.L., Brussels   131, 133
The Art Institute of Chicago   41
Asian Art Museum, San Francisco   136, 151
The Asia Society, Inc., New York   74
Françoise Aubin, Beaufort-en-Vallée   12
The British Library, London   77–8
The British Museum, London   14, 25, 37, 72, 99
Bulloz, Paris   65, 154
China Photo Service, Beijing   18, 30, 55
Cultural Relics Bureau, Beijing   2, 51, 63, 93, 100, 145, 152
Philippe De Gobert, Brussels   54
The Fogg Art Museum, Harvard University, Cambridge, MA   38, 92
Freer Gallery of Art, Washington, D.C.   40, 59, 140
Fujii Saiseikai Yūrinkan, Kyoto   155
Robert Harding Picture Library, London   50, 64, 94
Leo Hilber, Fribourg   5, 9, 33, 61, 116, 129, 134–5
Luc Joubert, Paris   86
J. L. Klinger, Heidelberg   3, 53, 149
Chantal Kozyreff, Brussels   83, 87
Linden-Museum, Stuttgart   26
The Metropolitan Museum of Art, New York   11, 13, 62 (photo: Cultural Relics Bureau, Beijing), 85, 113

The Minneapolis Institute of Arts, Minneapolis   144, 147
Musée Guimet: Bibliothèque, Paris   7, 16–17, 21–4, 31–2, 36, 57, 76, 95–6, 99, 101–2, 106, 111, 117–18, 123–4, 126–7, 143 (photos: Georges Routhier, Paris)
Musée Turpin de Crissé, Angers   82
Museum für Kunst und Gewerbe, Hamburg   153
Museum of Fine Arts, Boston   88–9, 115
National Museum of Korea, Seoul   75
William Rockhill Nelson Gallery of Art – Atkins Museum of Fine Arts, Kansas City   69, 103, 110, 137
New China Pictures Co., Beijing   4, 15, 35, 90, 146
Orion Press, Tokyo   112, 128, 139
Rapho, Paris   44 (photo: Brian Brake), 70
Réunion des Musées nationaux, Paris   1, 8, 46–7, 56, 60, 71, 97, 107–9, 150, 157
Rheinisches Bildarchiv, Cologne   39
Rietberg Museum, Zurich   105, 119
Rijksmuseum, Amsterdam   27–8, 45, 48–9, 58, 66–7, 142
Georges Routhier, Studio Lourmel, Paris   19–20, 29, 42, 52 a + b, 68, 79–81, 104, 114, 121–2, 125, 138, 141
Royal Ontario Museum, Toronto   84, 130
Seattle Art Museum, Seattle   34
Alain Thote, Paris   6, 10, 43
Ole Woldbye, Copenhague   73
Yale University Art Gallery, New Haven, CT   132, 148 a + b

Ingrid de Kalbermatten, using the indications provided by the author, was the photo documentalist for this book.

Index

236

238

This book was set and printed in September, 1982
by Kastner & Callwey, Munich.
Colour photolithography: c.l.g., Verona
Photolithography black and white: E. Kreienbühl + Co AG, Lucerne
Binding: Conzella Verlagsbuchbinderei Urban Meister GmbH & Co KG, Munich
Design and Production: Franz Stadelmann
Maps: Editions Buchheim, Givisiez
Editorial: Barbara Perroud-Benson

Printed and bound in West Germany